Corporate Performance Management

August-Wilhelm Scheer
Wolfram Jost · Helge Heß
Andreas Kronz

Editors

Corporate Performance Management

ARIS in Practice

With 145 Figures
and 5 Tables

 Springer

Professor Dr. Dr. h.c. mult. August-Wilhelm Scheer
E-Mail: augustwilhelm.scheer@ids-scheer.com

Dr. Wolfram Jost
E-Mail: wolfram.jost@ids-scheer.com

Dr. Helge Heß
E-Mail: helge.hess@ids-scheer.com

Dr. Andreas Kronz
E-Mail: andreas.kronz@ids-scheer.com

IDS Scheer AG
Postfach 10 15 34
66015 Saarbrücken
Germany

Original German edition published by Springer, 2005

Cataloging-in-Publication Data
Library of Congress Control Number: 2005936459

ISBN-10 3-540-30703-6   Springer Berlin Heidelberg New York
ISBN-13 978-3-540-30703-6   Springer Berlin Heidelberg New York

Springer is a part of Springer Science+Business Media
springeronline.com

© Springer-Verlag Berlin Heidelberg 2006
Printed in Germany

Cover design: design & production GmbH
Production: Helmut Petri
Printing: Strauss Offsetdruck
SPIN 11594000   Printed on acid-free paper – 43/3153 – 5 4 3 2 1 0

Preface

Over the years, the discipline of process management has been discussed in terms of a wide range of issues and approaches. When the concept was first mentioned in the media 12 years ago, discussions initially centered on whether sweeping changes along the lines of Business Reengineering or smaller, incremental steps would prove more successful, or the optimum form of the notation for documenting workflow sequences.

Since these beginnings, Process Management has become an important control instrument in many companies, because its practitioners realized that optimizing a company's capacity to create value in the form of processes has a direct and immediate effect on the bottom line. While process optimization is undoubtedly a highly effective method of cutting costs, over the last few years much greater significance has been attached to the subject of customer orientation.

If you think about the last time you were dissatisfied with your supplier or provider, and why this was so, you will very probably agree that the reason for your dissatisfaction had nothing to do with the product itself, but instead was related to the quality of service or processes: delivery dates that were not met, slow response times, the need to speak with multiple contacts etc.

The oft-quoted adage "If I can't measure it, I can't optimize it" applies equally to processes. It is therefore essential for companies to formulate their process objectives for times, costs, and quality in terms of concrete, measurable performance indicators. Then, the latent synergies in the company can be exploited to the full with benchmarking and process comparisons, and best practices can be identified.

This understanding has been called "Corporate Performance Management" by the Gartner Group, and it refers to the use of "Processes, Methodologies, Metrics, and Technologies" in order to create an inextricable link between corporate strategy, planning, implementation and controlling. In order to assure a company's agility, its management must use tools and methods that enable the consequences of decisions to be evaluated quickly, so that the company can respond with flexibility. Synonyms for "Corporate Performance Management" are "Business Performance Management" and "Enterprise Performance Management".

Besides its direct use for optimization purposes, the importance of monitoring processes has also increased as a result of initiatives and statutory regulations regarding corporate governance and risk management. For example, the Sarbanes Oxley Act requires that companies present proof of the effectiveness of their internal control systems as part of their periodic company reporting programs. This means that essential process checks and the associated processes must be documented and the suitability and effectiveness thereof must be tested regularly.

Even the trend towards outsourcing processes is predicated on a clear definition of what is expected of the service provider in terms of process performance, and necessitates the implementation of appropriate monitoring measures for testing compliance with service level agreements.

Disproving the old saw that builders' homes are the most in need of repair, IDS Scheer can demonstrate the remarkable success of implementing this process-oriented approach in its own house using ARIS Process Platform: among its other achievements, consistent process-orientation by a committed support team at the Customer Helpdesk cut enquiry processing time by more than half, and for this the team was honored with the "Helpdesk Award 2004", awarded by an independent technical panel at the end of 2004.

But have we reached the point where we can make sense of all these numbers, alerts and benchmarks and make the right decisions? What good is a whistling kettle if no-one knows how to turn the heat off? Process Mining methods have been developed and patented to ensure the consistent application of data mining techniques to process data, and which are available as part of the ARIS Controlling Platform, provide guidance in finding the important cause-and-effect relationships among millions of discrete items of process information.

Against this background, the trend towards attaching more and more importance to organizational knowledge and the analysis of organizational relationships, beyond pure key performance indicator systems, is entirely logical. In companies with flat hierarchical structures and knowledge-intensive processes, success depends to an ever increasing degree on ensuring that the right employees – often separated by time and geography – work together and communicate efficiently. Rigid supervisory responsibilities and reporting paths are losing their former primacy; adhoc interaction, collaboration and working in communities merge with well structured workflows.

It is here that exhilarating challenges await today's managers, as they are called upon to combine new levels of freedom and motivation for the individual with a results-oriented approach to meet their own expectations for effectiveness and efficiency.

This volume continues the "ARIS in Practice" series of articles published by the Springer Verlag. Contributions will focus on the use of the ARIS Controlling Platform in visualizing, evaluating and analyzing "actively lived" business processes in sectors such as the chemicals industry, telecommunications, energy management, logistics, and also banking and insurance. When these tools are combined with the requisite industry knowledge, they can be used to monitor company performance and set up a program of continuous optimization based on process-oriented key performance indicators.

The editors wish to express their sincere thanks to all the contributing writers, without whose technical skills and efforts this book would not have been written. All contributors are named in alphabetical order at the end of the book.

The editors also wish to thank Mr. Michael Linke, IDS Scheer AG, for his consummate management of the compilation of this book, and for his organizational support.

Saarbrücken, October 2005

August-Wilhelm Scheer   Wolfram Jost

Helge Heß   Andreas Kronz

Table of Contents

From Process Documentation to Corporate Performance Management

August-Wilhelm Scheer
Institute for Economic Information Technology, University of the Saarland

Wolfram Jost
IDS Scheer AG

Summary

Since its emergence in the early nineties as an innovative tool for corporate reorganization, Business Reengineering has evolved considerably, and even now its tenets are experiencing something of a renaissance. In the last few years, additional, dynamic methods such as activity-based cost calculation, the process-based Balanced Scorecard, or Process Mining have been introduced for use together with static process analysis. In this context, the term Corporate Performance Management is used to denote all the long-term, process-oriented modes of action and approach that have been adopted in companies. Specifically with regard to the ARIS methodology, a number of proven method-based and software solutions have been developed over the years, which enable perform-ance-based company controlling.

Keywords

Process documentation, ARIS, EPC, SAP R/3, reference model, ERP, key performance indicators, metrics, performance management, balanced scorecard, simulation, process cost analysis, target process, actual process, optimization measures.

1   The History of Business Process Management

In the early nineteen-nineties, when the notion of the "business process" was first used in academic circles in connection with BPR (Business Process Reengineering), no-one could have foreseen that, more than 10 years later, the idea would be more current than ever before. In the dynamic IT and consulting industry, where the half-lives of topics and trends shrink daily, this is an exception. The overall concept of the business process was developed in stages, and Corporate Performance Management represents the most advanced stage of its development.

The approach became the centre of interest in the 1990s, with the publication of Michael Hammer's book, "Reengineering the Corporation". Central to Hammer's version of the BPR approach was the idea that companies can increase their competitiveness by radically restructuring and optimizing the organization of their business processes. This approach was greeted with enthusiasm in Europe, although it tended to be interpreted in "softer" form. However, the one element that was entirely absent from Michael Hammer's approach was method-based and technology-based support for the BPR concept.

ARIS was the first development and publication ever of a standardized data and procedural model for business process management (see Figure 1). Shortly afterwards, IDS Scheer developed the ARIS Toolset, the first tool for (graphic) modeling of business processes. With the ARIS method and the ARIS Toolset, companies were now able to document their business processes, and to present them in comprehensible form to their employees in the technical departments. The transparency and shared understanding of the processes that this engendered also gave rise to the first process management usage scenarios.

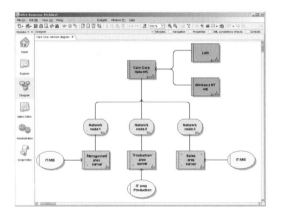 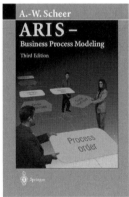

Fig. 1: Process representation and introductory publication to ARIS

2   Business Processes as the Link between IT and Organization

Soon afterwards, extensive analysis of the collected data was added to the simple modeling capability. Dynamic process simulation (ARIS Simulation) and process cost analysis (ARIS PCA) are two variants of process analysis that have lost none of their currency to this day, and which are still in use in many ongoing projects. The sustained success of the first large reengineering projects soon gave rise to the question of linking the process concept to the introduction of modern ERP systems. SAP identified this development early and decided to document the process logic encoded in its R/3 System on a business management level. This documentation (called the R/3 reference model) was based on the ARIS method and used the ARIS Toolset as its technology platform. SAP consultants and customers alike used this as the basis for reaching a consensus on the interpretation of business processes that were to be mapped with SAP.

3   Design, Implementation and Controlling as the Basis for Success

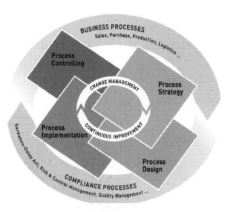

Fig. 2: Business Process Lifecycle

After the ERP wave came the Internet, which ushered in the era of e-business. After a brief period of confusion and missteps regarding the "what, how and when", it soon became plain that e-Business too would only lead to success if a fully consistent consideration of the value added chain were given due consideration, and a process-oriented approach were applied to this entire aspect of business. Ultimately, the primary aim of e-Business was to redefine business processes throughout the company, as is also attested by the recently coined terms e-Procurement or Supply Chain Management.

One of the most important lessons of the New Economy hype was that process orientation cannot continue to be limited to static documentation and analysis, that even the phases of process implementation, and particularly those of overall, i.e. "corporate" or "enterprise-wide" controlling must be incorporated to provide a complete picture of holistic process orientation. IDS Scheer has invested substantially in the development of new software solutions relating to all aspects of these three strategic areas (design, implementation and controlling), so that it can close the "Business Process Lifecycle" loop and offer its customers an end-to-end range of solutions (see Figure 2).

4   Increased flexibility thanks to service-oriented architectures

Fresh significance is now being attached to the subject of process-based software implementation and operation due to the paradigm of service-oriented application architecture based on interacting Web services. The ERP manufacturers have realized that their "old", monolithic system architectures are reaching the limits of their flexibility with regard to the support they can offer individual customer processes. New architectural approaches – e.g. SAP's "Enterprise Service Archi-tecture (ESA)" – serve to reinforce thinking in process terms, not only when the IT system is initially implemented but also when it is in continuous operational use (see Figure 3).

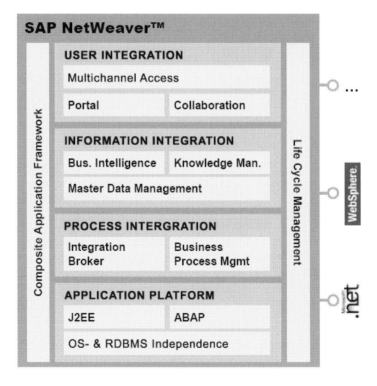

Fig. 3: ESA concept by SAP

5   Process Performance Controlling

Almost a decade after the initial development of the Business Process Management approach, the biggest problem in IT and reorganization projects is still the lack of sustainability in budgeting, planning and implementing process strategies. To be sure, substantive improvements are attained for a short while, perhaps 6-12 months after the end of the project, but after that, the subsequent stage of continuous optimization is neglected.

The same is true of the introduction and use of standardized software. Many customers hope that using the software will enable them to tap new areas of benefit potential. The oft-cited Return on Investment (ROI) is emblematic of this hope. Nowadays, this figure is used only too freely as a basis for decision making. Meanwhile, a test as to whether and to what degree this (theoretical) value – usually the result of much painstaking research – is actually realized, is often entirely omitted. In future, companies will not be able to afford not to test in this fashion, because it will mean losing the ability to act on substantial medium- and long-term improvement opportunities. Any company that makes a substantial financial investment in organizational or software projects must also deal with the question of continuous success monitoring long after the project has been completed. The "performance" of every process change, whether it is supported purely in organizational terms or also by the technological infrastructure, must be tested in terms of its actual effectiveness.

Performance Management and Process Controlling are the watchwords of the hour. The aim is to ensure that running processes are subject to constant improvement through continuous and – to the extent possible – automated measurement and analysis. Process key performance indicators thus serve as the basis for the sustained success of the project, and Performance Management and Process Controlling themselves become an important component of company-wide controlling. In the future, it will no longer be sufficient to use just the "classic" financial indicators as the basis for directing the company. These figures are generally backwards-looking and thus they do not lend themselves to rapid responsiveness. They also do not provide sufficient resolution to enable real corrections to the operational business to be derived. Legislators have also realized this. Thus for example the "Sarbanes-Oxley Act" has been passed in the USA. According to this legislation, all publicly listed companies must now prepare a report on the quality of business processes that affect financial reporting and balance sheet figures in addition to the conventional financial report. This report must be audited by an independent public accounting body. In other words, legislators are of the opinion that in future a statement of "bald" financial figures will not be sufficient to provide a true representation of a company's economic situation. A similar EU Directive is also being debated in Europe. This example is intended to provide an indication of the importance that will be attached in future to the measurement and continuous analysis of processes and process key performance indicators in the realm of corporate governance as well.

6   Flexible Software Platform as Basis for Corporate Performance Management

As a corporation with a worldwide presence, IDS Scheer implemented Corporate Performance Management focusing on the review and optimization of business processes, and has been using it successfully for many years. The ARIS Process Platform offers tools and method-based support covering all the enormously diverse aspects of Corporate Performance Management:

ARIS Balanced Scorecard (ARIS BSC) allows a strategic treatment and analysis of the company from various perspectives, ARIS Process Cost Analyser (ARIS PCA) enables processes to be evaluated in terms of their costs, and ARIS SOX Audit Manager supports SOX-compliant auditing of workflows pertinent to balance sheet preparation. ARIS Process Performance Manager (ARIS PPM) functions as the core component and enables the actual processes running in a company to be visualized, analyzed and compared with target processes entirely automatically. The "buried" treasures and undiscovered potential of the company, and thus also the key to its future direction, are to be found in the merging of process models, process key performance indicators and conventional financial figures. This future direction is also supported efficiently by the tools offered as part of the ARIS Process Platform suite.

From Corporate Strategy to
Process Performance –
What Comes after Business Intelligence?

Helge Heß
IDS Scheer AG

Summary

If companies are to succeed in today's markets, it is absolutely essential that their centralkey processes be designed efficiently. In issues of company analysis, traditional Business Intelligence projects have often not delivered the results that are required in order to be able to derive direct optimization measures in terms of times, costs and quality. The aim of Corporate or Process Performance Management is to optimize the process sequences at work in the company through computer-supported analysis of process structures in conjunction with key performance indicators, so as to organize them more effectively. New approaches in communication and activity analysis yield optimization options whose effects are felt far beyond those of conventional Business Intelligence solutions.

Keywords

Process Performance Management, process management, key performance indicator systems, service level agreements, process mining, right-time monitoring, organizational analysis

1   From Corporate Strategy to Process Management

The primary tasks of the management staff of any company will always be to organize its business as effectively ("Are we doing the right things?") and efficiently ("Are we doing things right?") as possible. Effectiveness concerns both the strategic decisions relating to business segments, products, markets and M&A. However, the imperative for constant reinvention is not limited to product developments, it applies most particularly to the company's processes: Amazon, Dell, Ebay and Ryanair have not achieved their extraordinary success merely by bringing new products to market, they also revolutionized their order processing and service processes.

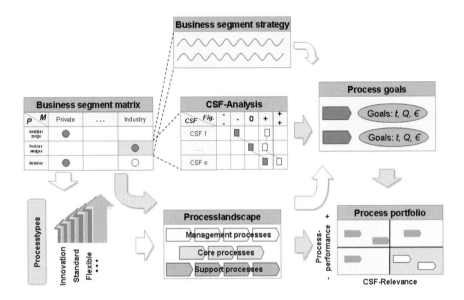

Fig. 1: Derivation of process objectives from success factors
for the business segments

Furthermore, decisions to position the company as an innovation or cost leader in the market, or to attract and keep customers with high quality of service result in the creation of entirely different key competencies and processes. Figure 1 shows how metrics and objectives are assigned to the key processes of any business segment from the analysis of critical success factors.

This renders the performance of the processes measurable. It then becomes possible to derive optimization potential from shortfalls in achieving objectives. This then leads to the creation of the classic optimization loop: Monitoring and Analysis – Optimization – Implementation.

Figure 2 shows how the core processes of a business segment can be evaluated with regard to performance and relevance. The processes in the top right quadrant are highly significant for the company, but demonstrate low performance (in terms of costs, quality, times etc.) so that a need for optimization literally becomes visible. The processes in the left half are candidates for outsourcing.

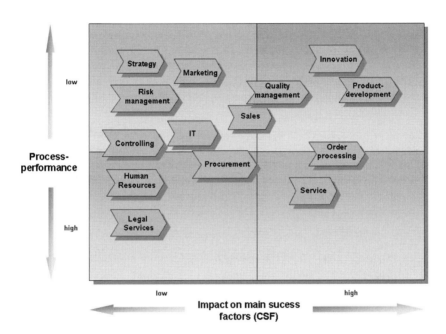

Fig. 2: Portfolio for evaluating corporate processes

Setting up a key performance indicator system that will assure such an evaluation effectively is no minor undertaking: to the outside world, the success of a company is shown by reporting of its profitability and financial indicators. But these indicators alone are not adequate to enable the company's operations to be directed truly successfully, because financial success is not generally revealed until some time after the commercial decisions and optimization measures have been made. Accordingly, monitoring must be instituted at the point where the value is actually added and the decisions are having a direct effect on costs, quality and throughput times. Put another way: "You are only successful in the long terms if you know why you are successful." (Rupert Lay)

2   Monitoring, Analyzing and Optimizing Processes

With the advent of concepts like the Balanced Scorecard, the last few years have seen a change of perspective towards constant monitoring of all company activities for the effects of the results, so that they can be manipulate and directed to specific ends. The intention is to create a system that evaluates its own performance on a continuous basis, and is able to respond flexibly to changes.

But value is added in the key processes of the company, which means that commercial success is entirely contingent on efficient process management. This transcends the purely internal company view, and involves customers and suppliers as well. To be successful, the pertinent key processes of the company (depending on the sector of industry, for example product innovation, product development, sales, order processing, service business, ...) must be designed efficiently with respect to the criteria of cost, quality and time such that they lead to high customer satisfaction and opportunities for reducing costs can be exploited to full advantage.

At the same time, the efficiency of the processes must be monitored constantly and close to real time, so that problems may be detected and optimizing measures may be taken as early as possible. To this end, it is indispensable to set up measurement procedures for the essential key performance indicators, so that the results can be objectified ("one version of the truth"); the axiom "what cannot be measured cannot be optimized" remains as true as ever.

2.1   Corporate Performance Management Takes the Place of Business Intelligence

In the past, typical Business Intelligence - and Data Warehouse – approaches often concentrated largely on financial analyses. Even though this has changed, a large number of these projects still do not really satisfy the informational needs of their users with regard to detecting optimization potential: The highly data-driven approach of many Business Intelligence projects entails enormous effort to extract the data and preserve its quality, and often it also fails to deliver information that can be used to derive optimization measures. The traditional Data Warehouse - and OLAP tools did not deliver the results that could be used directly for optimizing business processes or implementing strategy.

It is evident that analyses must be linked more closely with the company's value creation. Traditional Business Intelligence Systems are being replaced by process-oriented Performance Management solutions.

The phrase **Corporate Performance Management (CPM)** was coined by Gartner Group to describe the combination of "processes, methodologies, metrics and technologies to measure, monitor and manage the performance of the business" (see Buytendijk et al. 2004.).

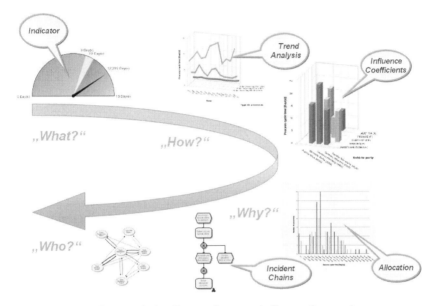

Fig. 3: Top-down analysis of key performance indicators for actual processes

CPM is thus directed at continuous monitoring of the effectiveness of the results of all company processes and the constant optimization thereof, i.e. its objective is a monitoring system that monitors the business performance of all pertinent business processes all the time, detects and reports weaknesses and problem situations, ideally even suggests optimization options, and evaluates the success of improvement measures. Substantive recommendations for action, including their chances of success, are needed so that better decisions can be made more quickly. **Process Performance Management** may be regarded as the heart of CPM.

To the confusion of many users, the abbreviation "BPM" is used for both **"Business Process Management"** and **"Business Performance Management"** (which is synonymous with **Corporate Performance Management** and **Enterprise Performance Management**).

At present, conventional business intelligence companies are competing for the CPM market with the providers of Business Process Management systems. BI tools are attempting to refine their traditional, data-oriented approach to emphasize the association between their analyses and business processes (see Chamoni, Gluchowski 2004). Upon closer examination, hardly any of these BI providers can really know anything about the company's business processes – much less analyze them. When BI providers talk about process orientation, they are usually thinking about their own analysis process, from the point when the data is extracted until it is processed in the frontend.

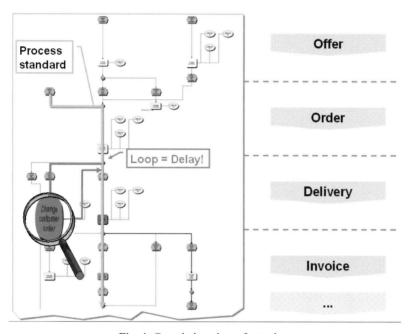

Fig. 4: Cumulative view of actual processes

Some Process Management providers have added monitoring and analysis components to extend the scope of their tools, which were originally intended for process modeling and documentation, to support the entire control loop of Planning – Execution - Monitoring. The most important insight is that pure indicator systems which are not associated with the business processes are inadequate. Instead, indices with their plan and warning values serve to direct attention to problem cases, which must then be investigated more closely with a process analysis. Figure 3 shows how index anomalies are detected at a high level of abstraction, then the influencing factors are identified, and the structure of the actual processes is analyzed for the critical combinations.

An analysis instrument such as ARIS Process Performance Manager (ARIS PPM) is able to generate the structure of actual processes automatically: process fragments are derived from the operational data that is extracted from the source systems (ERP, CRM, EAI, Workflow, Helpdesk systems etc.) and are combined to form a total process (see. Heß 2004). This can be done for single operations (process instances), but one of the more interesting aspects is that it can be used to generate a visual view of a set of operations, showing for example the probability that certain process paths will be passed through or the frequency with which certain loops are executed (see Fig. 4).

This means that a combination of both performance indicators and process structures is essential in order to obtain a meaningful analysis.

2.2 Corporate Governance and Corporate Performance Management

Besides questions of optimization, a series of legal requirements have also kept the subject of process transparency and evaluation under scrutiny:

Both the revised **International Capital Framework Agreement (Basel II)** and the **Law on Control and Transparency in Companies (KonTraG)** require a near real-time representation of business relationships and the risks associated therewith in addition to current business figures.

The **Sarbanes Oxley Act (SOX, SOA),** which was enacted in 2002 in a reaction to several high-profile stock exchange scandals and cases of fraudulent accounting practices, also demands the introduction of appropriate risk management and control systems in the company. This particularly requires that company management provide constantly updated information on the effectiveness of its internal control system as part of the periodic company reporting program. This means that decisions must be made as to which management, business and support processes are relevant for financial reporting purposes. For these processes, the pertinent risks and control activities must be documented and evaluated. In practice, the control system can only be tested effectively with system support.

2.3   Management-oriented Analysis of Process Performance

In many sectors of industry, customers' requirements regarding the quality of service provision have risen to the point that satisfying these requirements has become a key survival issue for companies: for example some logistics providers promise their customers free transportation and dispatch handling if they do not meet the agreed delivery date. The effect that this has on costs if serious delivery delays arise can only be surmised.

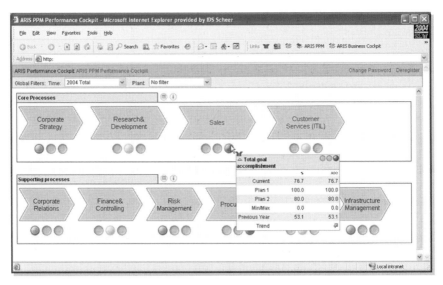

Fig. 5: Cockpit interface with management-oriented
processing of business performance

As a result, the managements of very many companies are extremely preoccupied with the performance of their key processes. Modern cockpit interfaces enable users to navigate without special knowledge of the system and thus provide an unprecedented degree of transparency (see Fig. 5).

Moreover, it is critically important for corporate managers to be aware of the link between the financial indicators and process performance. If financial indicators show negative trends, it is important to analyze them and adopt corrective measures (see Fig. 6).

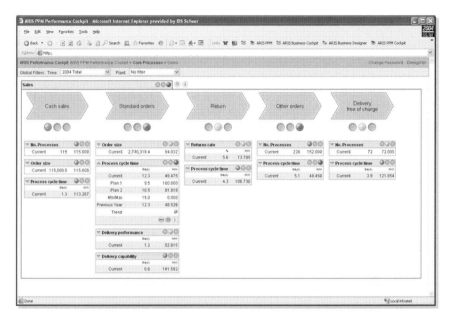

Fig. 6: Drill-down to key performance indicators along the value creation chain

Example: Failure to reach planned sales volume may trigger the following analysis chain:

- In the second quarter, sales increased by only 1.8% instead of the planned 4% compared with the same quarter in the previous year. Why was this?

- Orders received were on target but the number of credit notes rose dramatically. What was the reason for this?

- Question for SALES: Are we having quality problems?

- If not – question to SALES: Are we having problems meeting delivery deadlines?

- If yes – question to WAREHOUSING: Are we encountering many out-of-stock situations?

- If not – question to LOGISTICS: Are we making mistakes with supply or are there scheduling problems in Shipping?

- If yes – question to MATERIALS MANAGEMENT: Are we having quality problems with the materials delivered by our suppliers?

It becomes evident that financial indicators often reflect symptoms that require closer analysis of the processes (in the nature of a "root cause analysis"), because that is where the actual causes lie. The objective is to establish a consistent connection between financial and non-financial value drivers.

2.4   Six Sigma on the Path to Business Excellence

Six Sigma is a management approach that evolved in a practical environment for the purpose of drastically reducing process non-conformances (in terms of quality, times, etc.). "Sigma" is derived from the statistical standard deviation; "Six Sigma" means allowing only 3.4 errors per million error possibilities, i.e. executing 99.997% of all processes in compliance with the stated targets and specifications. The publication of successes by companies like Motorola, General Electric, Ford etc. has resulted in many other companies engaging in "Business Excellence" initiatives with Six Sigma (see Kieslich et al. 2004).

Six Sigma establishes a Total Quality philosophy in the company, which places the focus on the customer and translates the customer's specifications to measurable quantities. Six Sigma and Process Management are very closely related, because the familiar DMAIC cycle is ultimately established to achieve continuous process improvement. Clear process objectives are derived from the value drivers thus obtained; the degree to which these objectives are attained is continuously measured, and the reasons for non-conformances are analyzed – this is very similar to the requirements of a CPM system. Here too: The targets of cost reduction and quality optimization cannot be attained without measuring the results of processes.

The high level of attention demanded of managers in companies where Six Sigma is practiced, and its close association with corporate strategy are particularly interesting. Organizational implementation is usually carried out by special Six Sigma teams, which are attached directly to the executive management levels of the company.

2.5   Outsourcing and Service Level Agreements

The question of which processes constitute the key processes of a company and which can be contracted out to external service providers forces companies to deal with the evaluation of services: cooperation along a shared value creation chain cannot function efficiently unless the requirements the service provider is expected to satisfy have been clearly formulated and its services can be continuously measured and monitored. Particularly with regard to outsourcing processes, this means that **Service Level Agreements** must not only be defined, it must also be possible to monitor them on a continuous basis (see Fig. 7). A new process for managing outsourcing activities must be set up (see. Scheer 2004).

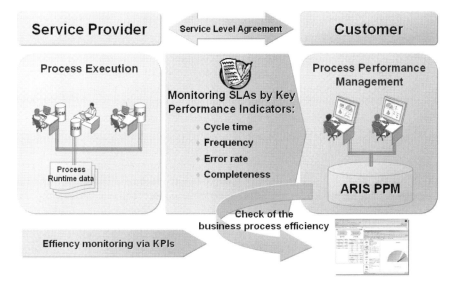

Fig. 7: Continuous monitoring of Service Level Agreements

2.6   The Path to the Process-oriented Organization

Corporate Performance Management is the foundation stone of permanent company controlling based on key performance indicators and processes, so that the process-oriented organization can respond cohesively, rapidly and flexibly to changed requirements and framework conditions, and can make decisions sooner.

Many companies are currently committed to incorporating a process-oriented approach in the structural organization as well. It is clear that the responsibility for processes must remain with the technical departments, but the decision must still be taken regarding assignment of the task of process management itself.

A "Process Management" Competence Center is very often set up for this purpose, with responsibility for horizontal tasks such as defining documentation conventions, supplying tools and assuring quality assurance and consolidation of project results, and fulfilling the roles of multiplier and coach in the company.

Even the role of the CIO is being completely rethought: Whereas this executive's key tasks were once the supply and operation of hardware and software, the focus of his duties is shifting more and more to ensuring the efficiency of the process infrastructure.

However, it must be added that in many companies where IT once served as the innovation engine and growth driver, IT managers are now most likely to be the first to be affected by cost-cutting measures. The question of the benefit of IT for the company has been given only secondary importance. The introduction of a new IT system was commonly regarded to be successful as long as it was completed on time and under budget. Other success criteria such as reduced costs, increased productivity or increased customer and employee satisfaction were often considered to be unquantifiable and therefore ignored.

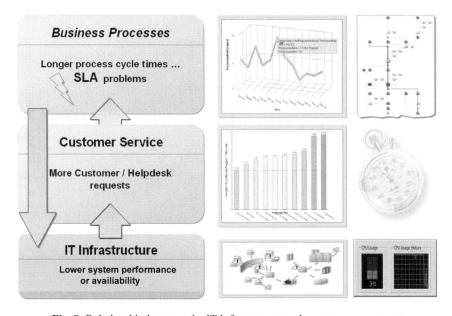

Fig. 8: Relationship between the IT infrastructure and process management

All that is now changing: the object is now to control the interface between the technical area and IT, so that the process optimization achieved with IT solutions can be measured and the ROI in software can be proven. Business and IT considerations collide in the question of monitoring: The IT manager, who uses system management support to measure the performance of his hardware, network components and applications, must now face the effects that IT problems have on running business processes, for example so that he can assign priorities for escalation and troubleshooting. Conversely, when investigating the root causes of weaknesses, the process manager is interested in whether IT problems were involved in the cause (see Fig. 8).

This means that monitoring the performance of a company must include a consideration of strategic aspects combined with process-oriented analyses as well as IT-related analyses (IT-service management) in order to yield an all-round view.

Service-oriented Architectures and CPM

In a very small number of cases, it is sufficient to carry out a manual analysis of business process sequences. Data gathering techniques such as interviews, workgroups etc. are useful for creating a generalized transparency for the business processes; but gathering data in this manner is not adequate to meet the requirements of currency and objectivity. Since most process-relevant data is now present on IT systems, it must be possible to extract this data from these "source systems" consistently and automatically, and ultimately to reconstruct the entire process performance chain, e.g. from customer inquiry to delivery and receipt of payment, from these individual items of information. This requirement applies particularly where processes transcend system boundaries (e.g. CRM – ERP – Legacy System).

In this context, it is evident that all approaches of a Service-Oriented Architecture (SOA) facilitate the extraction of process-relevant data, since the data then does not have to be extracted individually from each source system; it can be supplied by the middleware. As a result, the SOA approaches that are implemented to lend greater flexibility to business processes also make it considerably easier to monitor the workflows (see Krafzig, Banke, Slama, 2004).

3   Trends in Corporate Performance Management

3.1   Process Mining for Automated Weakpoint Analysis

According to some estimates, the volume of data held by companies is growing at an average rate of 90% per year. In companies where several hundreds of thousands of operations are executed every day, the process manager is often not in a position to detect weak points, because they are lost in the analyses of overall quantities for example because of data compression and averaging. But from the customer's point of view, every single delay or complaint is difficult to excuse. Special analytical techniques must therefore be used on process information in order to detect such situations.

Data mining techniques are able to provide information and insights, and to identify relationships from large volumes of data, and are being used more and more for analyzing process data (process mining). The objective in this case is to discern combinations of dimensions (e.g. customer groups, products, regions, sectors, plants, local authorities etc.) that have particular characteristics and special requirements in terms of optimizing times, costs or quality.

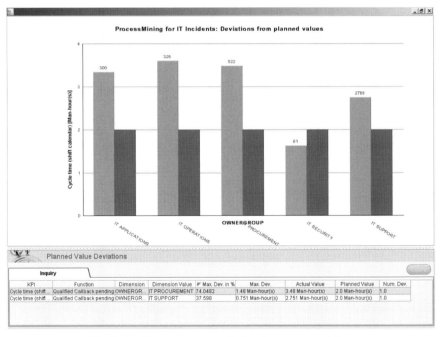

Fig. 9: Intelligent process analysis using process mining

Figure 9 shows how process mining techniques are used to perform **intelligent process analysis** instead of the usual "slicing and dicing" of data: ARIS PPM leads users directly to *those* processes and combinations of dimensions that show the largest deviations from plan values or the most significant anomalies. For example, the constellations are highlighted in which the largest discrepancies occur between regions in terms of throughput times, costs or quality key performance indicators. Then, the reasons why the throughput time is so much longer in region A than in region B must be investigated – again, this is done by an analysis of the process structure. Finally, the process mining capabilities can be used for internal benchmarking.

3.2   Proactive Instead of Reactive: Right Time Monitoring

Data relating to past events must be analyzed so that conclusions regarding weakpoints and optimization potential can be drawn. However, process managers need more information than this, because their chief concern is of course to detect and eliminate problems in ongoing processes. The ex-post perspective becomes an ex-ante view.

As products lend themselves more and more to comparison, even as the number of variations multiplies (for example, Daimler-Chrysler offers about 10^{27} variants and builds the same car only about 1.4 times per year), in many industries the time to respond to customer wishes has become a critical success factor. In the industrial sector, being able to fulfill customer requirements quickly and specifically means being able to manufacture in small batches. In service-oriented sectors, the challenge lies in determining and reducing the activities within the process that do not add value: The reason for the long throughput time for a life insurance application is not that the processor in question really needs that long to complete the processing steps for the application, but usually because of the complex and often uncoordinated communication paths between the insurance company and the other parties involved, such as brokers, the healthcare agency etc.

In both the industrial and the service environments, the need for near real-time analysis and information grows as throughput times become shorter. "Real-time" here does not necessarily mean millisecond processing, but rather the synchronization of the supply of information with the need, so that the term "right-time" or "true-time" monitoring is perhaps more appropriate: The supply of essential information to the right consumer at exactly the right time, to provide those responsible with every resource to obtain current information at all times, and to institute appropriate escalations and notifications upon the occurrence of all events that deviate from the process standard. True real-time requirements only exist in a few sectors, e.g. fraud detection in financial and banking transactions.

Right Time companies are process-oriented, because true time services cannot be provided unless processes are considered from end to end, i.e. from the customer requirement to completion of the order. Right Time companies are also event-oriented, because they can respond to external and internal events (triggers") at any time: new customer contact, entry into market by a competitor, supplier reports delivery bottlenecks, complaint from a high-priority customer, etc.

The term **Business Activity Monitoring (BAM)** describes the ability to detect such events (events = data from RFID systems, from barcode scanners, process events from ERP, CRM and SCM applications, etc.) to provide a right-time view of the business processes. In the previous example, this means for instance that a delayed delivery of goods is detected, the impact of the delay to the extent that it threatens the supply deadline for the final product can be assessed, and responses and notifications can be derived therefrom immediately. The old principle of the recipient's duty to look for information is thus turned on its head, and then it becomes the task of the information system to provide the necessary information in good time to everyone concerned.

The next step is to be able to look into the future: Predictive models are used to forecast future trends and identify problems ahead of time, while it is still possible to intervene and institute countermeasures.

3.2.1   From the Organizational Chart to the Dynamic Organizational Analysis

An analysis of the efficiency and effectiveness of processes entails more than just a consideration of the structure of the control flow, i.e. which activities are performed in what order. The following aspects are also particularly interesting for optimizing the business (see Fig. 10):

- Organizational analysis: Who works with whom, and how?

- Analysis of data and documentation relationships: What data and documents are used in the process?

- Analysis of system support: Which IT systems are used?

For analysis purposes, this means that the extracted process information is also used to make statements about these aspects. Just as target processes can be modelled and compared with real actual processes via CPM, this can now also be used for the organizational, data, document and system side (see Fig 11).

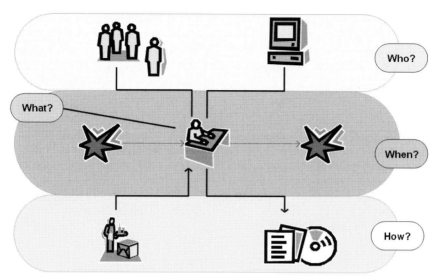

Fig. 10: Aspects of process analysis

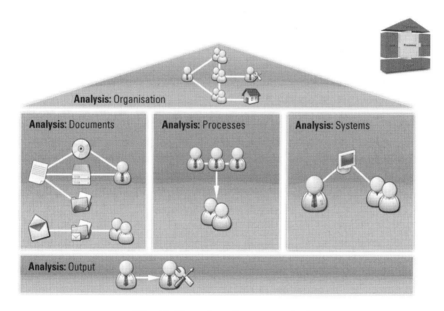

Fig. 11: Extension of process analysis

In the following, the analysis of organization and responsibilities will be dealt with in more detail with reference to an example: Classic organizational charts provide a static view of the structural organization of a company according to association with given disciplines. It does not offer a great deal of help in answering the question of how departments and employees interact in real life, and where communication can be improved. Meanwhile, transparency of this nature is becoming more and more important, especially in knowledge-intensive and cooperative processes, so that networks can be organized more efficiently, and ultimately to ensure efficient processing.

Questions that are typically asked in this context are for example:

- Which organizational units/positions carry out which activities? (How often? With what quality? With what throughput times? At what costs?)

- Which units work together closely? How often do organizational units O1 and O2 work on the same process instance? How often is work handed off from organizational unit O1 to O2? Where do friction losses arise between departments?

- Which employees and positions form the communication bridgeheads with other departments? Which organizational units / positions are holding up the efficient flow of the processes?

- Who needs what kind of training? Who is a special knowledge carrier and specialist?

- At what percentage of its capacity is a department working? How can personnel costs be reduced?

These activity and communications analyses spotlight the relationships of organizational units and employees among each other and also make transparent the link between structural organization and the procedural organization. As with the analysis of generated actual processes, now the real relationships among the organizational units can be reviewed. Figures 12 and 13 show what an organization-centered navigation may look like when it is based on dynamic relationship networks rather than static organizational charts. For example, the user can see what relationships the "Sales" organizational unit has with other units, whereby the nature of the relationship may be one of *cooperation, delegation, information* etc. The processes in which this organizational unit participates and the subsections for which it is responsible are also clearly revealed.

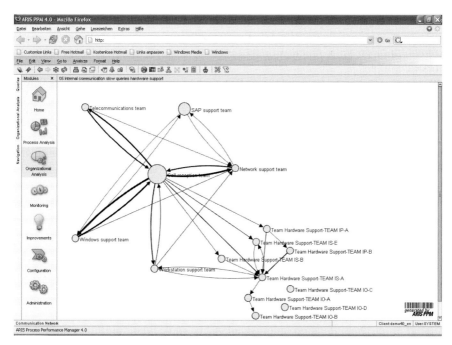

Fig. 12: Communication between organizational units

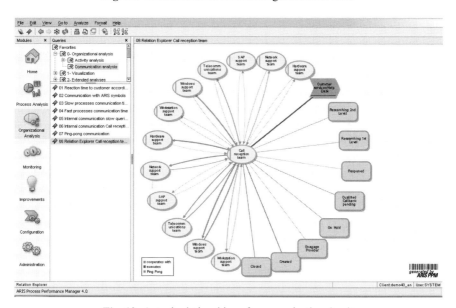

Fig. 13: Actual relationships of an organizational unit

This visualization is essential for revealing, analyzing and optimizing the real communication relationships during the execution of a process. Techniques are used (see Fig. 14) from a variety of disciplines, including statistics (correspondence analysis) and sociology (social network analysis etc., see Cross, Parker 2004; Kilduff, Tsai 2003).

In many companies, the boundaries between structured, well documented and ad-hoc processes are also becoming blurred: not infrequently, parts of an entire process are supported by mail systems and collaboration features, with no possibility to correlate these activities with the structured data. Examples are the bid phase of processing an order, schedule and deadline agreements, synchronization of innovation and development processes. This may require even these communication relationships to be analyzed and visualized, since they are a part of the workflows that are to be documented.

4   Integration in Business Process Portals

Business process portals serve to provide the employee with all the information he needs for the efficient processing of his role-specific workflows and activities.

This is particularly interesting when it is combined with the EAI- or SOA-based architectures discussed earlier. Process portals offer the capabilities an employee has by virtue of his role to define process sequences, execute them via a workflow, and to control or monitor them. Portals can also be used to integrated human interactions with the automated processing of activities so that they become the central user interface for all internal and external business processes. Cockpits for controlling process performance are the central component of process portals (see Fig. 15).

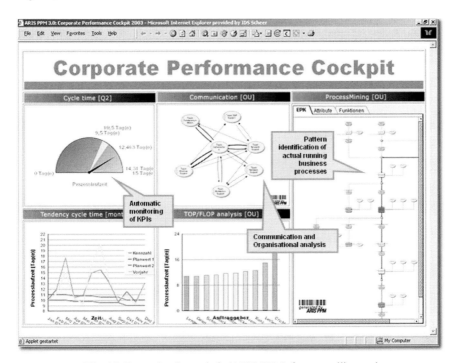

Fig. 14: Example of a cockpit (ARIS PPM) for controlling and monitoring business processes

Besides support for structured processes, efficient and effective support for work sequences and tasks that are not precisely defined also continues to gain importance. For this, collaboration features are needed that enable employees to communicate with colleagues, customers and partners. To this end, process portals provide the capability to efficiently use and share data, knowledge and applications in the manner of a project.

This is where process portals, virtual workspaces and business communities merge (see Hagel, Armstrong 1997; IDS Scheer [1]; IDS Scheer [2]): synchronous and asynchronous collaborative tools and services such as e-mail, chatrooms, discussion forums, blackboards, Instant Messages, Web conferences, combine manual interactions with collaborative business processes. In particular it is important to replace the undisciplined use of all these tools with an ordered integration in the value creation chain. At this point, the circuit is completed by thus synchronizing the supply and demand of information in the fashion of a right time company.

5   Literature

Buytendijk, F., Wood, B., Geishecker, L.: Mapping the Road to Corporate Performance Management, Gartner Report 30. Januar 2004.

Chamoni, P.; Gluchowski, P.: Integrationstrends bei Business-Intelligence-Systemen. In: Wirtschaftinformatik, 46 (2004) 2, Page 119-128.

Cross, R.; Parker, A.: The Hidden Power of Social Networks: Understanding How Work Really Gets Done in Organizations. Boston 2004.

Hagel III, J.; Armstrong, A.G.: Net Gain – Expanding Markets through Virtual Communities. Boston 1997.

Heß, H.: Marktführerschaft durch Process Performance Management: Konzepte, Trends und Anwendungsszenarien. In: Scheer, A.-W.; Abolhassan, F.; Kruppke, H.; Jost, W. (Hrsg.): Innovation durch Geschäftsprozessmanagement. Berlin et al. 2004, Pp. 119 -136.

IDS Scheer [1]: Business Communities – Status Quo und Marktmodelle. June 2001.

IDS Scheer [2]: Virtual Workplaces – Status Quo und Marktmodelle. June 2001.

Kieslich, T.; Lange, D.; Röttgermann, A.: Six Sigma – Methodik zur Business Excellence. In: Scheer, A.-W.; Abolhassan, F.; Kruppke, H.; Jost, W.: Innovation durch Geschäftsprozessmanagement. Berlin et al. 2004, Pp. 93 -102.

Kilduff, M.; Tsai, W.: Social Networks and Organizations. SAGE Publications 2003.

Krafzig, D.; Banke, K.; Slama, D.: Enterprise Soa: Service-Oriented Architecture Best Practices. Prentice Hall 2004.

Scheer, A.-W.: Unsere ARIS Methode öffnet die Tür in die Weltliga. In: Scheer, A.-W.; Abolhassan, F.; Kruppke, H.; Jost, W. (Hrsg.): Innovation durch Geschäftsprozessmanagement. Berlin et al. 2004, Pp. 1 -10.

Managing of Process Key Performance Indicators as Part of the ARIS Methodology

Andreas Kronz
IDS Scheer AG

Summary

Evaluating processes with the aid of key performance indicators continues to gain acceptance as an integral element of corporate controlling as well as process management. This article will first describe the tasks associated with process controlling, which will then be used as a basis for defining the objectives of a process-oriented key performance indicator management system. In particular, we will explain how the description of key performance indicators can be integrated in general process modelling. When KPI management has been assigned its proper place in the process management loop, roles that are needed to implement it in real terms will be defined.

Keywords

Process-oriented key performance indicator system, indicator, key performance indicator (KPI), eEPC, KPI management, business process controlling, monitoring of business workflows, collection concepts, process instance, Performance Management, dimensions, calculation rule, measurement points, functions, ERM attribute, measurement probes, KPI allocation diagram, key performance indicator tree

1   Introduction

In many companies, the controlling function is being increasingly expanded beyond its traditional intepretation to include active support for the control and optimization of company workflows. As a result, it assumes a new role in classic process management, not only because it occupies the key position of process monitoring, but also because it integrates workflow monitoring with corporate controlling. Collecting and analyzing performance-related key performance indicators is the first prerequisite for holistic process management and forms the basis for consistent and continuous process optimization.

This idea can be put into practice by using powerful tools in different areas of the company to collect data in a process-oriented manner and present it in the form of process key performance indicators that apply throughout the company. To this end, many companies have already selected the ARIS product family as their tool for the business process management environment in general, and ARIS Process Performance Manager (ARIS PPM) in particular for Business Process Controlling. The main objective in installing such a system is to set up an overall view of the company's core processes and to establish a cycle for continuously improving process efficiency.

At the same time, the efficiency of the processes must be monitored constantly and in close to real time, so that weak points may be detected in the nature of an early warning system and optimizing measures can be taken. Measurements must serve as the basis for deriving measures that will help to improve the company's performance. Standardized process descriptions that are applicable throughout the company represent the linchpin of the system, because they determine what is to be measured, how it is to be measured, the nature of the measurement and they serve as the starting point for new arrangements.

The principal tasks of process controlling are as follows:

- *Evaluation, analysis and continuous monitoring of business workflows* Monitoring is performed on the basis of manually or automatically collected data. Evalaution is done with reference to target values, which are set by management and validated by the technical departments.
- *The aim of process controlling* is to map the process reality in a task-oriented manner according to the issue and task. The viewpoint or also the viewing mode may be shifted in any number of ways, for example if Sales or Production are considering the same processes.

- The result of process controlling is transparency of the processes, in structural terms and for purposes of evaluation. Operational and strategic decisions can be made on the basis of information and process evaluations that are kept permanently current. This becomes all the more important as companies strive to keep pace with a volatile environment of constantly changing business processes and adaptations.
- The results of process controlling can also be used as the basepoint for process optimizations. In this case, process controlling can provide insight into weak points and some indication of the improvement potential. Derived measures are thus quantified in terms of their costs and benefts at the planning stage. After improvement measures have been implemented, their effects can be made transparent and the actual situation thus created can be evaluated with process controlling.

1.1   The Process-oriented Key Performance Indicator System

The basis for all process controlling is a process-oriented key performance indicator system that links the process perspective to the essential controlling aspects of the business. The key performance indicators must enable conclusions to be drawn regarding the effectiveness of the processes (e.g. customer satisfaction) and their efficiency (e.g. processing time, delivery reliability, process quality and costs). In addition, a process-oriented key performance indicator system is configured so that it is possible to make statements about the actual course of the process.

Since most process-related data is stored on IT systems in the majority of companies, a computer-supported system can be set up to extract the data from these "source systems" and to use these individual items of data to reconstruct an order processing chain, e.g. from the generation of a purchase order to receipt of the product and transfer of payment. For the parts of the process that are not yet fully mapped in computerized form, for example customer acquisition and consulting, the pertinent process information can be gathered by manual methods. In both cases, it is imperative to establish a clear connection between the process and its key performance indicators, without which it is practically impossible to interpret the KPIs or derive any meaningful measures.

By using the various data collection techniques, a global view of processes can be obtained and a comprehensive system of key performance indicators can be created.

2.   Objectives and Tasks of Process-oriented KPI Management

KPI management has three distinct objectives, which are reflected later in the spheres of responsibility of various roles.

The primary objective of KPI Management is to provide a consistent definition of the KPI system. The content of the KPI system must therefore be synchronized with a variety of areas (management, proceess manager, software development etc.) and it must obey unambiguous calculation rules. Besides this definition, target values and threshold ranges must also have been coordinated.

The KPI system must be documented in unambiguous terms and must be made accessible to the various groups concerned. It must describe how individual key performance indicators are calculated, and consequently how they are evaluated, how KPIs are interrelated, and the nature of their connection to the process. These essential features of the KPI system must be described unambiguously in the process models.

KPI Management is also responsible for the processes that trigger a change in the KPI system itself, and which much ensure that the consistency of the system is preserved, and that the KPI system documentation is also modified in accordance with release management for the process description.

A number of factors can trigger changes to the KPI system:

If the strategic alignment and subordinate objectives of the company are changed by its management, the control instruments and thus also the key performance indicators must be adapted. This can affect the targets, and also the definitions or priorities of key performance indicators in the KPI system.

Even a change in the processes themselves due to strategic realignments or optimization measures, can create a need to adapt the KPI system, for example because activities that needed to be measured no longer exist.

And not least, a change to the application system landscape can influence the key performance indicators, because changes are usually made to the IT systems in order to effect a change in processes, which in turn is intended to affect the KPI system.

2.1   Terminological Conventions

Several concepts must be defined as they relate to KPI Management, to provide the basis for a common understanding:

2.2   Measurement point

A measurement point defines a point in the process at which data is collected (by manual or automated means) for calculating key performance indicators. A measurement point returns one or more data items (point in time, information about the object concerned) every time a concrete processe (process instance) is executed. The measurement point has an equivalent (interface or data extraction) in an application system under consideration, which is characterized by the description of the format of the data records that are returned at this measurement point as a description of the change in status of application objects (creation, modification, completion, ...).

2.3   Key Performance Indicator (KPI)

The key performance indicator calculates one or more values from the data returned by the measurement point in accordance with the definition assigned to it. Fixed target values or target ranges that may apply only to specific products, services of business transactions can also be defined for the KPI.

2.4   Evaluation or Analyses

The evaluation interprets the key performance indicator with reference to various criteria – called dimensions – (time period; product; region) and possibly describes a relationship between the results and the predetermined targets or non-compliances therewith. The dimensions are also exported from the source systems in the form of features of individual application system objects, and are transferred as properties of the process instances. The user evaluates the level of performance of his business processes by considering the interaction between the KPIs and the dimensions.

A graphical representation and the representiation medium are also agreed as part of the analysis in conjunction with the corresponding tools.

3.   Description of Key Performance Indicators

For the purposes of process-oriented KPI management, the description of the key performance indicators must be embedded in the business process modeling in order to assure optimum support for the objectives of KPI Management. To this end, the structures of the KPIs and their connections to the processes must be documented as well as their definitions. Several descriptive techniques are used within the framework of the ARIS methodology. The following section includes descriptions of the most important model types.

3.1   Key Performance Indicator tree

The key performance indicator tree structures the KPIs by organizing them in individual, technically related KPI groups (e.g. Quality, Cost, Time, and also process-oriented groupings). It should be noted that there may be more than one key performance indicator tree. It is also possible for KPIs to be assigned to several KPI trees according to the target group.

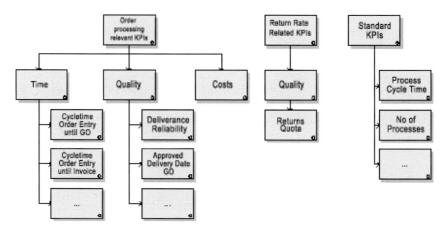

Fig. 1: Example of a key performance indicator tree

3.2   KPI Allocation Diagram

The KPI allocation diagram defines the measurement points and the data at the measurement points that is to be included for the purposes of the KPI. Linking multiple KPIs to a new KPI is also described in the KPI allocation diagram. This can be used to map key performance indicator calculation hierarchies. Changes to the names of KPIs, such as "Number of POs" instead of "Number of processes" can also be specified in the diagram.

A description of the calculation rule for a KPI is maintained within the KPI to which it applies. The KPI allocation diagram does not have to provide a mathematically precise or complete description of the KPI, but it does enable a technical specification to be made, from which an exact calculation specification can be derived as part of IT requirements management.

In the example, the key performance indicator is calculated from the Goods Outward Actual and Goods Outward (planned) measurement points (see Fig. 2).

In order to provide a full description of the KPIs, the point in the process sequence where the necessary data is collected must be defined. These points in the process define the measurement points and are used later in the specification of the interfaces required. Measurement points can return any amount of data simply by receiving or reading the data in question from the IT system that is involved in the execution of the function. Thus, measurement points return not only the specification for the systems from which the data is drawn, but also the time information regarding when the data relating to the process sequence is collected. This is especially important for data that is liable to change during the process sequence.

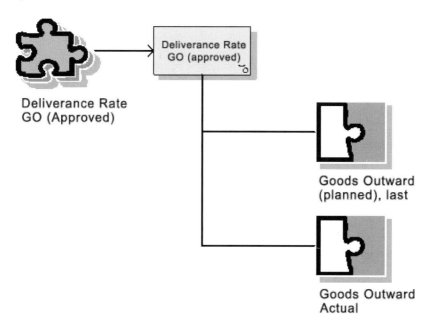

Fig. 2: Example of a KPI allocation diagram

There is another distinction between measurement points and key performance indicators. Whereas measurement points return data relating to a single point in the process, key performance indicators often rely on data from multiple measurement points. For example, when calculating a time period from function A to function B, the data from the measurement point at function A must be combined with the data supplied by the measurement point at function B. It is also evident that the KPI can not be calculated until the process has passed through function B.

Thus the separation of KPI and measurement point also enables measurement points to use, or reuse, data for multiple KPIs.

3.3   Technical Model Representation in ARIS

An event-driven process chain (EPK) is a model that is used to describe graphically the chronological-logical sequence of a service provision process. It is based on the following assumptions:

Every activity (operation, processing step, *function*) within a process is caused by a management-relevant change in the status of an infomation object. Every function can bring about a management-relevant change of status of an information object. The status of a management-relevant information object is described graphically by an *Event* type object. Accordingly, the event is chosed as the reference point for the measurement point. The information is not available to the measurement point until the information object's change of status has been stored in an IT system.

A cross on the event indicates that the event represents a measurement point for the process controlling system (see Fig. 3).

The measurement point returns one or more values that can be used for calculating different KPIs, so N-M relationships can be drawn between measurement point and KPI. The data returned by the measurement probe is represented as *ERM attribute* type objects and can therefore be reused from data models and integrated in other data models. Besides the technical description, information about the specific URL or the original database table and data type information can also be stored in the ERM attributes. The EPC can also be elaborated with organizational units. The organizational unit describes the groups of processors in the company that perform the function. Organizational units are connected to the respective function by non-directional connections (*informational* connection type). Measurement probes can also return information about organizations on the basis of the information that exists in the IT systems. These are often reflected in the form of dimensions.

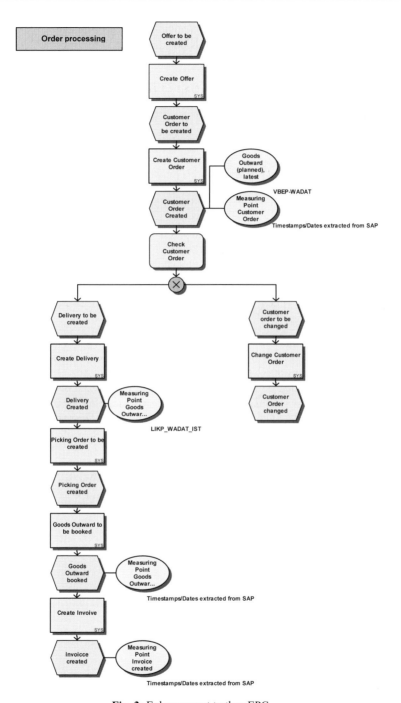

Fig. 3: Enhancement to the eEPC

4   Integration of KPI Management in the Process Management Loop

KPI Management intersects with Process Management at many points; it may also be defined as a component thereof. The KPI Management tasks assigned to the roles concerned can be derived from this integration.

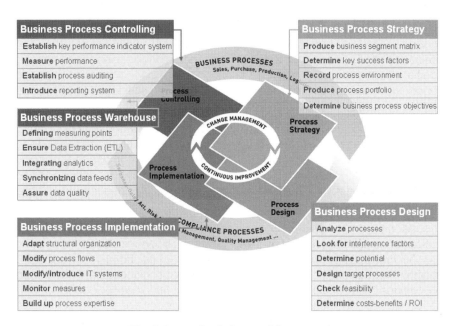

Fig. 4: Integration in Process Management

The description of key performance indicators must be embedded in Business Process Design. The definition and structure of the KPIs as well as the relationship between the KPIs and the processes are described here. Adaptations to the processes necessarily cause adaptations to the KPI structure.

When processes are strategically realigned or new services are designed (Business Process Strategy), the KPIs must necessarily be adapted as well, because the reflect what management expects of the processes. Changes to the KPIs in turn mean that measurement points must be redefined or reconfigured, and they must be submitted to requirements management for the application systems.

In order to ensure efficient, cost-effective controlling, the implementation of measurement points must be taken into account in the implementation and support of the processes by IT (Business Process Implementation). Interface management of the measurement points has the effect of gathering the data in a Business Process Warehouse, which holds the data in readiness for all process questions regarding times, quality and costs, also for the purposes of process cost analysis. The Business Process Warehouse also contains the clearing point and ensures the consistency of the data from the measurement points. The controlling tools are integrated as components of the Business Process Warehouse.

Business Process Controlling uses the data from the measurement points for process-oriented evaluations analyses with ARIS PPM. These analyses are combined with traditional controlling approaches as necessary to obtain an overall picture of company performance or to add process auditing to the auditing function.

The results can be made available in a central access platform so that they can be prepared in a manner most suitable for the target group. This platform should be integrated in the company portal so that it can be included in the single sign-on access and authorization arrangements. The controlling scenario can be supplemented and rounded out to good effect with special reports for different user groups.

Besides the purely operational use of process controlling, key performance indicators can also be accessed by process analysts. In particular, analysts can also use the functionalities of the process controlling tools (Process Mining, ABC Analysis etc.) to detect weak points in the process sequence and derive improvements. Some of the analyses are carried out in the controlling tools (for view of just the Actual situation), and process modeling is used as well for Target-Actual comparisons. The KPIs can also be used as the basis for defining new target ranges for KPIs.

5   Tasks and Responsibilities as Part of KPI Management

Besides the tasks associated with KPI Management, responsibilities must also be defined for the individual activities. This definition results in a series of roles, which must be integrated as a role concept in the Process Management role concept (not further described here). Therefore, only the roles of KPI Management will be described explicitly in the following section.

5.1   Management (Mmgt)

Management is responsible for the targets and the strategic alignment of process management as part of the KPI Management function. This includes establishing rough key performance indicators and target values that support the strategy and enable its implementation to be controlled.

The KPIs are also defined in coordination with the Controlling departments, which embed them in the overall controlling infrastructure and/or use them for interdepartmental comparisons and benchmarks.

5.2   KPI-Manager (KPI-Mgr)

KPI Managers are responsible for the routine operation of KPI Management. They convert the KPI targets received from management to calculable key performance indicators so that they can be implemented operationally. To this end, they coordinate with the technical departments and prepare a consistent detailed specification of the KPIs. Since the KPI Managers also serve as the collection point for KPI requirements from the operational technical departments, they reconcile these requirements with the targets supplied from the Management level in consultation with Process Management.

At the same time, they work with the IT departments to determine available and required measurement points, from which the required key performance indicators can be calculated. They also define the criteria and dimensions that are necessary in order to be able to evaluate the key performance indicators. The consistency of the dimensions themselves must also be ensured, for example so that performances for different KPI areas can be evaluated uniformly.

After feasibility testing, the KPI Managers cooperate with IT Requirements Management to draw up suitable release plans for realizing the measurement points and adapt them to the release plans for process modeling. With regard to the KPIs themselves, their implementation is coordinated with the IT managers of the controlling tools. The KPI-Mgrs also use KPI trees and KPI allocation diagrams to document the KPIs in process modeling.

Besides the changes to the KPI system due to new targets set by Management, the KPI Managers determine the effects of the system changes on the key performance indicator system. Since system changes may be either IT or process changes, they must be integrated in the corrsponding requirements or change processes (this is a required input from the respective change manager).

5.3   Process Managers

As part of KPI Management, Process Management has the task of confirming the respective KPIs for the processes in consultation with Corporate Management. Process managers receive the decision criteria from the KPI managers, who have translated the targets into process-compatible KPIs in cooperation with the technical department. The process managers and corporate management share joint responsibility for ensuring compliance with the KPI target values.

5.4   Technical Departments

Together with the KPI managers, the technical departments work out the detailed specification of the key performance indicators and contribute new KPI requirements for operations as necessary.

5.5   IT System Managers and Requirements Management

IT system managers work with the KPI managers to harmonize new or changed measurement points. The requirement for new measurement points must be included in Requirements Management and synchronized as necessary.

Requirements Management itself must consider measurement points for all new IT plans, and clarify changes as necessary with the KPI managers.

The IT System Managers are thus reponsible for the stability of the measurement points, particularly in the event of IT changes, and for the corresponding information from the KPI Managers.

The IT Managers of the controlling tools implement the key performance indicators according to the specifications defined by the KPI managers. Depending on the changes, they may also be required to cooperate in adapting the process modelling.

5.6   Use of the KPI system

The following table summarizes the possible usage scenarios of the key performance indicator system for the various roles.

	Use
Management	• Corporate leadership using highly aggregated data • Notifications in the event of significant deviations • Control of implementation of the strategic target values • Derivation of new strategic alignments
Controlling	• Use of the Process KPI system as a module in overall controlling • Interdepartmental comparisons and benchmarks
Process Management	• Operational control and continuous monitoring of the managed processes • Notification in the event of deviations • Derivation of measures
Process Analysts	• Cause tracing, structure analyses and target/actual comparisons • Derivation of structural changes from processes
KPI Mgr	• Control and support of the KPI system
IT Management	• 1st and 2nd level support for KPI tools (3rd with technical management) • Continuous monitoring of business management processes from the technology perspective

Fig. 5: Use of the KPI system

Operational, Tool-Supported Corporate Performance Management with the ARIS Process Performance Manager

Markus von den Driesch
IDS Scheer AG

Tobias Blickle
IDS Scheer AG

Summary

In ARIS Process Platform, and particularly ARIS PPM, users have a professional tool for Corporate Performance Management. Consistent alignment with process analysis, combined with the ability to analyse process-external data at the same time, enables users to detect weak points in the process organization with comprehensive and easy-to-use analytical methods (Process Mining, ABC analyses etc.). Beyond the evaluation of key performance indicators, the graphic visualization of actual processes is a patented method for identifying patterns in the execution of processes and pinpointing optimization potential. The system has been applied successfully, its flexibility and effectiveness proven in widely differing real-life situations for many customers in vastly different sectors of industry.

Keywords

Key performance indicators, process mining, process visualization, weak point analysis, scalability

1.   The Path to Corporate Performance Management

A comprehensive Corporate Performance Management (CPM) system is not possible without the collection and evaluation of objective key performance indicators for the most diverse aspects of a company's life. Most conventional reporting and business intelligence applications focus on financial indicators and do not take adequate account of the company's business processes.

Yet it is precisely an evaluation of the performance and efficiency that yield these financial indicators which is so important for detecting problems and enabling the introduction of optimizing measures as early as possible. Only an overall view of the performance of the processes in the context of other aspects makes it possible to reveal weak points and define measures for correcting them.

Thus the collection of key performance indicators that enable the quality of the business processes to be evaluated is essential for Corporate Performance Management. A one-time "snapshot" for evaluating process performance, e.g. in the form of a manual collection and analysis, is no longer sufficient, because the workflow sequences in the company are evolving constantly and are constrained continuously by external influences.

1.1   Requirements for Process Controlling

Accordingly, a procedure is required that enables process-based key performance indicators to be evaluated on an ongoing basis. It should be possible to collect the process-relevant information automatically, techniques and aids should be provided for weak point analyses, and it should be possible to prepare the information appropriately for the target group (management, process manager, process participant).

The set of key performance indicators to be calculated must be defined flexibly, and in such a way that it can be expanded to meet changing requirements of the company's specific processes. Besides calculating key performance indicators, it is also necessary to be able to visualize the structure of actual processes, since this is the only way to obtain generalized explanations for their performance behavior.

Since processes very often extend across the boundaries of multiple heterogeneous systems, it must be possible to analyze workflows "from end to end". Since processes are very often included that are performed hundreds of thousands of times a day, the analysis component must be scalable so as to be able to assure consistently good behavior both when the information is imported and while the information is being analyzed.

2. Process Performance Management with ARIS PPM

With ARIS Process Performance Manager, IDS Scheer offers a software solution that is purpose-built for controlling and analyzing business processes. As part of this solution, a patented procedure is used to collect process-relevant data from the operational IT systems, reconstruct process automatically and calculate key performance indicators for these processes. An extensive list of options for analyzing the key performance indicators online and particularly for presenting the actual process measurements in the form of event-driven process chains (eEPC) place the system in a class of its own.

2.1   Visualizing the Real Process Structure

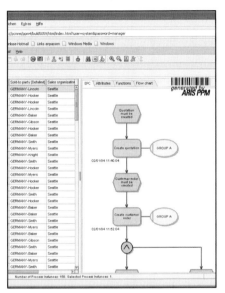

Fig. 1: EPC visualization of a process instance

Process analysis using ARIS PPM is based on "process instances", i.e. the individual, concrete operations that belong to a process type, e.g. order processing, purchasing or maintenance. The chronological-logical sequence of each individual process instance can be displayed graphically in the form of an event-driven process chain. The EPC representation has now become established as the industry standard for mapping business processes, and is very easy for users to understand. Unlike the design components of the ARIS product family, with which processes can be modeled by the users themselves, the process chains and their graphical presentation are automatically generated by ARIS PPM are the data has been imported from the operational system.

The corresponding EPC is created for each individual business transaction and supplied with the appropriate instance information (i.e. dimensions such as customer, times of execution, executing person, region, etc.). Since these models are generated dynamically, the process structure may appear differently for each individual instance, depending on the sequence of activities that have actually taken place. In particular, parallel processing operations and processing loops provide important clues regarding potential optimizations. With this presentation, the precise workflow sequence and structure of the business transaction can be recorded very quickly. Deviations from the target model can be identified.

An especially interesting analysis option is obtained when several of these actual workflow sequences are combined and visualized as an EPC model. This "compressed EPC" represents the average behavior of the underlying process instances that have actually been passed through. To do this, the selected process instance models are virtually "superimposed" on each other (see Fig. 2). During compression, all the objects and connections of the selected process instances are incorporated in the compressed EPC. Objects (e.g. functions, organizational units, events) and connections that fulfill specified equivalence criteria are combined to form one object or connection. The logical workflow sequence is retained by incorporating connectors ("AND", "OR", and "XOR" branches) in the process workflow sequence.

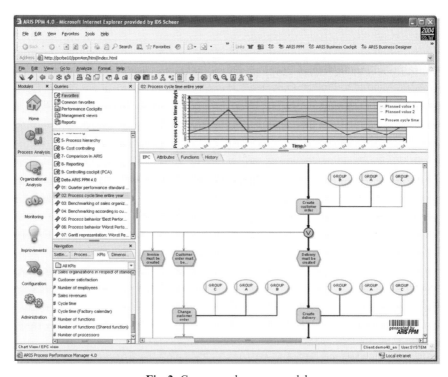

Fig. 2: Compressed process model

This visualization of the compressed model is highly suitable for performing a structural analysis of the process, because it clearly shows the user which are the most important paths and activities in the process. The probabilities of various paths are expressed graphically by different connection thicknesses. This enables various behavior patterns in business processes to be evaluated and structural differences to be analyzed. For example, the user can thus test whether optimization measures affect the main path, or whether secondary paths that are traversed less frequently are disruptive and should be eliminated.

The compressed process model thus represents an actual model, which can be compared to a target model (modeled with ARIS components wherever possible) to determine structural differences (see Fig. 3): Paths in the target model are not passed through in reality, probabilities differ from expectations, activities must be passed through several times, unplanned organizational interruptions occur during processing because several organizational units are involved, etc.

This information serves as the reference point for continuous optimization of the process.

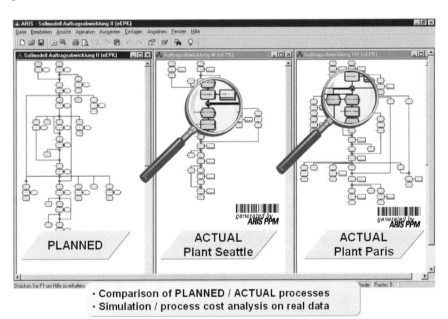

Fig. 3: Comparison of a target model with actual models

2.2   Key Performance Indicators and Analyses

Process visualization in the form of aggregated process chains is a primary aid to explaining and correcting structural disruptions and bottlenecks. Anything that is considered to be a "bottleneck" or "disruption" in a process is expressed in the corresponding key performance indicators, e.g. unsatisfactory "delivery relia-bility". Key performance indicators thus serve to *reveal* weak points in the huge number of individual business transactions, while the EPC presentation serves to *explain* the weak points.

In general, *key performance indicator* is understood to mean the interpretation of a numerical value that is returned by a key performance indicator definition under specified framework conditions. Let us consider the example of a "Process run-time for purchasing processes in August 2004" key performance indicator that has the value "5 days". The key performance indicator definition should be understood as a key performance indicator for the purposes of ARIS PPM, in this instance for example "process runtime". Limiting the range to "Purchasing processes in August 2004" serves as a filter for a "dimension". A dimension is a process-relevant var-iable that is used for catagorizing processes. In the example described, the "point in time" (= August 2004) and the "process type" (= Purchasing process) are di-mensions.

Straight way, a comparison of the key performance indicator value (5 days) with a reference value reveals a weak point. Reference values can be plan values, the previous year's figures, or even key performance indicators from comparable processes (e.g. benchmarking between different sales organizations, plants, regions).

The "Process runtime" key performance indicator can be calculated for each individual business transaction (process instance). There is a whole range of generally applicable key performance indicators which can provide useful information for each process type, such as throughput times, processing times, frequencies and the number of employees involved. Besides these, key performance indicators are needed that are only meaningful for certain process types, or which are based on given structures in the process sequence. For example, very frequent use is made of key performance indicators that measure the time period between two given activities in the process (time period key performance indicators). Another example would be delivery reliability key performance indicators, which evaluate whether a specified activity is completed by a desired point in time. These key performance indicators vary from one usage scenario to the next and must be defined specifically.

ARIS PPM therefore has a flexible rules mechanism which enables key performance indicators to be defined without any need for programming (see Fig. 4). All key performance indicators are calculation from information that is present on the process instance. A calculation rule defines which attribute values are to be used and how the various values are to be related to each other via operators. As well as providing simple arithmetical links, these operators enable complex condition checks. The user creates the rules mechanism with a graphic editor, which hides much of the complexity of the calculation rules.

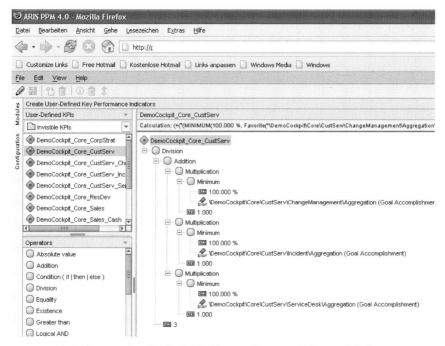

Fig. 4: Example of an individual key performance indicator definition

Like the key performance indicators, dimension values can also be calculated with these rules so that the process instances can be classified. The key performance indicators and dimensions calculated in this way are saved in the database for each individual process instance. The consideration of the key performance indicator values for individual process instances is used in monitoring scenarios. For monitoring purposes, the user receives targeted alarms regarding critical conditions in the individual business transactions so that operational counter-measures can be instituted.

On the other hand, in overall process management a number of process instances of the same type is used. Here, it is desirable to reveal systematic errors. For this purpose, the key performance indicator values for a set of process instances are aggregated. The aggregation type is usually an averaged value (e.g. for time periods) or a cumulative value (e.g. for quantities, costs).

The aggregated key performance indicator values often need to be calculated in terms of new key performance indicators. In the example of the rate of returned goods, the ratio of goods returned to the total number of purchasing operations is calculated. Returns are often separate business processes. The "return rate" key performance indicator must then be calculated from the number of returns divided by the number of purchases, i.e. two aggregated key performance indicator values are calculated against each other. This subsequent reconciliation is enabled by ARIS PPM via "user-defined" key performance indicators, which the user can define directly in the user interface and which are then immediately available for use.

All the indicators that have been described up to now are based on data which is present directly on individual process instances. For a complete overview, however, some information that is not associated with individual workflow sequences is needed. For example, an evaluation of customer satisfaction is often conducted with a representative survey of a random sample. The number of people employed by the company is also independent of individual business transactions. Carrying out a complete evaluation of processes or the entire company also requires key performance indicators of this kind. In ARIS PPM, they can be saved as "instance-independent key performance indicators", which can be analyzed by the same methods as all other key performance indicators.

2.3   Documentation

To avoid misinterpretations or misunderstandings in the analysis, accurate documentation and descriptions of the key performance indicators and dimensions is essential. For this purpose, a description of how the key performance indicators are obtained is defined at the technical level. The corresponding measurement points can be modeled in a process chain, for example, using the description methods that apply throughout the ARIS product family.

Besides the modeled description, the end user can also access a brief description in layman's terms. In ARIS PPM, the user can view a description of the key performance indicator in a tooltip and can also refer to freely defined HTML documents with an explanation directly from the application.

2.4   Weak Point Analysis

It may seen, therefore that ARIS PPM is able to yield a large quantity of information (process structures, key performance indicators and dimension) that is essential for measuring and evaluating the company's performance. The user can start a simple analysis by querying a single key performance indicator. First results are shown in the speedometer diagram (see Fig. 5).

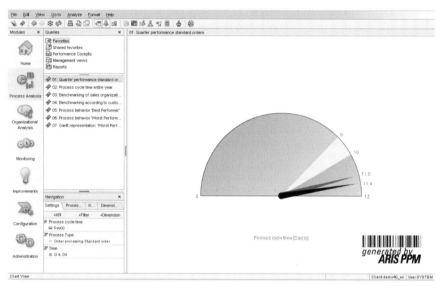

Fig. 5: Speedometer presentation

Here, the needle shows the process runtime as an average of a time interval. Comparison values (warning and alarm values) are also shown, so that the current value for the process runtime can be evaluated. Plan values can be set for each key performance indicator. From the simple average for a key performance indicator, the user can switch to the trend analysis by adding the Time dimension. Iteration is performed over the Time dimension, i.e. the time is plotted along the X axis of the diagram (in freely definable increments). With this display, the trend of the key performance indicator over a period of time can be reviewed, and noteworthy time intervals can be pinpointed (see Fig. 6).

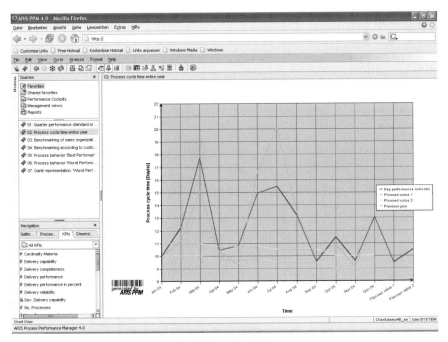

Fig. 6: Trend analysis

All key performance indicators depending on various dimensions can be visualized in the same way. Noteworthy deviations of the key performance indicators
for specific dimension values can also be identified.

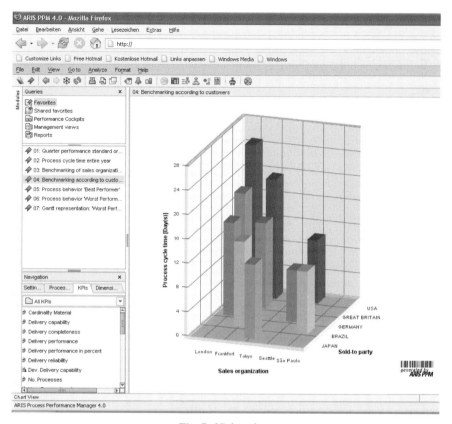

Fig. 7: 3D bar chart

The analyses can be represented with a number of different diagram types. For example, line diagrams lend themselves particularly well to indicating tendencies and trends. A 3D bar chart (see Fig. 7) presents combinations of the dimensions clearly for evaluation. Percentage distributions are often displayed with pie charts. In all cases, the mode of presentation is highly flexible and can be freely defined to provide the best possible conditioning of the information. It should also be noted that all data can also be presented in tabular form and exported to Excel.

2.5   Process Mining: Automated Weak Point Analysis

In practical use, 15-20 dimensions and a similar number of key performance indicators quickly become necessary. In order to be able to determine the significance of a key performance indicator for a dimension value here, the combination of each indicator with each dimension would have to be checked – a very time-consuming task if it is undertaken manually.

With the Process Mining feature in ARIS PPM, all such tasks can be automated. The system checks the combinations of key performance indicators and dimensions automatically and returns a list with the most significant noteworthy features. The "noteworthy feature" is determined from the maximum deviation of a key performance indicator value from an average in a given iteration step.

The chart on the right in Fig 8 shows the average process runtime for several facilities. Evidently, all values are fairly similar, the "noteworthy feature" or deviation width is correspondingly low at 4%. One may therefore draw the conclusion that different facilities have little or no effect on the key performance indicator - the dimension "Plant" is therefore not a noteworthy feature. Similarly, a dimension is noteworthy if it has a large fluctuation width (Fig. 8 left). The process runtime varies very considerably from one customer territory to another, which indicates that customer behavior also varies between territories.

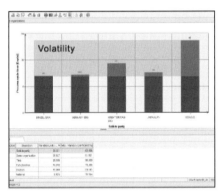 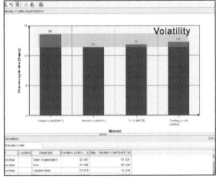

Fig. 8: ProcessMining by noteworthy features

ARIS PPM provides further support for analyzing the data with ABC analysis and Top-Flop displays. In a top-flow diagram, a specified number of "best" and "worst" values are presented (see Fig. 9). This enables best practices and optimization opportunities to be detected very quickly. The ABC analysis is a method for establishing priorities, separating the critical from the non-critical and determining the respective cost to benefit ratios in individual areas. For example, ABC analyses can be used to determine which products and services are the most important for a company's sales, who are the most important customers, or what efforts are having a financial effect. The objective of an ABC analysis is to direct the company's attention more actively towards the important areas and to identify starting points for targeted measures.

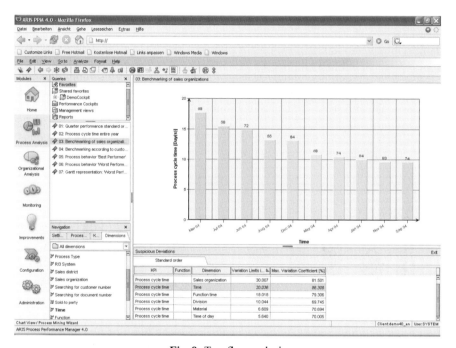

Fig. 9: Top-flop analysis

2.6   Management Views

Management-oriented views in ARIS PPM enable the occasional user to obtain a quick overview of the critical key performance indicators and the most important analyses. The content and conditioning can be configured individually without difficulty (see Fig. 10).

This display is particularly suitable for integration in a company portal, to provide a large group of recipients with access to current analysis results. A management view logs into the ARIS PPM server automatically, enabling further, interactive analysis to be started simply by clicking on one of the displays with the mouse.

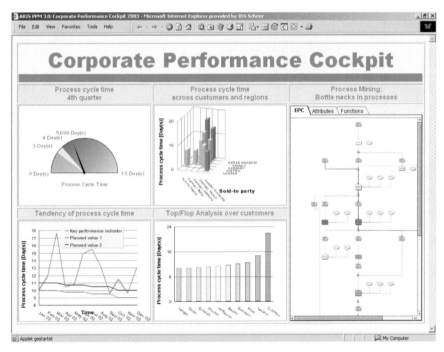

Fig. 10: Management view for quick overview of the most important analysis results

2.7   Offline Reports

Besides the online analysis described in the preceding, evaluations on paper are also needed for some user groups. For this purpose, reports can be defined that generate a PDF document, for example. Report generation can be automated on the server, so that daily or weekly reports are created automatically at specified intervals.

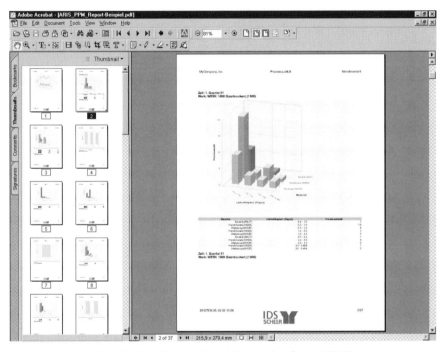

Fig. 11: Sample report in Adobe Acrobat format (PDF)

3   Technical Aspects

3.1   Process Generation

As has been explained, the calculation of key performance indicators requires data on individual process instances. A process instance contains information about the activities performed, the points in time when the activities were carried out, the processors in the process, and the structural sequence of the activities.

ARIS PPM uses the function, event, links, and organizational unit object types to map a process instance as an event-driven process chain. Unlike the static ARIS models, in ARIS PPM these object types represent measured operations at the instance level or an aggregated level (see Fig. 12).

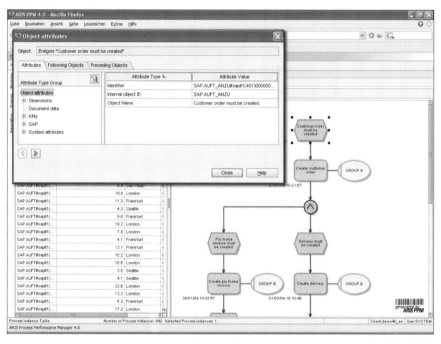

Fig. 12: Sample EPC from ARIS PPM

The information about process sequences must be extracted from the application systems that support the business processes operationally. Some process-based systems, for instance workflow systems, can then provide the workflow for a business transaction directly as an instance EPC. For these systems, ARIS PPM specifies an XML-based default import format. Each individual process instance is imported and stored in its entirety, and the configured key performance indicators are calculated.

However, in most application systems it is not possible to fully extract a complete process chain, because their operation is document or record-driven. But they often hold a change history for the documents. ERP systems are typical examples of such application systems. In these cases, then, a procedure is needed that can reconstruct the correct process sequences from an enormous number of individual items of information. ARIS PPM enables this by linking the occurrence of given event in the source system (e.g. creation of a new record) to a "process fragment". A process fragment represents a "mini-process" that consists of a function, a start event and an end event.

All additional information about the event that is stored in the application system is also exported, e.g. the date and reasons for a change, name of the creator, etc. The associated process fragments are instantiated while the events are being imported to ARIS PPM, i.e. the objects of the process fragment are supplied with real data and stored in the database. These process fragments, which are initially unconnected, are then combined with the aid of rules to form complete process instances or process chains. This operation is called merging and is a core functionality of the application (see Fig. 13).

In the first step of merging, all process fragment instances belonging to a given business transaction are collected. In many cases, this is facilitated by a unique identifier, which can be extracted from the application system for each system event. This may be an order number or a transaction number, for example. If one unique identifiier is to be used for all substeps, the directly preceding or following substep can also be identified. This mechanism enables a gradual compilation of all the process fragment instances.

At this point in the processing associated process fragments are found as the import progresses; but they are not yet linked to each other. There are a number of routines for placing the fragments in the correct order.

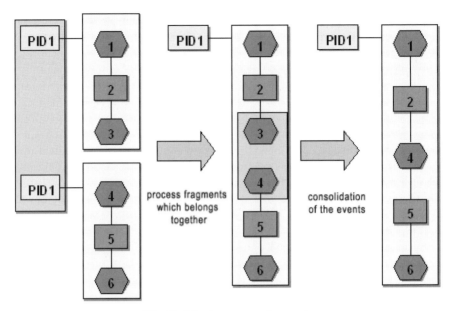

Fig. 13: Merging process fragments

The "sort merge" sorts the fragments according to a definable ordering criterion, e.g. the time of execution. The individual fragments are connected to each other via the events. The subsequent event in each case is deleted and the function is then connected directly to the preceding event of the subsequent function. In the key-based merge, on the other hand, more complex connection rules are possible. In principle, a rule is defined for the equivalency of events. The events can have attribute values just as functions do. For example, two events are considered to be identical if they have the same name in the same process instance. These identical events are consolidated, that is to say they are fused into a single event, the connection relationships to the functions are changed accordingly and another link is added to the process chain.

In real situations, not all fragments of a process instance will be included in an extraction operation. The mechanisms just described will also function if associated process instance fragments are imported into ARIS PPM at different times; this means that a process instance can continue to grow with the passing of time.

3.2   System Architecture

A system for continuous process measurement must be able to process and store extremely large volumes of data. For the simplest of processes, data on 10 or more measurement points is returned so that the system can generate a process instance. And the process instance data must be available for prolonged periods of time.

Depending on the process type, access and analysis capabilities are required for several months or even several years; as result, the number of process instances to be managed can quickly grow into the millions.

As a rule, various operational IT systems are integrated for returning data. These are often located in a computer center and their integration must satisfy certain security considerations. This is why an application like ARIS PPM is designed with a client-server architecture (see Fig. 14).

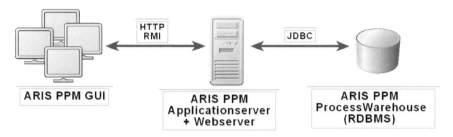

Fig. 14: Client-server architecture

ARIS PPM has a three-tier architecture consisting of the frontend, the server application, and the relational database. The frontend provides the functionalities that are needed for analyzing and navigating. This is the presentation layer for the process data that is supplied by the server application.

Queries are formulated in a special metalanguage by the frontend. During the analysis operation, the server application converts these queries into SQL retrieval queries for the database. The application server also provides the extended analysis functionalities such as Process Mining, ABC analysis etc. Both the frontend and the application server are programmed in Java, so they are largely platform-independent.

3.3   Scalability

As was explained previously, very large volumes of data can flow into the database. But the volume of data has direct implications for the performance of the system, during both the import and the analysis. To achieve acceptable times, the computing capability should be configured correspondingly, especially in the case of the database server. The scaling concept of the ARIS PPM enables the system to be expanded incrementally. According to this concept, the data can be distributed among several individual PPM systems or "subservers", each with its own database. The data is imported directly to these subservers, so the import operation can be carried out in parallel.

The user only needs to log into a master server, so he is completely unaware as to whether the data is held on one system or is shared among several (see Fig. 15).

The master server submits the analysis queries to all the subservers in parallel and consolidates the partial results as a total result, which is presented to the user.

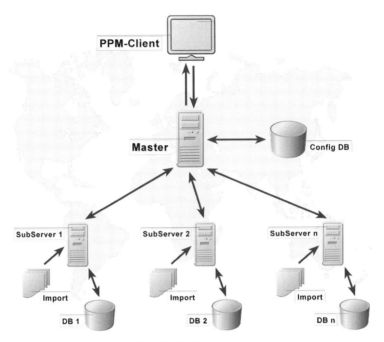

Fig. 15: Scaling concept

This scaling concept enables solutions to be implemented in which additional computers can be added incrementally as the volume of data grows, while significantly reducing the cost of the initial investment.

Successful Process and Performance Controlling in the Power Supply Industry by SÜWAG Energie

André Dreißen
IDS Scheer AG

Rainer Heinrichs
Süwag Energie AG

Summary

SÜWAG Energie AG took the decision to implement a program continuous process and system optimization of its business processes based on ARIS Process Performance Manager. The service processes at four different locations were selected for Performance Monitoring with a standardized, software-supported process controlling system. After just two months, the first substantiated analysis based on SAP IS-U were available, so that process improvement measures could be initiated.

Keywords

Quality key performance indicators, complaints quota, energy industry, SAP IS-U, process mining, implausible meter reading results, customer segments, disruption factor analysis, anomaly analyses, process controlling tool

1   Introduction

Süwag Energie AG is based in Frankfurt am Main and was founded in mid-2001 as the result of merger of four regional power supply companies. From the outset, the new company has been keenly aware of the new competitive landscape in the energy market, and today, in the electricity sector for example, it supplies energy to more than two million consumers.

The company was faced with the challenging of making the right strategic decisions to combine the differing corporate elements and cultures. At the same time, it was important to distill out a series of best practices and introduce them as standards in the company – without allowing the customer base to experience any loss of the quality they had come to expect.

Today, the business model has barely changed, but the company's structural and procedural organizations have both been completely redesigned. Corporate processes and IT were examined from the points of view of cost savings, flexibility and future-proofing.

2   Redesign of Processes and IT

In order to standardize the hitherto highly heterogeneous IT landscape, it was decided to expand the existing ERP platform (SAP R/3) as part of a new IT strategy. In the design phase, a business process model was developed around the SAP solution for the energy supply industry, SAP IS-U (Industry Solution Utilities), which covers many of Süwag Energie AG's core processes, from customer contact to meter reading, billing, device management, accounting, and supply management.

As part of the implementation of the new IT strategy – in addition to various support systems – the eight billing systems that had been used by the four former companies (one each for standard and special contract consumers) were replaced with SAP IS-U, CRM, EDM (Energy Data Management) and BW (Business Warehouse) in a project that lasted two years.

The most important consideration when introducing the new IT architecture was to ensure efficient mapping of corporate workflows. Because Süwag employees are based at four different regional sites, standardized processes are particularly important for interdepartmental cooperation and to ensure a uniform public face.

All phases of setting up the new company were guided by a professional process management system, which divides the lifecycle of a business process into three phases:

- Process design

- Process implementation

- Process controlling

In this context, the development or refinement of a business process is to be viewed as a closed loop: If needs to adapt the current corporate workflows (organizational change requirements, optimization potential, etc.) are identified as part of the process controlling program, procedures for redesigning and implementing the changed workflow are triggered directly afterwards. Following on from that, particularly the structure and implementation of the process controlling program at Süwag Energie AG are analyzed in detail.

2.1 Process Controlling as a Means to Protect Investments

Introducing a highly-integrated IT infrastructure that enables both departmental and company-wide processes to be executed efficiently is often a highly complex undertaking, associated with considerable costs. In many cases, the company's expectations of new IT systems are disappointed despite the high cost in terms of money and work. The main reasons for this are:

- the specifications from the process design phase are not implemented consistently

- the overall view is lost in the implementation phase and optimization is carried out in an unbalanced manner from the point of view of one area

- insufficient account is taken of the fact that the system is dynamic and continues to evolve

- the integration of the new software in the existing IT landscape is only partly successful (e.g. because of its complexity or interface problems)

- the decisions made in the design phase are not checked or reviewed.

Accordingly, it is important and wise to protect this investment. This includes a critical examination of the objectives of a larger conversion process - even after the software has been installed. One common management error is to concentrate on planning up until the new software becomes operational (including a brief phase of operational guidance by the project team). Then the project team "returns to the ranks", the successful project director is assigned new tasks, future change requests are managed via a contact person in IT – continuous monitoring of the application and processes is neglected.

The negative scenario: In future, the software solution is modified in the areas of responsibility of the individual technical departments, more or less necessary additional developments are integrated, modules that are not needed are not removed, a whole range of new reports is developed. For processes that were once lean and standardized, variants are created for different sectors, customer segments, products, locations, etc.

The result: Process and system performance are compromised. The level of dissatisfaction among users rises. Within a few years, the first reengineering project is begun. In the worst case, this results in a new, expensive software solution.

The long-term success of any process and IT landscape is based on three major factors:

- The ability of the defined processes and selected IT solution to continue to operate in the future
- The transfer of the project organization for an implementation project to the structural organization of the company
- Continuous, active review of the workflows and IT

Modifications to processes are being made constantly in the daily business of a company: A planned process (target design) seldom matches the process as it is introduced, and this in turn is not the same as the process that is actually running every day. To actively control the form of the process and to protect the investment in process and IT architecture, Süwag Energie AG introduced a modern process controlling program.

The advantages are obvious: After its employees, a company's business processes are the most important decision-making criteria on the market. Process controlling is a continuous procedure; regular discussion of their own processes by employees promotes the culture of process optimization in the company. Besides, evolutionary changes in small increments have a much better chance of being accepted in the organization than revolutionary reengineering projects, whose success is further threatened by political and budgeting resistance.

3   Process Controlling at Süwag Energie AG

3.1   The Objectives of Process Controlling

Besides the overriding objective of investment protection described previously, process controlling is used at Süwag to pursue a number of specific subordinate objectives, as illustrated in Fig. 1.

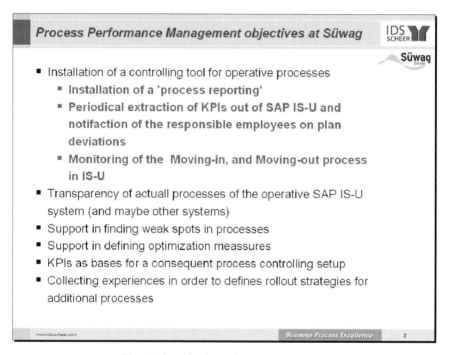

Fig. 1: The objectives of process controlling

Controlling is viewed as a continuous corporate task, in which a standardized control system ensures transparency by regular process reporting. Transparency is also assured in the sense that the paper trail of the process performance in daily business transactions can be verified or disproven with substantiated analytical data in the technical departments. The analysis tool ARIS PPM (Process Performance Manager) was introduced as the platform for continuous process and system optimization.

Since most midsize and large energy suppliers in Germany now use SAP IS-U, and this suite has established itself as the de facto industry standard, the analysis capabilities of ARIS PPM have been tailored specifically to the situation in energy supply industry. We were therefore able to build a software-supported process controlling system in a short period of time.

3.2   Project Content

With the introduction of SAP IS-U, particularly the customer-related processes at Süwag Energie AG were completely restructured. Because of the large number and multiplicity of processes, and their direct effect on the perception of the company from the outside, the Customer Service department was chosen as the department for introduction of the process controlling pilot project. Süwag customer service employees work on the various customer segments (Private and Commercial Customers, Industrial, Retail & Services, and Public Sector) at four different locations. Processes that are essential for carrying out business on a day-to-day basis are supported in SAP IS-U by a central user interface (the SAP CRM Customer Interaction Center).

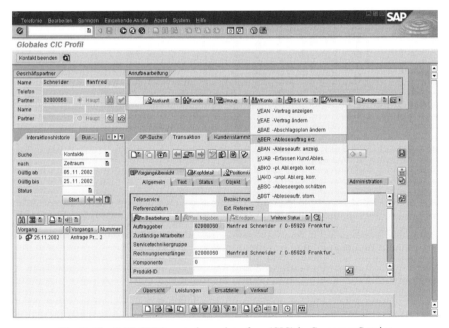

Fig. 2: The SAP CRM central user interface (CIC) in Customer Service
(German version)

Information relating to customers such as addresses, current supply contracts, open invoices, complaints etc, can be displayed very easily.

Customer-related processes such as contract modifications, moves, changes to banking data or bill checking, can be carried out as needed. When ARIS PPM had been installed, the wide variety of single transactions were merged in SAP IS-U to obtain complete and comparable workflows, prepared for graphical display and made available for analysis.

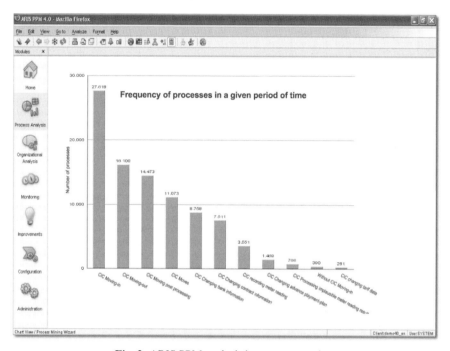

Fig. 3: ARIS PPM analysis by process numbers

Here, ARIS PPM functions as a stand-alone software package – with no effect on the performance of the operational SAP system that represents the direct contact with the customer. In the design phase of the project, the processes selected for performance monitoring included these high-volume processes:

- Moves
    - Moving in
    - Moving out
    - Moving post-processing
- Changing bank information
- Changing contract account

- Recording meter reading
- Changing advance payment plan
- Processing implausible meter reading result
- Changing tariff data

Fig. 4 shows an individual evaluation of the process data analyzed in the ARIS PPM user interface – in this case the frequency of processes in a given period of time.

4   Examples of Use

Following the launch of the pilot project in the Customer Service department, ARIS PPM was installed and key performance indicators were defined. The success of this kind of process controlling is decided in large part by two factors:

- complete and accurate evaluation of data
- integration of the process controlling task in the organization

With this in mind, all the data and key performance indicators that had been gathered were tested in the project team and also validated by the technical department. After just two months, the project team was able to provide the first substantiated evaluations based on SAP IS-U. The quality of the data and the results of these first evaluations were so promising that it was possible to release the application for operational use with a few adjustments. Indications of non-optimal use of SAP transactions (e.g. Move in/Move out) meant that the first process improvement measures could be instituted in very short order.

It was also revealed that some processes are associated with high post-processing effort. Based on these findings, further evaluations can now be made to determine and correct the reasons for the post-processing needs.

Moreover, regional differences were identified and used in the definition of best practices to improve the average process performance of the entire company.

To simplify process controlling, adapted evaluations were developed for the various target groups. The target groups for process controlling (management board, divisional management, process managers) can receive canned reports either in hardcopy or electronically via the intranet (HTML format) and email (PDF format) as necessary. Direct access to ARIS PPM with a browser is possible from any workstation, provided the user is logged in with the corresponding, user-specific authorizations.

ARIS PPM has been measuring customer service processes successfully since early 2004. And now for the first time, substantiated and documented analyses can be received regularly and automatically from the core IT systems without any additional effort.

By setting up role-specific information views (called Management Cockpits) the pertinent data can be combined in such a way that the respective process controller can call up an overview of the entire area for which he or she is responsible with a click of the mouse. If the predefined parameters such as process quantity and throughput time, or the quality key performance indicators such as error rate and complaints quota within the desired tolerances, the manager can be assured that performance in this area is satisfactory. If individual values fall below the benchmark, a value – depending on the significance of the key performance indicator for that division of the company – can be observed more closely, or a more thorough analysis can be carried out directly (Process Mining). Fig. 4 shows a jump from the Management Cockpit used by the head of the Süwag front office.

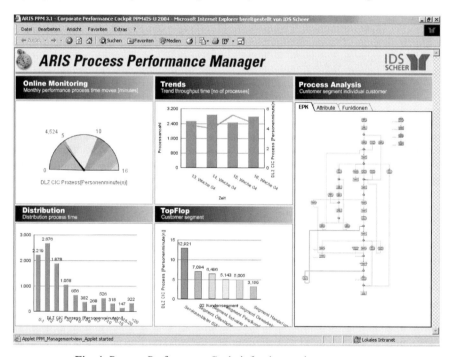

Fig. 4: Process Performance Cockpit for the moving core process

The moving core process was selected from manager's entire area of responsibility. Five different aspects of the business process are combined in a standardized way in this display. The head of the front office is informed about:

- the average process throughput time for all moves (monthly view)

- the trend by number of processes and throughput time (weekly view)

- the distribution of the individual processes and their throughput times

- the distribution of throughput times by individual customer segments

- the actual progress of the the moves in SAP IS-U

All graphical displays are generated automatically by the Performance Management software, so that the user can concentrate exclusively on analyzing the data. The display of the system process workflow (on the right in Fig. 4) is particularly noteworthy.

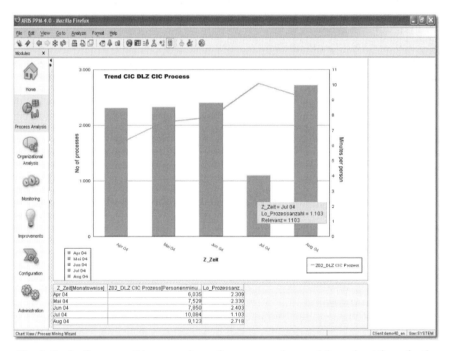

Fig. 5: Evaluation – monthly comparison of process numbers and throughput times for the moving core process

The target workflows developed in the design phase can very easily be compared with process shown here, as it is actually running in SAP. It can be particularly interesting to superimpose all the occurrences of a business process for a given analysis period, as has been done here. This shows the individual variants of the processes particularly clearly. It often shows that a process is not executed as "cleanly" as was envisioned in the blueprint, but possesses considerably more variants or is delayed by more loops or unnecessary wait times than was anticipated.

If the development of certain aspects of a process is categorized as critical, a disruption factor analysis is triggered. The extreme versatility of the tool we are using enables the various views of the process under consideration to be displayed in more detail simply by marking them.

A concrete example of a process analysis is shown in Fig. 5. Here, the process number graph (bar) and the process throughput times graph (curve) for the Moving process are compared with each other by month. Besides the clear fall in the number of moves in July (due to vacation time) the initial processing time for Moving as shown here rose significantly, from 6 minutes in April to 9 minutes in August. This value also peaked at 10 minutes in July. Because of the frequency of this high-volume process (generally > 2000 moves per month) and the fact that its performance has worsened by about 50% is would seem that a more thorough analysis of this point is merited. This analysis does not always lead automatically to optimization measures, since the figures returned may be singular events or due to seasonal influences.

Conclusion and Forecast for the Future

Based on our experiences to date, the task of process controlling should not be restricted to a central unit (except for interdepartmental control), it should be embedded in the respective technical areas. On the one hand, those affected will then be directly involved, and on the other, the analysis will be simplified because the substantive technical expertise will be immediately available.

Following our initial positive experiences with Process Controlling, we have instituted a coaching and know-how transfer program, led by the technical consultants of IDS Scheer. In the medium term, the employees of Süwag will refine processes and the apparatus for controlling them independently. As a result, the task of process controlling will be appended to the job description for department heads and process managers.

At Süwag, this new task will also be integrated in the existing meeting structure. In future, managers will be required to report on compliance with key performance indicators/benchmarks at the divisional level every 4-6 weeks. Measures for optimizing the processes will be defined and controlled based on the results of the anomaly analyses. Urgent process adaptations will be implemented in parallel with and independently of these measures.

ARIS PPM is a highly suitable process controlling tool in this context. For all the automated data conditioning and the high degree of user support, there should be no mistake but that the success of process controlling is thanks to the employees who make draw the correct conclusions from the data they receive.

No Business Intelligence Without Process Intelligence

Helmut Kruppke
IDS Scheer AG

Tino Bauer
IDS Scheer AG

Summary

More and more companies are asking themselves how they can gain demonstrable, measurable benefits from innovations in communications and IT technology. By providing information that can be used as the basis for decisions, Business Intelligence serves as the means. At the moment though, the major hurdle is that the information needs to be structured before it can be used. This can only be achieved by management-instituted measures to bring about an improvement in the way services in the company are performed. These service performance processes must be designed in such a way, taking into account the internal and external information base in the company, that the service (process output) results in an improved competitive position for the company. The link between Business Intelligence (information supply function) and the competitive service performance processes is the management cycle. This cycle ensures that the available information is transformed into targetted measures. It further guarantees that the implementation of these measures also brings about more competitive service performance processes via the control and monitoring of target achievement.

Keywords

Business Intelligence, controlling, business process management, business process optimization, management process, management cycle

1   The Challenge: Use Information Deliberately to Raise Operational Performance!

Information management is not just an operational task, it has now become a strategic tool in setting the company apart from its competitors. The rising level of electronic support for operational business processes by IT means that the company can draw on more and more data. As a consequence, pertinent information is becoming more and more important for generating knowledge. Meanwhile, many corporate decision makers are drowning in data and starving for information.[1] They have data cemeteries, but no information on which to base their decisions, or to institute an effective decision-making process. When considering the benefit that flows into the company routine from the existing data stock, the objective observer is often prompted to wonder about the way of doing business: "Business as usual or Business Intelligence?"[2] In order to generate information from unstuctured data, companies are turning more and more to Business Intelligence systems as planning and control tools. But the derivation of concrete measures leading to a measurable improvement in the company's profitability often does not happen. In order to make this step, the information obtained must be transformed in the respective phases of the decision-making and control process – referred to in the following as the management cycle – into measures that will remain effective for the long term.[3] The fact that this transformation often does not take place is usually due to two reasons:

1. Nowadays, decision-relevant information is often stored in different locations, so its results have to be combined in Excel spreadsheets. This impedes consistent access to information for the analysis of cause-and-effect relationships between strategic target variables and operational performance processes.

2. Either the available information is not processed further to obtain targetted measures with an optimized cost-benefit ratio, or defined measures "drain into the sand" because there is no institutionalized control of their implementation to ensure a continuous Target-Actual deviation analysis.

---

[1] Gentsch, 2000.

[2] Grothe, Gentsch, 2000, P. 10.

[3] See Wild, 1982, P. 37.

The current "second" Business Intelligence wave represents an attempt to counter the first cause. Unlike the first, primarily technology-oriented wave, this new wave places "Business" firmly in its focus. And with the objective of achieving measurable improvements in the factors that contribute to competitiveness.[4] This approach will be presented in the following chapter 2. To combat the second cause, company decision makers must first define objectives from the "right" information and then derive measures for achieving those objectives. One way to transform the information advantage thus gained into measurable, sustained improvement in the performance of business processes is explained in chapter 3. Finally, the solution approach is illustrated in a concrete, real-life example in chapter 4, then future development possibilities in the company's operational life will be examined in the conclusion in the last chapter.

2   Business Intelligence as a Basis for Providing Targetted Information

The start of the Business Intelligence movement was represented by the technological opportunities that arose from the Data Warehouse systems. These provided the necessary conditions for a standardized, company-wide information base for evaluation and analysis purposes, despite the various, differing source systems in the company. But as its name suggests, a Data Warehouse is just a "storage facility" for consistent information. This is associated with the following problems:[5]

1. Transferring data from the operational systems to a Data Warehouse is extremely labor-intensive and rigid. Any significant organizational change usually means that the interfaces to the Data Warehouse have to be reconfigured.

2. The available analysis methods are not capable of handling the enormous volumes of information that will be available in the future. Most importantly, the procedures to enable comparisons if changes are made to the product, customer or organizational structures are not in place.

3. The user interfaces in Data Warehouse systems can usually only be used by specialists. However, these are not usually the same people as the decision makers who actually need the information.

4. Methods for "matching" the operational information from the business processes of a company with the strategic targets are not available. It is thus not possible to make a success comparison.

---

[4] See Scheer 2004, P. 12.
[5] See Kieninger/ Mayer, 2002, P. 234f.

Business Intelligence is intended to make up for the shortcomings of classic Data Warehouse systems. "Business Intelligence" (BI) refers to the analytical process, that transforms – fragmented – company and competitors' data into action-oriented knowledge about skills, positions, activities and objectives of the internal or external spheres of activity (actors and processes) under consideration."[6] In order to ensure the required, consistent supply of information, the Business Intelligence approach of the future must meet the following requirements:[7]

1. Preconfigured, powerful analysis models capable of handling very large data volumes

2. Central information models (point of reference)

3. Central methods which are also used in the operational systems (plausibility checks etc.)

4. Configurable generators for transferring data from legacy systems

5. Powerful, customized user interfaces.

Constantly changing data as well as changes to the environment and surroundings mean that flexible analytical approaches are essential. This necessary adaptation is enabled by the Business Intelligence process. Three phases must be passed through so that knowledge can be distilled from base data by identifying associations and relationships:[8]

1. Provision of structured, unstructured or qualitative and/or quantitative base data

2. Identification of correlations and relationships with or without a hypothesis

3. Communication of the conditioned results to the corresponding decision makers.

By expanding the object of analysis, the use of Business Intelligence places much higher demands on the managerial qualification of the users. Without excellent methodological knowledge, Business Intelligence solutions cannot be implemented to any good effect.[9] The Business Intelligence approach consists of the following central modules:[10]

1. Multidimensional models (e.g. data cubes made up of sales regions, customer segments, product groups and time sequences) are suitable for mapping structured, quantitative data. A list-oriented data analysis

---

[6] Grothe/ Gensch, 2000, P. 19.

[7] See Kieninger/ Mayer, 2002, P. 235.

[8] See Grothe/ Gentsch, 2000, P. 19ff.

[9] See Klieninger/ Mayer, 2002, P. 234f.

[10] See Grothe, 1999, P.7.

method does not reflect reality, nor does it serve an explorative analytical procedure.

2. Expansion of the influence factors is served best by the most comprehensive treatment perspectives possible.

3. It is possible to avoid being overwhelmed with data by focussing on the respective core questions and analyses of the areas under consideration. Each core analysis must establish a connection between key performance indicators that are important for the bottom line and execution processes. This enables you to advance rapidly to the causes of possible "anomalies". Analysis time is reduced, even as the quality of the analysis gets better.

Use of new technologies improves the controlling and optimization of all business processes that are relevant for a company. Because "Information alone does not equip a person to act."[11] Information systems must be assessed primarily according to whether and how they affect the behavior of people.[12] In and of itself, an information system does not provide any benefit. Often, an informational competitive advantage mechanism is assumed implicitly in company practise. In order to be able to actually convert the consistent supply of information to a raised level of corporate performance, this information must be used in a directed manner so that business processes are also improved deliberately as operational drivers of company performance. Accordingly, one can only really talk about "information conduct performance" if the information supply system is directed at providing the correct information in each phase of the decision making and control process.

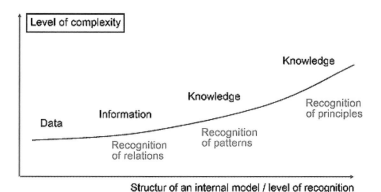

Fig. 1: Complexity reduction – Evaluation of data[13]

---

[11] Gabriel, Dittmar, 2001, P.19.

[12] See Weber, 2002, P. 97.

[13] See Grothe, 1999, P. 3.

Management decisions must be made in the face of constantly changing conditions. Expanding the scope of consideration and the accompanying complexity of the decision situation means that new controlling instruments and methods must be used so that optimization potential can be identified quickly and objectively.[14] As a result, the role of the decision making process is becoming more and more critical in implementing defined strategies. Optimization decisions can no longer be made centrally by individual departments on the basis of static, canned information from standard information systems. Too much important, decentralized information from the technical departments would be ignored. But this integration inevitably leads to a greater degree of complexity. In order for the decision makers to be able to process this plethora of information for the purpose of achieving their objective, the decision making process must be supported by information technology. This is the only way to prevent important criteria from being neglected due to "information overload" or too much attention being paid to minor problems.[15]

Handling this task properly requires purpose-built tools and methods, so that potential can be identified and isolated even in a complex decision making environment. To this end, IDS Scheer has developed an approach that provides methodological and technical aids for decision making. Substantiated results or optimiza-tion potential and the measures required to achieve them can be developed in the consideration of end-to-end processes, not centrally and top-down. For this, key players have to be integrated. It is evident that the information supply function of Business Intelligence must be seen as a precondition for an objective-oriented decision making and control process. The results of this management cycle are business processes that are aligned optimally with corporate objectives.[16] The next chapter will deal in more detail with the interplay between Business Intelligence, the management cycle and business process optimization.

---

[14] Even in the company-wide consideration of the order processing process, complexity increases because of the many departments involved.

[15] For an approach regarding objectivity failures that occur in the decision making process and which task areas and the reference points for controlling it yields, see Otto 2003, Pp. 52 to 85.

[16] Ultimately from this design of business processes, it is possible to derive configuration options for the structural organization, IT support and staff development.

3 Directed Optimization of Business Processes with Business Intelligence

With the support of technological development, Business Intelligence offers the capability to supply all management processes with the decisive information. The result is a technologically sophisticated and networked method of decision making and corporate control (Information Supply Chain).[17] This Information Supply Chain supports the entire management cycle, from strategy development and the corresponding derivation of objectives to the analysis, setup and evaluation of alternatives, all the way through to monitoring the defined measures. A range of tools are available in the individual phases of the management cycle, including data and process mining, agent-supported analyses and automated target-actual comparisons. The management cycle enables corporate objectives to be realized by the directed design of business processes and objective achievement to be monitored continuously.

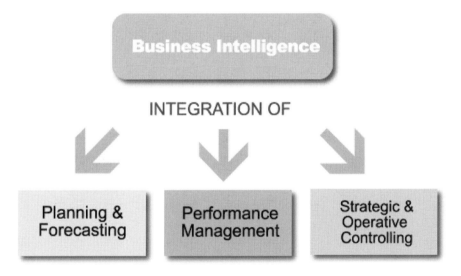

Fig. 2: Global Business Intelligence approach[18]

---

[17] See Alff, Bungert 2004, P. 157.
[18] See Alff, Bunger, 2004, P. 157.

Phases of the Management Cycle

The management literature includes a wide range of phase models to describe the management cycle. In the abstract, it is possible to talk of the following phases: planning and decision making, and implementation control. In general, planning is understood to be "a systematic, future-oriented examination and definition of objectives, measures, means and routes to achieve an intended objective.[19] Besides the design of the executing processes, this also includes the breakdown of objectives and the assignment of responsibilities. The purpose of planning is to design company activities and processes with the aid of specific information and using special tools. In such a way that corporate processes are aligned with the achievement of company objectives taking into account changes in the environment and surroundings (see chapter 2). Implementation control then includes all the activities that are necessary for implementing the measures defined in planning. In the next step, the results of realization are compared with the objectives defined initially. This check yields new knowledge for the next management cycle. The ongoing realization check enables control results to be fed back into the current management cycle.[20]

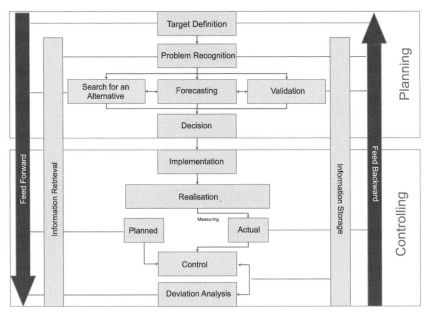

Fig. 3: Management Cycle (according to Wild 1982, P. 37)

---

[19] See Wild, 1974, P. 13.
[20] See Weber, 2002, P. 32f.

3.1.1 Information Requirements in the Phases of the Management Cycle

Different information needs arise for each phase of the management cycle: In the planning phase – from objective definition to realization of the decision – decision makers must be supported by interactive control systems. Interactive control systems are at the heart of the organizational awareness, so that decision makers pay constant attention to them. In this way, the awareness of Management is directed to the diagnostic part of the system, which is associated with a particularly high level of strategic uncertainty.[21] In the second part of the management cycle (control) – which deals with monitoring the implementation of the defined measures – diagnostic control systems are particularly important. These control systems provide Management with confidence without requiring constant attention.

Like a thermostat, ideally the system regulates itself with negative feedback loops and does not need to be attended to when it is running.[22] The task of Management is to define the execution and thus the business processes to be as efficient and effective as possible beforehand, as part of the planning phase. This requires a profound knowledge of the activities involved in the execution (business processes) and their conditions. This knowledge may be available in various forms: In the form of quantitative statements (figures), qualitative statements (technical and layman's terms), which is referred to as explicit knowledge, and in the form or non-verbal, implicit knowledge.[23] The purpose of the Business Intelligence approach is to supply the management cycle systematically with information. This means collecting, storing, processing and communicating the information that is needed in each phase.[24] In practice, it has been revealed that some of these phases are run through relatively often. For this reason the somewhat more abstract model, the Business Process Lifecycle, has proven useful and includes all the steps listed previously:

---

[21] See Simons, 1995, P.91ff.
[22] See Simons, 1995, P. 59ff.
[23] See Weber, 2002, P. 91f.
[24] See Weber, 2002, P. 93.

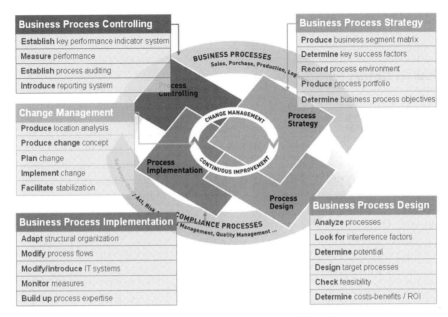

Fig. 4: IDS Scheer's Business Process Lifecycle

The next section will deal with each phase of the Business Process Lifecycle and the IT support for ensuring that all phase-specific information needs are met:

Process Strategy Phase

In this phase, the business sector-specific critical success factors (CSF) relative to the competition are identified from the corporate objectives and the market and resource situation. In conjunction with the business sector strategy, the business processes are determined from these critical success factors and are then used as operational drivers. The objective is to adapt the executed business processes in the company to changing economic framework conditions. This necessitates integrating realtime data in the planning processes. The basis for carrying out the planning are the business process objectives, which are derived from the business sector strategy. The primary considerations at this point are the customers' needs and the question of how they can be met.

To support this process as fully as possible with the appropriate information, the existing IT systems must be combined in a consistent platform. In many companies today, this concept is pitted against a situation of data islands, caused by IT landscapes created to serve individual departments. What is required is a portal as a "single point of access and contact".[25] The IT realization is made possible with a global Business Intelligence concept ensuring that all information

---

[25] See Alff, Bungert 2004, P. 157.

that is decisive for the management cycle is available from the distributed IT systems in a closed information flow.

Process Design Phase - Analysis

Since business processes are understood to be the operational drivers of a company's results, they always end in a measurable performance. This performance can be measured with respect to one or more process objectives. If a company wants to research the reasons for not achieving process objectives, the business processes that are responsible for creating this performance must inevitably be analyzed. Because this where the causes of the factors that disrupt the business process are to be found. Disruptive factors are higher-level weak points in a business process, which prevent a defined process objective from being achieved. The causes of disruptive factors may extend across several subprocesses or departments. Therefore, disruptive factors must always be described as relating to a complete end-to-end process. These causes must ultimately be eliminated specifically with measures that are optimized in terms of the cost-benefits ratio. In order to be able to make valid, reliable statements about the causes of a disruptive factor or the extent of its implications, process-related knowledge is essential before any action can be taken with regard to the cause.

In Process Performance Management, the efficiency, quality and financial viability of all pertinent business processes except the process instance level are measured continuously during ongoing operations, and the information thus obtained is made available for analytical purposes. This enables disruptive factors in the business processes to be detected and their effects to be evaluated and analyzed both qualitatively (location in the process) and quantitatively (additional commitment in terms of time or expense). Cause tracing is speeded up by a detailed analysis of the process with automated modeling of the actual process sequence on the basis of process-related information. This information is obtained from the company's own in-house IT systems using Process Performance Management solutions.[26] This is where the Business Intelligence modules described in chapter 2 - multidimensional models and agent-supported analysis methods – come into play. The it is possible to evaluate the disruptive factors with concrete costs by quantifying the effect caused. This in turn enables disruptive factors to be prioritized using an 80/20 analysis, so that attention can be focused on the important disruptive factors in an end-to-end business process.

---

[26] ARIS PPM reads all the business events to be investigated into a repository from one or more source systems via application-specific adapters. The process-relevant runtime information that is thus obtained on the activities performed is used to generate event-driven process chains (EPCs) automatically (see IDS Scheer White Paper, 2004, P. 24f.).

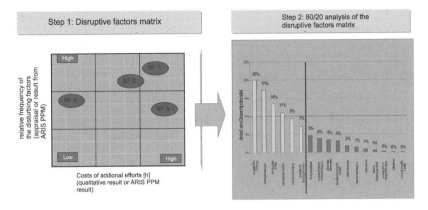

Fig. 5: Prioritization of disruptive factors according to the 80/20 rule

3.1.2   *Process Design Phase - Optimization*

Based on this, in the next step measures can be determined using creativity techniques to optimize the business processes affected. At the same time, the measures to combat the cause are developed to be as wide-ranging as possible. Measures to minimize the effects are only worked out when there are no more approach options here. The alternative measures can then be evaluated for their effect in eliminating a disruptive factor. The effort required to implement them must all be assessed.

In IT terms, this phase is supported with the evaluation of the optimum cost/benefit ratio in the selection of alternative measures. Them the selected measures can be refined and combined in bundles of measures. This enables refined implementation planning and a fairly exact estimate of the Return on Investment for each bundle of measures.[27] As a result, a reliable decision making basis for implementing the packages of measures is provided, as well as an implementation project plan for immediate adaptation of the business processes concerned.

---

[27] See Bauer, 2004, P. 226f.

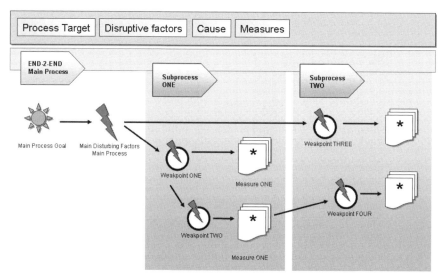

Fig. 6: Disruptive factor diagram for analysis and display of cause-and-effect relationships

Process Realization Phase

In the literature, realization of measures is considered to be an execution action, not a management action, and falls within the responsibility of the line managers.[28] But here too, important and challenging tasks such as physically changing and adapting the structural organization and process sequences, changing or introducing IT systems, implementing the defined KPIs in the system, building up process expertise among employees and all the elements of Change Management must be mastered. The realization phase and Change Management are each associated with their own constellations of tasks, which are beyond the scope of this article. At this point, then, the transition is made to implementation controlling of the measures.

Process Controlling Phase

The purpose of the Process Controlling Phase is continuous monitoring of the effectiveness of the measures implemented by means of a permanent process monitoring system. Whether the target objectives defined in the Process Strategy Phase are indeed achieved in the Process Realization Phase is monitored continuously by means of target-actual comparisons referring to the KPIs that have been set up. IT support enables the efficiency, quality and profitability of all pertinent value-creating business processes to be measured continuously. At the

---

[28] See Weber 2002, P. 32.

same time, in the event of deviations the causes can be tracked as far as the business process level at a glance. This it is ensured that both levels – the management level and the execution level – are controlled in coordination with each other.[29]

Supporting the management cycle with a Process Performance Management tool provides access to the following IT-related capabilities: [30]

1. Automated measuring and evaluation of the current process performance with plan-actual comparisons of the defined KPIs

2. Automatic notification in the event of deviations (management by exceptions)

3. Cause analysis with detailed process analysis and automated, tool-supported visualization of the actual process sequence by OLAP (Online Analytical Processing) and Mining methods

4. Compression of process instances that have actually been run to identify in-house best practices

5. Benchmarking with industry-typical reference data and reference processes.

Based on the principle of the management cycle as a control loop, the process design phase now follows again with analysis and optimization of the business processes using the information that has been gained.[31] In real-life operation, interaction between targeted information supply and business process optimization leads to significant improvements in operational capabilities, as will be explained in the following example.

---

[29] This is typically referred to in the literature as strategic and operational controlling (see Horvath, 2002, P. 254ff.).

[30] ARIS PPM enables the automated calculation of process key performance indicators, notification of deviations, trend analyses and cause analyses down to the detail process level (see IDS Scheer White Paper, 2004, P. 26ff.).

[31] If it is determined that the defined target objectives are impossible to realize, for example because they are not consistent with the company's own in-house capabilities, or the external framework conditions have changed, the objectives must be adapted with a target correction.

4   Approaches for Solutions to Increasing Operating Performance Capability with Business Intelligence in Practise

A SAP R/3 rollout did not lead to any increase in the efficiency of the order processing process. The result was often more work instead of simpler process sequences. What was called for was a solution approach that was capable of dealing with the enormous complexity of order processing at BASF AG: The company employees about 40,000 employees to fulfil not quite 1 million customer orders per year. The following functional areas are involved in the order processing process: Sales (inhouse/field sales), Materials Management Center, Filling/Production, Warehouse, Scheduling, Shipping/Transportation and Transport Providers. This alone may provide some idea of the complexity of the field under investigation. To tackle this complexity, IDS Scheer took over both the structuring of the management cycle phases in the course of the project and the supply of information to these phases with its proprietary Business Intelligence solution for the analysis, measurement, design and continuous controlling of corporate business processes.[32] Among other things, this included ensuring that the "correct" information was collected as the basis for decision making and the "correct" methods were used for processing this information.[33] In the next section, the case example will be presented with reference to the phases of the IDS Scheer Business Process Lifecycle:[34]

Process Strategy Phase

Besides a demonstrable increase in the efficient and effectiveness of the processes, the primary objective of the initiative was to ensure that company workflows were strictly aligned with internal and external customer requirements. In this context, delivery reliability was to be measurably improved in terms of delivery times, quantities, quality – for both long-term and 24-hour orders – and thereby lowering the complaints quota. However, overall order processing costs must also be cut at the same time. The following preconditions for the progress of the project formed the design guideline for realizing these objectives:

- Transparency in the order processing process must be preserved with regard to the individual activities. Moreover, efficiency, complexity, error rate and throughput speed must be rendered measurable with Key Performance Indicators (KPIs).

---

[32] See also Approach to rationale-oriented controlling at Weber 2002, P. 48ff.
[33] See Seuring/ Bauer 2003, P. 5f.
[34] See Bauer 2004, P.224ff.

- This transparency should then be used so that potential could be quantified and evaluated using internal and external benchmarks.

- Potential realization was then enhanced using measures that were optimized in terms of their cost/benefit ratio.

In the course of realization of these objectives, the following questions were then answered during the phases of the management cycle:[35]

- What disruptive factors prevent the interdepartmental workflow of the order processing process?[36]

- What costs are caused by these disruptive factors?

- What measures for realizing the optimization potential identified are suggested by the best cost/benefit ratio?

Process Design Phase – Analysis

Important disruptive factors in the order processing process were identified from a comprehensive, system-supported analysis. With propriatary Business Intelligence systems and ARIS Process Performance Manager, the interviewing effort could be reduced while at the same time increasing the validity and reliability of the results. In this phase, a calculation was made of the theoretical savings potential associated with the extra effort when the disruptive factor occurs. For this, the effects of the 30 disruptive factors were analyzed and quantified. Each disruptive factor was described with a Key Performance Indicator (KPI). These KPIs could be integrated in operational processes with the ARIS Process Performance Manager. ARIS PPM is an IT solution manufactured by IDS Scheer that enables decision-relevant information to be made available quickly and according to the situation. In this way, the additional effort that is associated with the occurrence of a disruptive factor could be quantified with an algorithm and evaluated in terms of cost and time. Since the development and implementation of measures consumes resources, only the most significant disruptive factors were pursued further.

These were the disruptive factors that were responsible for 80% of the theoretical total savings potential. For example, it was revealed that changes to the delivery date or delivery quantity that were received shortly before the scheduled shipment caused additional coordination effort totaling up to almost 2.5 hours. The top disruptive factors could then be investigated in more detail for their causes using ARIS PPM.

---

[35] See The management cycle according to Wild 1982, P. 37.

[36] All potentials identified in a screening phase are clustered and combined as disruptive factors (DF). DF are cost drivers in that they hinder the normal execution sequence of a business process. The resulting additional cost can be measured using the effects that appear after the DF has occurred. The sum of all disruptive factors yields the *theoretically* realizable savings potential.

For example, it was possible to analyze not only when delivery dates and delivery quantities had been changed shortly before shipment, but also how often and in what time period these changes were made. The source of the order to change and the administrator who made the change could also be identified. This made it possible to delimit the object of the investigation exactly and define a specific countermeasure.

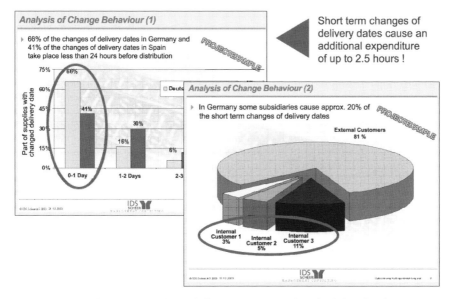

Fig. 7: Example of an analysis result from ARIS PPM: Short lead time for changes to delivery date and quantity and source of the order to change

Process Design Phase - Optimization

Remaining with the example of the order changes at short notice, the measures developed to counter this included the following: It was determined that the design of a special process "Change to customer order processing" would assure the flexibility required to remain competitive and still cut processing time. Both the organizational implementation with clear rules and responsibilities, and the computerized implementation so that the change process could be automated were defined in a measures plan.

Example

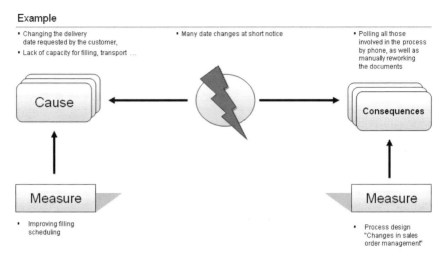

Fig. 8: Measures definition: Every disruptive factor is in a cause-and-effect relationship, which must be made transparent

The effects of these measures were predicted to be fewer manual processing steps and less communication effort. In the end, when the measure plan was implemented fully, well over 50% savings in processing effort for each short-notice order change was determined. The prioritized measures were presented to the steering committee inclusively as part of a business case.

Process Realization Phase

With this approach, BASF AG and IDS Scheer together defined measures that enabled about 65% of the costs caused by the disruptive factors to be saved. This was simply by concentrating on a few top disruptive factors and developing targetted measures to combat them. On the other hand, the costs of implementing the measures were just a good 10%. With the reduction method, it could be ensured that the resources were used specifically for eliminating core problems. This meant that the cost of the measures was significantly reduced. This design assured the highest possible rationality in the optimization of complex business processes. BASF now plans to apply the measures developed gradually to other business units.

Process Controlling Phase

Following the successful implementation of the project, BASF continues to use ARIS PPM so as to be able to monitor the effectiveness of measures subsequently using target-actual comparisons, identify any deviations and – if necessary – institute countermeasures as early as possible.[37]

5   Conclusion

As the example shows, targetted use of all the information available in a company unlocks access to considerable benefit potential. However, it is essential to carry out the analysis in a targeted manner, conduct a structured evaluation of the improvement potential, draw up a definition of highly effective measures that optimizes benefits, ensure continuous control of the implementation of measures for changed processes, and to put in place a permanent system of target-actual comparison of the effectiveness of the measures. Unfortunately, very few companies are tapping into this potential yet, although the methods and technologies required are available today. Companies that are able to align their business processes on the requirements of their environment and surroundings will not only gain a competitive advantage, they will also be able to manipulate this alignment better and faster than their competitors. The prequisites for this are the supply of decision-relevant information and the ability to transform this information quickly and effectively into sustained measures for the targeted alignment of business processes.

---

[37] See related discussion 2004, P. 30.

6   Literature

Alff, S./ Bungert, W. (2004): Business Intelligence; in: Scheer, A.W. (Ed.): Innovation durch Geschäftsprozessmanagement, P. 155-167

Bauer, T. (2004): So steigerte die BASF AG mit Supply Chain Controlling und – optimierung die Effektivität und Effizienz ihrer Auftragsabwicklung – schnell umsetzbar und toolgestützt; in: Scheer, A.W. (Ed.): Innovation durch Geschäftsprozessmanagement, P. 219-229

Gabriel, R./ Dittmar, C. (2001): Der Ansatz des Knowledge Managements im Rahmen des Business Intelligence; in: Business Intelligence, HMD 222, 12/2001

Gentsch, P. (2000): Wie aus Daten Wissen wird; aus der 20. Saarbrückener Arbeitstagung; www.sapinfo.net/goto/stra/1498/DE, last access: 27.05.2002

Grothe, M. (1999): Aufbau von Business Intelligence; www.competence-site.de/bisysteme.nsf/46392449EEAEF6FCC12569540059EB71, last access: 29.09.2004

Grothe, M./ Gentsch, P. (2000): Business Intelligence – Aus Informationen Wettbewerbsvorteile gewinnen, München.

Gentsch, P. (2002): Controlling, Stuttgart

IDS Scheer AG (2004): ARIS Controlling Plattform – Aris PPM – Aris Process Performance Manager, White Paper, September 2004, http://www.ids-scheer.com/germany/15097, last access: 29.09.2004

Klieninger, M./ Mayer, T.L. (2002): Informationssysteme für das Controlling der Zukunft; in: Gleich, R./ Möller, K./ Seidenschwarz, W./ Stoi, R. (2002): Controlling Fortschritte, Munich, P. 223-243

Related discussion (2004): Kein Process-Management ohne Monitoring; in Computer Woche, 31. Year, No. 27, July 2004, P. 30

Scheer, A.W. (2004): Intelligentes Business; in: technologie & management, Issue. 3-4, P. 12-14

Seuring, St./ Bauer, T. (2003): Information Needs in Supply Chain Decisions; in: Supply Chain Knowledge, Paper for SCM conference 2003 at Cranfield University, November 2003, www.sck2003.com

Simons, R. (1995): Levers of Control, Cambridge, Mass.

Weber, J. (2002): Einführung in das Controlling, Stuttgart

Weber, J. (1974): Grundlagen der Unternehmensplanung, Reinbeck b. Hamburg

Wild, J. (1982): Grundlagen der Unternehmensplanung, Vol 2., Reinbeck b. Hamburg

Monitoring with Key Performance Indicators at E.ON Bayern AG Sales Service

Robert Reif
E.ON Bayern AG

Andreas Kronz
IDS Scheer AG

Klaus Miksch
IDS Scheer AG

Summary

Within the space of just seven months E.ON Bayern AG implemented a Corporate Performance Management System based on ARIS PPM. The aim of the Sales Service project was to achieve holistic controlling of selected business processes using source data from SIEBEL CRM and SAP IS-U IT systems. The focus was on making business processes better and more directly controllable, generating more transparency in procedures and reliable automation of reporting. The results of this project contributed in various ways to the consistent identification of weak points and greater standardization of business processes, and provided significant support for the optimization of resource planning, deadlines and response times.

Keywords

Energy industry, SAP IS-U, Key Performance Indicator, automatic weak point analysis, Siebel CRM, XML dataflow, Business Process Management, throughput time, backlog analysis, ACTUAL processes, complaint processes, resource planning, response times, factual basis for discussions, insourcing system knowledge, warning values, frequency distribution

1.   The Need for the Project

1.1   The Company

With annual sales of more than EUR 46 billion and 66,000 employees, E.ON AG is the world's largest private energy service provider. With its two strong pillars electricity and gas, E.ON is clearly focused on energy business. Munich-based E.ON Energie AG is the largest private energy service provider company in Europe. It supplies some 21 million customers with electricity and gas.

As part of the merger of predecessor companies VEBA und VIAG to form E.ON AG, and also of PreussenElektra and Bayernwerk to form E.ON Energie AG and the parallel umbrella brand strategy adopted by the E.ON Group, the autumn of 2001 saw the start of the merger process for five regional Bavarian utilities. This led to the founding of E.ON Bayern AG as an E.ON Energie AG subsidiary in November 2001 (see Fig. 1), at which time a key performance indicator-based Process Monitoring System using ARIS PPM was successfully introduced.

E.On Bayern is part of the successful E.ON merger process

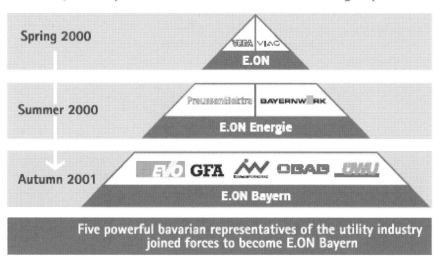

Fig. 1: E.ON AG merger process

E.ON Bayern is the largest regional utility in Germany. Its electricity sales amount to some 30 billion kilowatt hours (see Fig. 2). Within its territory, Regensburg-based E.ON Bayern serves approximately 2.2 million customers.

Electricity sales of German regional utilities
in billion kwh

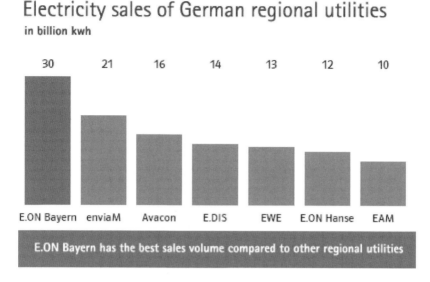

Fig. 2: Electricity sales of German regional utilities

E.ON Bayern is particularly active in the fields of distribution (medium and low-voltage grids) and sales. Sales are differentiated by commercial and industrial customers, local authorities, private customers, and redistributors. In both segments, 3,500 employees generated sales of EUR 2.6 billion in 2003, with a cumulative grid length of more than 175,000 km.

Company figures 2002

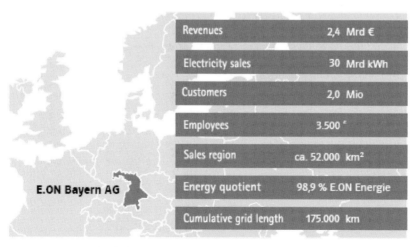

Fig. 3: Company figures E.ON Bayern AG (2002)

1.2   The Sales Service Mission

With some 2.0 million customers throughout Germany, the "Private Customer" segment is the largest customer group within E.ON Bayern and is supplied with professional and friendly service for all aspects of electricity, charges and billing by an in-house central sales organization, the "Sales Service".

At the beginning of electricity market deregulation, the sales service was restructured as a centrally managed organizational unit so as to achieve a uniform, central approach to customer support. Today, all private customers are supported from a total of four locations, differentiated by products under one disciplinary responsibility. Unlike with the former, decentralized regional approach to customer responsibility, this gives customers active in more than one region one central point of contact.

In order to provide logistical and methodical support for operative front-end units, horizontal functions that deal with common tasks such as quality management, process management, project coordination, order management, training, system support and IT coordination were bundled in Sales Service. Altogether, Sales Service has a headcount of about 580, making it one of the largest units in E.ON Bayern.

Sales Service is thus responsible for quality- and cost-optimized processing and support for E.ON Bayern's private customers (general pricing, product customers and employees' electricity) and also business and multi-site customers with annual settlement.

The large number of customers means that this is a typical mass consumer business. For example, the number of relocations alone amounts to some 200,000 p.a. In addition, there are some 4,400 telephone calls a day and approx. 3,500 items of mail from customers (letters, faxes, emails), at peak times this can rise to 8,000 items per day. A professional mail system geared for efficiency was set up to achieve fast mail turnover and near real-time processing times for customer issues.

As in Sales Service as a whole, benchmarking is carried out regularly at the company and process levels to increase transparency within and across the Group's regional utility companies. This permits a continuous improvement process that identifies and eliminates weak points in both structures and processes and enables units to learn from the best in class. The core element is continuous monitoring at the business process level, as established at E.ON Bayern with ARIS PPM.

1.3   Situation before Project Start

Over the past few years, the E.ON Bayern organization and the Sales Service have been consistently improved and optimized. About 3 years ago, a project initiative was launched to optimize corporate processes on the basis of a wide range of aspects, with quality- or cost-based goals being set for various projects. The outcome can be described as an "organized, future-proof, forward-looking and flexible" organization. Various challenges had to be overcome en route:

SAP IS-U and CRM Rollouts

Even before merging as E.ON Bayern, the five utilities had decided to migrate to SAP IS-U (R/3). Apart from one company, all had been using the R/2 version of IS-U. The fifth company had a proprietary system which was to be replaced. All five were subsidiaries of the former Bayernwerk, so while they did not immediately function "as one company" they did begin to pool their IT development work via Bayernwerk's IT subsidiary. This resulted in a joint IS-U migration plan which envisaged switching the individual predecessor systems to SAP IS-U (R/3) in 4 – 6 week intervals over a six-month period.

The SAP IS-U (R/3) rollout also led to major changes for the employees involved, especially the front-end units. Comprehensive training measures for a large number of employees led to bottlenecks in operating resources. Familiarization with the new system and the initial technical teething trouble led to longer process times, in some cases twice as long, as with the old system.

Besides the SAP IS-U rollout, a front-end CRM system from Siebel was introduced for comprehensive contact documentation and thus better customer service. This necessary action also led to longer process times in the beginning as additional activities now had to be established in the process. Both systems also encountered acceptance problems.

The system rollouts, longer processing times, employee problems caused by migrating to completely new software, and the additional resource stress from employee training sessions, for example, ultimately led to processing backlogs.

Centralization of Customer Support

In the wake of market deregulation and the increasing competition, the Group had to carry out organic consolidation of customer support practically at the same time as the system rollouts.

Until then, some of the predecessor companies had had their own autarchic, stand-alone customer support at their own sites or in their regions. In part, the organization comprised an integrated, general support structure within which the teams were responsible for a certain number of customers or a given territory and provided "their customers" with everything from classic 1st level or front office services through to highly complex and time-consuming 2nd level or back office services. Reminders/debt collection and supply blocks were normally handled by specialist teams.

Other companies had organized their customer support with specialization and strict separation of 1st level / front office und 2nd level / back office by means of a typical call center organization, albeit without territory- or customer-specific assignment. Every employee was responsible for every customer as long as the customer calling had an issue within his or her field of responsibility.

The differing organizational forms led to differing employee structures and pro-files in the various units. Whereas the one unit fostered a more generalized qualification of employees, another preferred to deploy employees with particular expertise to the pertinent area. As a result of the heterogeneous organizational structures, the employee structures were just as heterogeneous and differentiated. Reorganization thus faced a "human" challenge of merging the various organizations and cultures.

Development of Backlogs

Processes that had not yet been fully synchronized, four IS-U migrations and the rollout of a CRM system very quickly led to a significant extra workload for the operational units. The resulting bottlenecks in operational processes could not be offset with efficiency actions during the initial phase and thus resulted in the buildup of a backlog in dealing with customers' issues. In service areas, backlogs normally result in increased customer contacts and complaints on all contact paths as customers assume their issues have not been received by their electricity utility and so submit more letters or complain. The effect of a rising backlog can therefore be gauged by the reduction in contactability and TSF (telephone service factor).

Lack of Transparency

Rising backlogs also lead to a rising volume of short-term status information on individual cases. Results for reports were usually generated manually and were often challenged so that they needed to be reconfirmed several times. The workload for research and clarifications rose out of all proportion because of the migrations and restructuring programs.

Given this complex situation, the need was identified to introduce a Performance Monitoring System in order to improve processes and make them directly controllable, to generate more process transparency and to reliably automate reporting.

2   Project Description

2.1   Project Brief

The *ARIS Process Performance Manager* (ARIS PPM) project was launched in mid-January with a planned duration of seven months before the monitoring system went live. In the run up to the project, E.ON Bayern critically reviewed the ability of the ARIS Process Performance Manager (ARIS PPM) tool from IDS Scheer before opting to deploy it. The project contents were, in detail:

Development and Definition of Key Performance Indicators for Reference Processes

As there was no definitive concept for a Performance Management System at the start of the project, an incremental approach was agreed for the technical realization. First of all, all the Sales Service core processes were described in technical terms and the appropriate key performance indicators defined. Following this analysis, two reference processes were selected for technical realization as a first step. The results were then leveraged to draw up a rollout plan based on the already defined key performance indicators as part of a specification and thus minimize project risks.

The two "most important" processes were chosen as the reference processes to be implemented. Importance was defined as "mass critical with a high degree of standardization", which led to the relocation process with approx. 240,000 runs a year being chosen.

On the other hand, the complaint process was chosen as a reference process with a high degree of complexity and little scope for standardization in order to exploit the range of the selected system and business of the Sales Service. Technically, the selection of the reference processes required an interface from ARIS PPM to both IS-U and Siebel.

Creation of a Specification (Requirements Definition and IT Concept) and Documentation

The project brief entailed not only implementation but also an intensive know-how transfer that would enable E.ON Bayern to maintain and develop the Process Performance Management system itself. The objective was the greatest possible independence from external service providers; as a result the contents of the project documents that were created extended from data export and import procedures within the interfaces, customizing settings for ARIS PPM and the frontend through to detailed algorithms for calculating the key performance indicators.

Technical Realization of a Basis System for the Reference Processes

Three different tasks were defined for realizing the basis system:

- **Adapting the ARIS PPM Frontend to E.ON Bayern requirements**

  The aim was to develop a user-friendly, intuitive system because ease of handling was identified as a driver for acceptance by users. Thus the preferred approach was to limit the analysis functionality, eliminate what was unimportant and provide full functionality only when actually required.

- **Mapping key performance indicators for the two reference processes Relocation and Complaints**

  This involved the precise definition of the key performance indicators and the evaluation criteria (dimensions such as customer group, team assignment) and the definition of the processing logic for the data received from the various interfaces.

- **Designing the ARIS PPM connection to SAP IS-U and Siebel**

  The objective here was not only the functionality but also an interface design that permits flexible and low-cost expansion for monitoring other processes.

Automated, Recipient-Oriented Reporting

As the Sales Service value-added chains involve a large number of employees at a number of levels, there are differentiated demands on the reports and reporting system. Top management has different expectations for processing and aggregation of data than middle management or coordinators and process analysts. Middle management and process managers need the ability to analyze not only highly aggregated data views but also highly detailed individual views. Therefore, the reporting system must comprise a mix of predefined, regularly called or distributed reports and "ad-hoc" analyses generated on demand. The project attached particular importance to maintenance-free automation wherever possible.

Conducting Training Actions

Without correct and efficient use of the system there is after all no benefit for the company. Therefore, particular value was attached to training actions at E.ON Bayern right from the beginning. In the run up to the project, the project team produced a "user guide" as support material so that attended training could be reduced to half a day per user. As efficient analysis has a highly individual character however, individual appointments were agreed with participants where required so that the most important queries could be discussed individually. The support team used this to derive standard queries in the system. This resulted in high integration with the system and the support team.

Institutionalization of Process Management in the Organization

Sustainability is only achieved if operation and use are ensured on a lasting basis after the end of the project. Thus not only technical but also organizational implementation of process management is very important for generating benefits from the project. To this end, the project team carefully selected key personnel to act as multipliers and opinion shapers in the company and so inject process thinking into the company. They were established from the project phase on as the central contact partners in their areas for process-oriented analyses.

Inter-unit reporting for top management was restructured along process-oriented lines and centralized to ensure data consistency and plausibility. This was used to modify the intra-unit reporting, which the technical unit produces for its management with unit-specific data. This is individually designed with respect to content and appearance following the logic of process-oriented analyses and queries (favorites).

To handle any problems or questions arising, the ARIS PPM Support was established as a central contact point for users and so provide support for the institutionalization of process management. It offers a hotline service for users with questions about key performance indicator contents and analysis possibilities or with improvement suggestions. It also houses the entire technical service for problems with data delivery, error messages and system problems of a technical nature.

Intensive Integration of all Technical Departments

As the introduction of a monitoring system is a highly sensitive project, the early integration of all those involved internally or externally is a critical success factor.

At E.ON Bayern, tasking of service providers for projects with an IT background is triggered by the CIO Department. Accordingly, a representative from the CIO Department was integrated even at the project planning stage. Likewise, internal units such as the works council and data protection representative were involved from an early stage and informed of the objectives of the project.

As both internal and external service providers were involved, they too were included in the planning phase. This meant that service providers could plan their resources in good time and also "signed on" to the project. The outcome is realizable solution approaches and realistic project plans by all involved with high planning reliability for all performance packages.

2.2   Phased Approach

The project itself was carried out in several steps:

Conducting Technical Workshops

The technical workshops with the affected departments were primarily designed to determine the information requirements with respect to the processes. In the project run up, there was a requirement of communicating 4-6 meaningful core key performance indicators per process so that the workshops could focus on the core questions. With regard to the budget, it was also decided that it would be better to add key performance indicators retrospectively rather than offer secondary or redundant key performance indicators during the first step.

The workshops were moderated by IDS Scheer. The workshops were run along strict process-oriented lines, in that the processes were discussed in the order that they arise and then their technical realization in the IT systems was discussed before a second step formulated the questions to be asked about the process and the measuring points and key performance indicator entailed by such questions.

The goal was to structure the workshops as efficiently as possible from the viewpoint of the technical departments and so avoid the additional workload of a large number of workshops or interviews. The one-day workshops each discussed one process in its entirety, which included not only the two reference processes, relocation and complaints, but all Sales Service processes so that the results could be applied seamlessly for the rollout.

Conducting IT Workshops

The results and requirements generated by the technical workshops were used by the two service providers involved, IDS Scheer AG and the Group IT subsidiary, to define the key performance indicators in concrete terms. Both the exact algorithms (e.g. throughput time without post channels) for the key performance indicators and the data extraction from the systems were defined.

As the Group IT subsidiary is also responsible for operating all the systems within the E.ON Group and thus Siebel and IS-U as well, it was responsible for extracting the data required in ARIS PPM from the upstream systems. Therefore the IT defined a precisely documented interface between the systems and the monitoring system, in particular the semantic definition for the data to be transferred. This enables the impact of data-level changes in the systems on the monitoring to be estimated. The semantic analysis covered only the two reference processes.

Development and Initial Customizing of ARIS PPM

Data extraction was conducted differently depending on the system concerned so that the existing software components and the technology of the source system could be optimally exploited and hence reduce development costs.

On the SAP side, a configurable software module from IDS Scheer AG was chosen that permits customizing so that any data can be periodically read out from the SAP system. This module also permits flexible reading of other data from the SAP system in future. As the SAP system does not log all the data required for process monitoring, a decision was taken to implement special routines in SAP IS-U that record this additional data and save it for subsequent extraction.

Extraction on the Siebel-PKS side was realized directly using the script options available in the Siebel system so as to permit faster development. All the system extractions end up in an XML data stream that can be used as input for the ARIS PPM system. XML technology permits system- and platform-independent data transfer that can be directly used for further systems or modules.

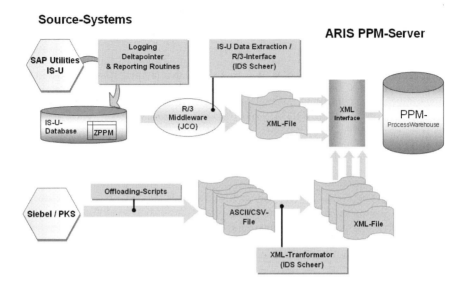

Fig. 4: Architecture of the data transfer interfaces

Parallel to the development work, the two service providers updated and expanded the technical part of the specification in exemplary cooperation so as to provide complete documentation.

Commissioning of ARIS PPM

A highly iterative process with prompt handling of error logs and usability experience was chosen for testing and development, whererin the tests were all conducted by E.ON Bayern employees. During the final test phase, the planned training sessions with a total of approx. 20 employees were staged so that their experience could be used as feedback for the final cycle. The employees were familiarized with the system, its navigation and typical analyses in groups of 3 to 5. Individual favorites were created for each employee in a one-on-one session. These sessions were also used as personal discussions to foster sustained conviction and acceptance. All these one-on-one sessions were carried out by E.ON Bayern support team employees.

Integration of the Systems/Outline Sketch of the System Landscape E.ON Bayern

The Sales Service has two core systems in addition to the standard office applications. The main system is SAP IS-U as the billing system in which all the business transactions from changes to customer master data, billing, metering, reminder/debt collection through to supply blocks are handled by Sales Service employees. In addition, there is a Siebel CRM system that is used as a documentation tool for all customer contacts and as a workflow system for the employees. Both systems interact and are linked by an EAI interface (Enterprise Application Integration). The typical business transactions workflow is as follows:

Fig. 5: General "Customer support" process model

During case processing, there is a customer-related "jump" from the corresponding Siebel screens to the IS-U entry screen. Customer master data is periodically transferred via EAI from IS-U to Siebel.

ARIS PPM monitoring is based on the reconstruction of the actual processes from the runtime data of the operative systems. As a result, a documented snapshot of the actual process is created for each business transaction and is saved in the process database. The process data is then used to calculate the key performance indicators. This requires time stamps on the process steps that determine the key performance indicator.

The general process flow shown in Fig. 5 combines the processes from Siebel and IS-U fragments. The interface concept realized for ARIS PPM enables an actual process picture to be created with Siebel and IS-U fragments for each business transaction (see Fig. 6).

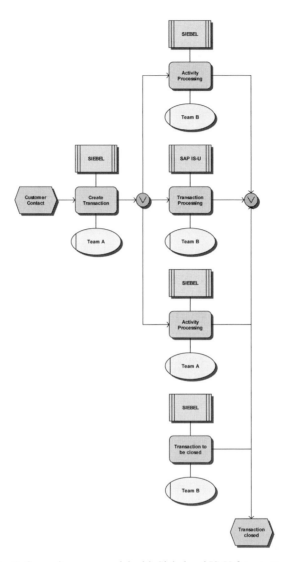

Fig. 6: General process model with Siebel and IS-U fragments

The ARIS PPM data-technical integration is completely automatic. Every night, the delta information of the last 24 hours is extracted from the upstream systems and made available to ARIS PPM as an XML data stream. All the routines are time-activated and run automatically without manual intervention. This minimizes operating and maintenance costs and also rules out error sources from manual data enrichment or even manipulation, which has significantly increased the acceptance of the system.

Interaction of Several Service Providers in the Project

A key and elementary factor of the project was the efficient coordination of the service providers involved. The Group IT subsidiary operates practically all the IT systems within the entire E.ON Group, involving hardware and software (computer center and support) through to IT and process-near consulting services. The IT subsidiary is the preferred provider so that synergy effects in the group are optimally exploited. Nevertheless, external service providers can be directly commissioned in justified cases, e.g. if the Group IT subsidiary does not have the required experience or references for the service required. This option was used for the Sales Service project.

In IDS Scheer, a service provider was commission that provides the ARIS PPM product, ARIS PPM integration know-how and many years of proven experience in business process management. The IT subsidiary is responsible for operating the IS-U and Siebel systems and has programming capacities with special knowledge of the systems and in particular their configuration. Thus, modifications to the productive system may be carried out solely by the responsible system operator.

Accordingly, the performances to be rendered by the service providers and the expected outcomes for the project were exactly specified and put down in writing. IDS Scheer took on responsibility for ARIS PPM introduction (ARIS PPM database and frontend), customizing the frontend, data import of the Siebel and IS-U files and their processing in ARIS PPM (import interface) and lead-managed the production of the specification. The Group IT subsidiary was to provide the necessary data as per the IDS Scheer requirements in an appropriate format from the upstream systems (export interface) and cooperate in the production of the specification.

3   Results and Experiences

The following presents typical ARIS PPM system screens used by E.ON Bayern and explains how the system is used for the various analysis and report requirements.

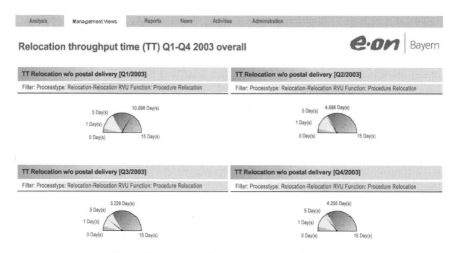

Fig. 7: Speedometer for relocation throughput time

This Management Cockpit for throughput times (DLZ) in the relocation process presents a speedometer – here as a quarterly comparison – which shows deviations at glance. The speedometer has three different colours that represent the threshold values:

Comment Screenshots
In order to preserve the original character of the project, the original screenshots (German) were only slightly modified for a better understanding. "realistische Beispieldaten" (German) is translated to "realistic example data".

Green area: Is the ideal area (planned value), from 0 days up to a defined warning value. In this example, the ideal (goal) throughput time for relocation is a maximum of one day, not including internal postal channels. In reality, however, this value is scarcely achievable as an average value.

Yellow area: A target range (planned value), between warning value and a defined alarm value, here between 1 and 5 working days. No response is required from management in the yellow area.

Red area: If the actual value in the period under review is above the alarm value it is in the red area. This shows management that there is a need to take action.

Fig. 7 shows how the Q1 2003 DLZ of approx. 10 days (red) was improved in the subsequent quarters to approx. 4.3 days (Q4).

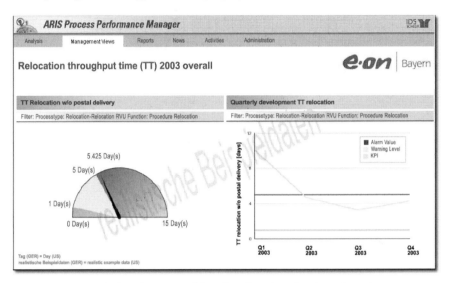

Fig. 8: Speedometer and line chart for relocation throughput time

The DLZ improvement during the course of 2003 is shown once again in Figure 8. Here it can be clearly seen that the alarm value, marking the beginning of the red area, was no longer crossed after Q2 and thus the process is within the tolerance range.

This insight was used to analyze what specifically led to the increase in DLZ in the period under review. One cause was a general increase in business transactions resulting from internal group reorganization which extended the Sales Service's scope of responsibilities, with the average DLZ rising on the back of unchanged resource input (see Fig. 9). These analyses are just two examples of the further tracing of causes that could be carried out.

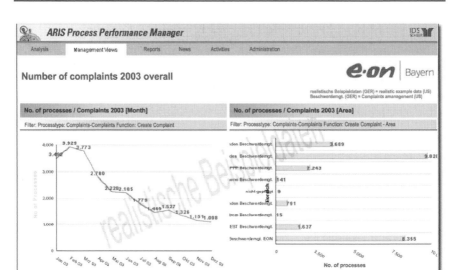

Fig. 9: Line chart number of complaints by month and
bar chart number of complaints by area

The frequency distribution was also analyzed. For example, Fig. 10 shows that more than 95% of all cases were dealt with within the yellow range (DLZ 5 days or fewer). The problem is then a few to very few extreme anomalies that could not be completed within 3 months or more, thus increasing the total throughput time. These anomalies could now be easily displayed and quickly identified in a further analysis as shown in Fig. 12 (Process list) for clarification and completion by the relevant units. Internal controlling was then modified so that extreme anomalies are reported individually but not included in the general analysis so as not to distort the overall picture.

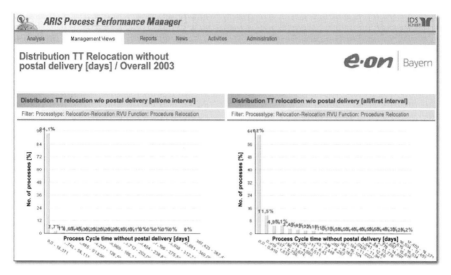

Fig. 10: Frequency distribution by time intervals

Another analysis approach is the controlling of processing backlogs. A Backlog Analysis Cockpit (see Figure 11) immediately shows the size of the current backlogs and their distribution across the individual teams. This can be analyzed further, leading perhaps to the temporary reallocation of staff from teams that are up to date to those with a particularly high backlog. This provides optimum support for operational personnel management.

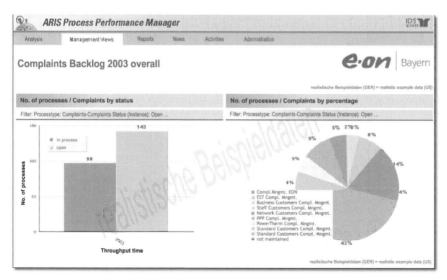

Fig. 11: Column chart of complaints backlog by status and
pie chart of complaint backlogs by team

The appropriate process list can now be generated, for example so that individual concrete business transactions can be identified ready for discussion in the units involved or for further detailed analysis. This results in a list of the ACTUAL processes that form the basis of the query just executed (see Fig. 12). The individual processes can then be called up as a diagram in EPC format (see Fig. 13). This option is also available to the operational units.

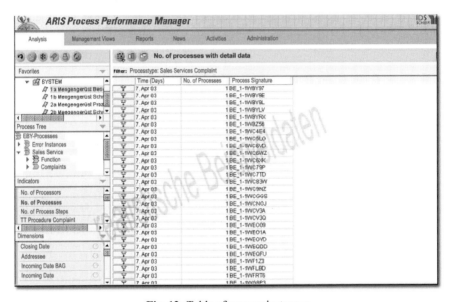

Fig. 12: Table of process instances

Every row of the table shown in Figure 12 represents an ACTUAL process read out from the upstream systems. The column diagram in Fig. 11, which displays the backlog of open complaints (96 complaints) in the left-hand dark blue column, can be used to drill down to and display the list of these 96 complaint processes (see Fig. 12). In other words, ARIS PPM always preserves the connection between the numbers in the analyses and the actual processes.

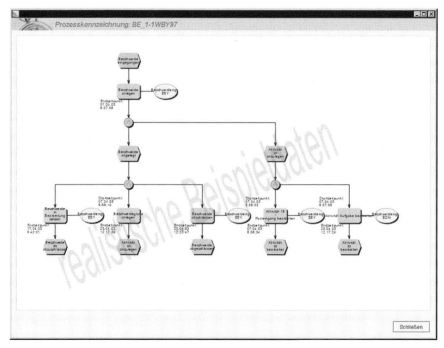

Fig. 13: ACTUAL process in EPC format

4   Benefits

The many benefits arising for Sales Service from the projects are described below.

Monitoring Deadlines and Reaction Times

The Process Monitoring System can be used to monitor and track deadlines and response times in handling customer issues. "Overdue" business transactions are displayed proactively and can be broken down to the data level using drill-down so that the case can be identified in the upstream system and dealt with. Corresponding automated reports and evaluations can be selected for these specific cases.

Support for Resource Planning

Although ARIS PPM itself does not have a forecasting component, it is ideal for drawing conclusions about team utilization and spotting peaks and excess capacities. For example, after the mass dispatching of invoices, the figures generated by ARIS PPM can be used to plan the additional HR requirements required to handle the higher level of customer queries expected 1-2 days later with the usual quality and efficiency.

Identification of Weak Points

The process presentations available can be used to analyze processes at the structural level. This enables questions about the actual status of standardization efforts, TARGET/ACTUAL deviations, or the degree of task delegations that have had no effect to be answered. Identifying weak points is thus a key basis for optimizing structural and process organizations.

Standardizing Business Processes

Even actual processes with a high degree of standardized tend to take on a "life of their own" and drift away from the target. ARIS PPM can be used to "superimpose" and compare variants of actual processes. This enables steps to be taken, which in turn generate more standards.

Factual Basis for Discussions through Concrete Figures

When figures are presented by various parties in an unverified manner, this generally leads to the numbers being challenged rather than a discussion of their significance. One goal achieved by the project is a reporting system based on a coordinated data basis that precludes interpretation by its complete automation, thus adding a new "fact-based" quality to discussions.

5   Lessons Learned

Insourcing System Knowledge

Right from the start, projects with external service providers call for a strategy for the collecting of the knowledge generated so that the know-how is available in a defined location for use after the end of the project. With an outsourcing approach, the knowledge of systems and internal structures remains with the service provider, who may is only engaged again when needed. This dependency on the service provider is justified using perceived or apparent cost advantages of outsourcing, also with respect to the costs for training and providing in-house resources. Arguments in favor of greater independence include greater control over the IT system, cost advantages in the event that the system is upgraded, and the use of IT resources already in place.

E.ON Bayern opted at an early stage for the insourcing solution. Although both service providers enjoyed full trust, the know-how for interfaces, customizing, key performance indicator calculation and technical support (hotline) is to be developed internally.

This does not apply to operating the system, as this is governed by the contracts with the Group IT subsidiary. Services and remuneration are laid down in appropriate service level agreements (SLAs).

It was decided to include the appropriate employees in the project from an early stage so that know-how could be built up continuously. During the transition to live operation, this enabled employees to take over responsibility from their experience as project members ("flying" change). This smooth transition to the operational phase ensured that the project benefits would be retained.

Technical Feasibility Proven

As was indicated earlier, it was decided to adopt a phase-oriented approach so as to evaluate in a first step the way in which the data is to be extracted from Siebel and IS-U and compiled in inter-system processes. Then a milestone was defined that provided the option to terminate project activities if a discussion showed that the first step had not produced any usable and reasonable results.

This approach was necessary because although IDS Scheer had comprehensive experience with data extraction from a very wide range of upstream systems, the high level of customizing required for the Sales Service's two systems and the individually developed linkage between the systems entailed a risk that the required workload might be excessive.

Interface Flexibility

As the interfaces to Siebel and IS-U were developed as configurable software modules, further measuring points and key performance indicators can be "docked" with relatively little effort. Despite a slightly increased workload for developing the interface concept and the interfaces themselves during the first phase of the project, the costs of developing further interfaces during rollout can now be minimized.

Data Volumes are "Processable"

Another uncertainty before the project started was the extraction of the data sets that are processed by Sales Service every day and the resulting performance of the ARIS PPM system. The proper dimensioning of the hardware and the networks used combined with appropriate scaling of the system and interfaces ensured highly effective monitoring. For some 2 years now, about 13,000 process steps including additional information have been exported and imported at E.ON Bayern with no performance problems.

6   Key Success Factors

E.ON Bayern regards the ARIS PPM project as a major success because the expected project benefits have materialized. There follows a summary of the key success factors for the project. These may also be regarded as a recommendation for many other projects.

6.1   Involvement of all Concerned Right from the Start

Identification of Key Players and Opinion Shapers within the Company

They can drive the project by forming a positive opinion and proactively avoid critical situations through open dialog and solution-oriented behavior. Together with and under the leadership of project management, problems can be tackled head-on without outside time pressure. For this project, the timely involvement of the works council and data protection representative was of major importance.

The technical and other departments affected are also of critical importance and must be intensively involved as they carry the project through their support and deployment of their employees and ultimately generate its added value.

Integration of the Service Providers Involved

Needless to say there is a defined client-contractor relationship between the project management and the external and internal service providers. Nevertheless it is important to create a climate of open dialog and to obtain and heed where possible the opinion of these service providers. After all, all those involved in the project must act as a team in which company boundaries are not apparent. This means treating and respecting service providers as equally entitled partners. At the same time the service partners must regard the client as a project partner.

6.2   Interdisciplinary Cooperation

The team staffing is very important for a successful project team. You need the right people with the right skills. The project had the right mixture of technicians and managers who complement each other and contribute their own particular expertise to the project, thus meeting the technical and organizational demands of a monitoring project of this nature.

6.3   Exact Task and Role Allocation among Service Providers

A clear and razor-sharp definition of the tasks and roles is an absolute basis on which service providers can act and cooperate. This avoids time-consuming discussions during the project itself about the allocation of tasks and budgets. It is important that this is defined in joint discussions attended by *all* the service providers affected – and documented *in writing*.

6.4   Project Marketing

Project marketing is part of any project. Do good – and talk about it. Or even better: Do good – and have others talk about it. Project marketing should not be addressed to the project organization and hierarchies alone. Also decisive is the marketing beyond the project, e.g. internal sponsors reporting positively on the project and the project team at higher levels via their network.

6.5   "Pragmatism"

Finally, a healthy portion of pragmatism is called for so that practical relevance is ensured at all times and to guard against overly ambitious demands that are demotivating and unrealistic. Here are some often quoted rules that proved to be invaluable during the project and very much recommended here:

- Projects should be simple so that they can be understood (keep it short and simple – KISS)
- Identify the project benefits clearly
- Do not overload the project. Better 80 or 60 actually achieved percent than the envisaged 100%, which is never achieved (80 / 20 rule)
- Pick the low-hanging fruit to generate a positive attitude towards the project (quick wins)
- Think big, start small

Performance Management Based on ITIL in IDS Scheer AG Customer Interaction Center (CIC)

Gregor Loes
IDS Scheer AG

Summary

The IDS Scheer Customer Interaction Center (CIC) has significantly boosted customer satisfaction by rolling out a Corporate Performance Management system based on the ARIS Process platform. The ISO 9000 certified Support Helpdesk, which looks after worldwide support for all ARIS products, used the Process Mining technology of ARIS PPM to carry out a reorganization to the ITIL standard very rapidly, reducing the processing times of 1st Level Support queries by more than half, which earned it a "Helpdesk Award 2004" from an independent jury.

Keywords

Service process, service quality, key performance indicator system, process definition, SLA monitoring, call volume, hotline, solution times, IT helpdesks, problem management, net processing time

1   Environment

Just imagine you were sitting in a restaurant on a Friday evening having just finished an excellent meal with customers you have invited to celebrate the successful conclusion of a project. When you ask for the bill, you realize that your wallet has been stolen.

You are in a very embarrassing situation and need help as quickly as possible. As you work for a very well-known company you agree with the restaurant owner that the bill will be sent to your company. But all your bank and credit cards were in your wallet. So you call the Information and ask for the telephone number to block your cards. The friendly voice on the other end of the line tells you the numbers you need and puts you through to the call center for blocking your cards. After a few minor hurdles, which you have to negotiate in the Interactive Voice Response system, your cards are safely blocked, in other words after a few minutes you can be confident that nobody can withdraw any money from your account.

This situation or one like it is no doubt familiar to many people. As bank customers, we expect rapid help in such a situation. Immediate blocking of the card and the assurance that any money withdrawn will be reimbursed by the bank is now regarded as the absolute minimum level of support that a bank must offer.

Such service levels are also now regarded as absolutely normal in other areas too. How would you react if you had been told that it was Friday evening and the service center cannot block your card until Monday morning and any debits until then would be at your expense?

Nowadays, impeccably organized service provision is expected from what are widely known as IT hotlines. That is why issues such as ITIL (IT Infrastructure Library) have been growing more and more important in the past few years. These are standards designed to help align IT processes to a company's core business. This pressure has long been experienced by product hotlines, for example. After all, customers pay a sizeable annual fee for optimum support. Providing optimum support in turn calls for optimization of the underlying processes. With more than 1,000 customer contacts per day this is much like a production-line activity. Fast solutions for customers can only be achieved if each work step is clearly defined, if there are model solutions and every employee can directly see what the next steps are. Comparisons with industrial production are thus quite appropriate. For example, if optimizing process workflows and interfaces reduces the average processing time per call by only one minute, a typical service hotline can save one employee, or create scope for new issues that have to be taken on by the service department without having to recruit new staff.

2   Description of the Problem

As described above, we are talking about the industrialization of service management particularly in the service environment. Service processes must be fast and efficient without impacting the highest possible quality for the customer. Some 70% of all customers change providers because of poor service (Source: Rockefeller Institute). Therefore it is important to establish a detailed key performance indicator system that identifies changes in service quality and helps to implement actions for improving this in service quality.

In addition, service units must increasingly be able to make their performances transparent. Not least, to protect themselves from the ever greater cost pressure they are subjected to. After all, many controllers cannot see why service units have such a large headcount and in addition the service spectrum is often very opaque for outsiders.

3   Procedure

The aim of most organizational changes in a company is ultimately to boost profits, i.e. if areas such as service or sales are to be reorganized, the corporate goals have to be broken down the service level and used to derive a key performance indicator system that provides meaningful support for controlling that area. The key performance indicators are assigned target values that are continuously measured. In a service unit, which as mentioned above can be compared with an industrial production unit, this means providing clear process definitions as a basis for achieving the target values. These process definitions in turn also help to establish what target values (e.g. target value for SLA compliance) are possible given the available resources. These process definitions can also be used as the basis for implementing a helpdesk/CRM system.

A balanced scorecard simplifies the presentation of the objectives and their key performance indicators and enables users to drill down to the underlying processes (see Fig. 1 - Balanced Scorecard for Customer Support).

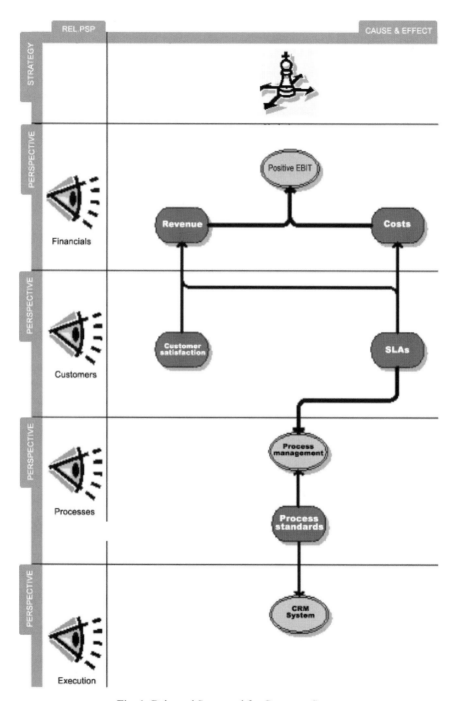

Fig. 1: Balanced Scorecard for Customer Support

4   The Solution

For many years now, IDS Scheer has had its service unit certified to ISO 9000 and later to ISO 9000:2000. Right from the start, a great deal of attention was paid to process standards, which were also used to implement a CRM system. With more than 4,000 service agreements, it is absolutely essential to monitor the defined service level agreements on a continuous basis, with computerized support. ARIS PPM is used for SLA monitoring. Besides SLA monitoring, it also analyzes workload, throughput times and wait times. For example, our analyses in 2003 showed that our call volume was rising steadily at a rate of about 20%. They also showed that about 13% of all queries accounted for 46% of our total hotline workload (see Fig. 2 Workload versus number of complex queries), i.e. a handful of difficult queries tied up a relatively large amount of resources. This in turn led to longer throughput times for the "simple" queries.

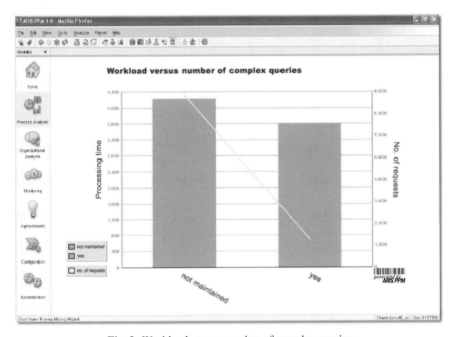

Fig. 2: Workload versus number of complex queries

Therefore, a decision was taken to launch an internal project that would reorganize the hotline area in line with ITIL principles. The goal was to reduce throughput times by faster processing of the much larger volume of "simple" queries and to assign the more complex queries to a special team formed for that purpose.

The aim was twofold: to reduce solution times and thus also waiting times for customers, and at the same time to reduce the number of open questions by direct processing at the 1st level. Unlike classic IT helpdesks, product support at IDS Scheer involves specialist support. Most incoming queries are relatively complex. Hence the 1st level solution rate cannot be compared with that of an IT hotline.

Following the ITIL definitions, a 1st level team was formed that tries to pass on help or solutions to customers as quickly as possible. Starting in Q2, more than 40% of queries on average were to be solved by the 1st level, rising to about 55% by Q3. The goals are part of the target definitions for the 1st Level team. The redefined 2nd level is responsible for deferrals and testing issues that cannot be clarified at the lower level. As for the 1st level, the target starting in Q2 was that an average of 60% of queries reaching the 2nd level should be solved at that level. Starting in Q3, the target level was set for 70%.

The remainder of queries are difficult and time-consuming problems that must be referred to problem management. ARIS PPM is used to continuously monitor the newly defined targets (see Figs. 3 and 4 Target definitions for 1st and 2nd level support).

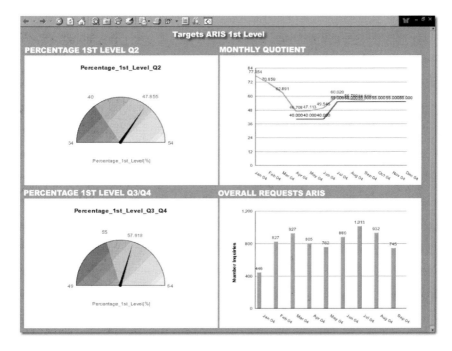

Fig. 3: Target definitions for 1st level support

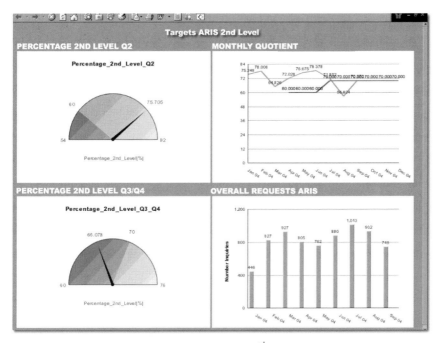

Fig. 4: Target definitions for 2nd level support

5   The Results

What has the ITIL-based reorganization really achieved?

- The throughput times for 1st level queries (i.e. technically simple queries) have been reduced considerably

- Customers' queries are therefore solved faster

- The number of open queries has fallen thanks to the faster throughput times

- The average net processing time per query has been reduced

- The throughput times for 2nd level queries have also be been reduced

- Here too, net processing times have been shortened

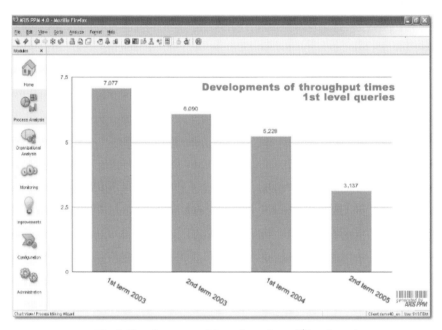

Fig. 5: Developments of throughput times 1st level queries

As a result, the growing number of queries was successfully mastered without additional staff, and the faster processing and throughput times have led to a drop in costs per query. The 1st level net processing times rose briefly because the new team had to be trained in the new tasks. ITIL-based reorganization is useful not only for IT departments. Wherever a high degree of service is demanded, it is advisable to test the ITIL Best Practice Model for its applicability and deploy it if this is the case. Post-reorganization analyses revealed that there was a very low overlap of similar knowledge in 2003 (see Fig. 6: CIC 2003 know-how distribution). Absences due to illness or vacation were thus a perennial problem for the unit.

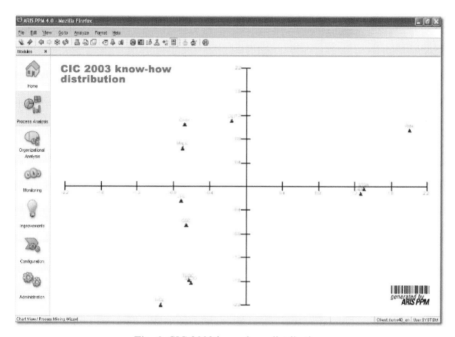

Fig. 6: CIC 2003 know-how distribution

The alignment with ITIL created teams with similar knowledge that covered a wide range of know-how. Vacation- or illness-related absences were now less disruptive for daily operations.

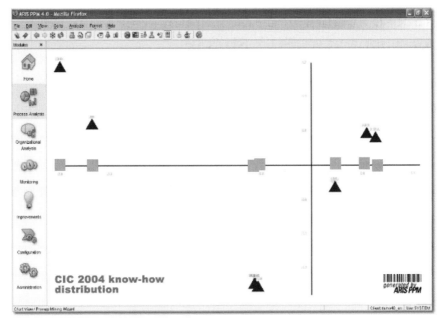

Fig. 7: Know-how distribution in CIC, 2004

6   Conclusion

For IDS Scheer, alignment to ITIL has paid dividends. Along with the desired cost reductions, throughput and processing times have been improved, thus leading to further optimization of support. Our success in endeavoring to improve customer satisfaction in a sustainable way with our helpdesk services through Corporate Performance Management was recognized in November 2004: The Helpdesk Award in the "External Support Service Provider" category awarded each year by a jury of experts and companies in the field of customer support has confirmed that IDS Scheer has a leading market position not only in software and consulting but also in support services.

Process Performance Management in Securities Operations at CREDIT SUISSE

Olaf Klein
Credit Suisse

Dirk Kogelschatz
Credit Suisse

Summary

Credit Suisse is following an ongoing initiative to implement a complete process orientation in its securities operations applications. Part of this initiative forms the monitoring of processes with the intention to obtain more information about executed process instances and thereby identify opportunities for continuous process improvement. Therefore, ARIS Process Performance Manager first was evaluated in a pilot study and subsequently implemented into the existing application landscape for securities processing. Today, the operations unit monitors its compliance to the time standards for execution defined in the service level agreements (SLA) between the different business units. Moreover, loops in the execution of processes or the cost drivers, like required manual interventions or delays due to communication with external parties become transparent.

Keywords

Business Process Management (BPM), Business Performance Management, Process Performance Manager (PPM), Key Performance Indicator (KPI), Service Level Agreement (SLA)

1   Motivation and Approach

Credit Suisse is one of the leading banks in Switzerland and internationally well-known for its private and investment banking services. Its securities operations unit in Switzerland is responsible for the custody and transaction services offered to Swiss and international clients through the different business units that represent Credit Suisse in markets all around the globe as well as through external asset managers who rely on the services.

For retail clients in Switzerland these services are offered by independent retail banks (Credit Suisse and Neue Aargauer Bank); for private clients world-wide by the private banks (Bank Leu and Hoffmann, as well as the private banking unit of Credit Suisse); for pension funds, investment funds, insurance companies and governments by Credit Suisse Asset Management, which is part of the investment bank Credit Suisse First Boston. Thus all the services offered by securities operations are provided for other entities of the Credit Suisse Group.

Around 50% of this business is cross border with more than 400 external custodians all over the world. This involves more than 50 currencies and roughly 20 million transactions per year.

Securities services include safekeeping and administration of securities (corporate actions), securities transfers as well as the clearing and settlement of trades. This wide range of activities is supported by 27 applications/application areas.

In 1997, within a first initiative of modernizing of the existing application portfolio for securities handling, the idea was born to identify the processes which were hidden in these applications. The goal was set to break up the monolithic black box applications and in a new design to separate processes and business rules from the underlying services providing the actual business functionality (see figure 3). For the execution and control of process instances a central engine was needed, hence "Auftragsmanager" (order manager) development was initiated. Event driven process chains, which are designed in ARIS Toolset and afterwards imported into the Auftragsmanager via a direct interface, form the basis of this approach.

In 1998 Auftragsmanager became ready for deployment and two different areas were chosen for the new application architecture. The booking system for stock exchange trades was one of them, while the other one was the application which supports securities transfers inbound and outbound of Credit Suisse. Following these two first successful implementations a strategic initiative called SEC2000 and aimed at the modernization of the entire securities platform was launched. Besides process control oriented architecture, emphasis was placed on the closing of around 450 functional gaps which over the years had come apparent in the applications. Closing these gaps leads to an increase of the straight-through processing rate and thus to a decrease of operating costs due to automation.

Auftragsmanager was declared the central element of the entire SEC2000 philosophy. Its implementation became mandatory for all applications. Thus for all existing applications an assessment was undertaken to reveal the processes within them in order to derive a master plan for continued implementation of a process oriented application architecture. This master plan guides ongoing activities for rebuilding the securities applications.

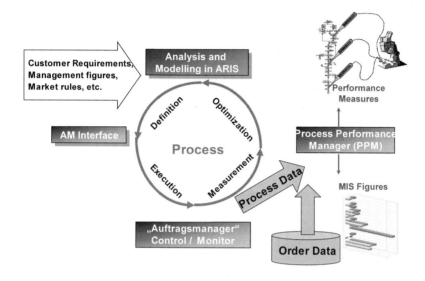

Fig. 1: Vision of a closed process control cycle

As explained above with ARIS Toolset the software solution for process design was found and with the development of Auftragsmanager the engine to actually execute and control them was built. Still one piece was missing to close the process control cycle envisioned (see figure 1). Although Auftragsmanager provides some means to monitor process instances in a quasi real time manner its ability to serve as a process measurement tool are too limited to exploit the potential of process optimization. Hence the need for an additional component became apparent. At the end of 2002 Credit Suisse's contacts with IDS Scheer led to the evaluation of the Process Performance Manager (ARIS PPM). A pilot study was started to find out, whether and how ARIS PPM could be connected to the existing environment. This pilot provided further insights concerning the prerequisites for a successful implementation of ARIS PPM.

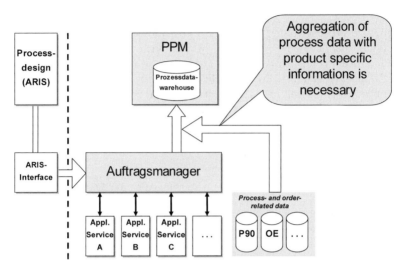

Fig. 2: Data feed ARIS PPM

Upon the termination of the pilot study the implementation of ARIS PPM into the process driven architecture was designed. Two essential lessons were learned in the pilot study. First, in order to obtain the insights for business process management from ARIS PPM, plain process data need to be enriched by order details (see figure 2). For instance the path an inbound or an outbound securities transaction follow through the widely ramified process chains is identical. Only additional order details permit their distinction. Second, the considerations on the performance indicators to be defined for a process need to be made in the process design phase. Otherwise the attachment of the "probe heads" for automated process measurement may not be possible as precise as necessary because of e.g. nonexistent granularity of the underlying models. Furthermore, developers at IDS Scheer were challenged to tune the performance of ARIS PPM, in order to cope with the daily volumes which are processed on Credit Suisse's securities processing platform.

2   Process Control and Modularization of Applications

In order to process control applications now modularized by disintegration into functional services the processes within the applications needed to be (re)identified. As it is the case with most legacy systems 15 to 20 years after their initial implementation, these applications had undergone major changes implementing more and more functionality into them. This had blurred business' understanding for the processes captured in the applications and de facto had led to a situation where understanding and responsibility between business and IT was entirely split up.

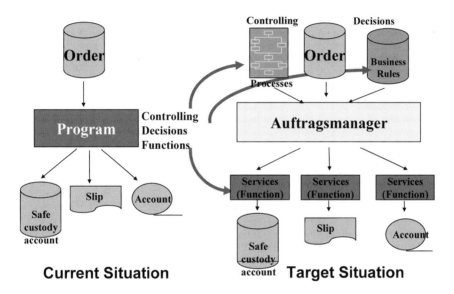

Fig. 3: Application modularization

By "digging out" the processes out of the applications again and identification of the interfaces, where users and applications interact, complete control over these processes was regained. Not to mention the improved communication between business and IT due to mutually improved understanding of each other. It was this front-to-end modeling of processes and execution of process instances, which made it possible to build a business case yielding a net present value and by this showing a positive return on investment. As important as this business case is, emphasis has to be placed on the level of collaboration between IT and business which will prove even more valuable in the long run. Essentially this can be ascribed to the fact that the process models can serve as the basis for the definition of future functional requirements.

3   Derivation of a Master Plan through Application Assessments

Figure 4 presents an overview of an assessment scheme which was followed for all the applications under investigation. In a kick-off meeting in which all parties involved were identified the developers for each application were informed about the new design approach and the goals to be achieved. Structured interviews followed. The interviews covered the typical questions about volumes processed, media brakes in the process flow and the interfaces involved. The results were transformed into a first process to give the stakeholders a first idea what process modeling actually means. The evolving discussions on these preliminary processes combined with the information obtained in the interviews then were documented in a report which included a recommendation.

The combined outcomes of all assessments led to the derivation of the master plan for the separation of processes from functional services. All together, more than 50 processes were defined. After approval of the master plan implementation could begin. For every application a concept was written including the final version of the process and detailed descriptions of the functions within this process. At the same time business requirements regarding process measurement were collected followed by the assignment of the necessary measurement points to the process.

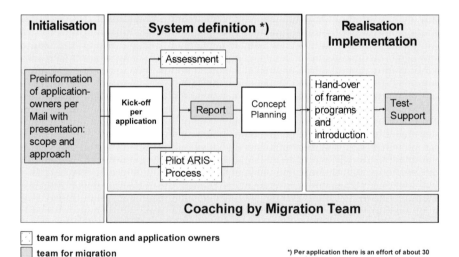

Fig. 4: Approach to application assessments

Coverage and Volumes Today

Right now about 35% of the 27 applications are controlled by the application Auftragsmanager. Process controlled order flow covers already the business areas of securities transfers, part of the process of OTC and stock exchange trade settlement, parts of corporate actions handling, securities lending and borrowing, as well as some support processes. Daily volumes of executed process functions currently vary between 350.000 and 800.000.

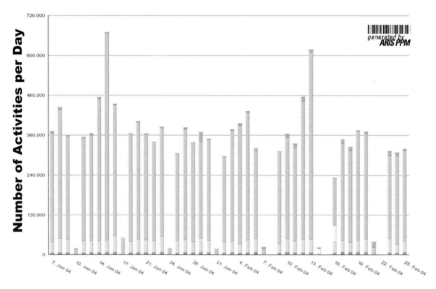

Fig. 5: Daily volumes

4   Architectural Setup

As mentioned before, ARIS Toolset is the preferred software and the Event-Process-Chain (EPC) is the method used for the modeling of the processes. All the processes then are imported into Auftragsmanager. At runtime these processes facilitate the communication between Auftragsmanager and the individual services providing the actual business functionality.

Services may be automated process steps, manual activities or online interfaces where the user interacts with the application (e.g. data entry). A service invoked by Auftragsmanager must communicate its termination. For automated process steps this is done by the underlying services, for manual/online steps this information must be delivered by process participants, i.e. the users. Upon termination of one step Auftragsmanager knows form the underlying process models which step to invoke next (see figure 6).

This communication setup assures that Auftragsmanager, as the central engine, obtains all information related to process execution and stores it in the process log file. Log data are imported into ARIS PPM every night. Simultaneously the import data are combined with order details, which are collected from other databases.

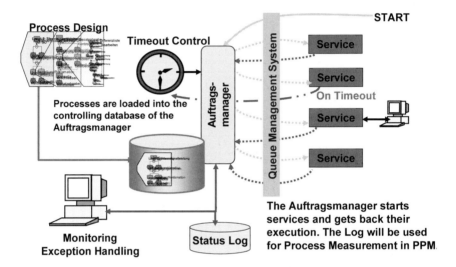

Fig. 6: Architecture and connections

5   Examples and Business Benefits

Securities transfers were the first process controlled orders. These processes had already been running for some years but processes were not yet measured due to the lack of an appropriate tool for automated process measurement. With the commissioning of ARIS PPM time was ready for the formulation of key performance indicators for securities transfers as shown below in figure 7.

Business Volume Related Measures (per Time Period)

Name	Description	Business Benefit
number of orders	measures the overall number of securities transfer orders	flexibilisation of reporting cycles; basis for dynamic allocation of workforce
number of cancel requests	measures cancelled orders (own and on customer request)	volume number not extractable from system until now
number of orders entered by employee	measures employee production	allows for differentiation of complexity of order constellations (pricing)
number of orders controlled by employee	measures employee production	allows for acknowledgement of secondary tasks

Process Performance Related Measures (per Time Period)

Name	Description	Business Benefit
percentage of orders fulfilling time related settlement standards	measures fulfilment of quality standards	quantitative quality assurance, allows for analysis of weaknesses in process setup
number of critical staff occurred in work flow	measures orders needing supplementary manual intervention	accounts for costs for order processing, allows for analysis of failure prone delivery constellations
number of orders overdue	measures orders settling after specified settlement date	quality check, allows for improvement through analysis
number of manual interventions	measures manual interventions during delivery process	accounts for costs of order processing, helps to increase STP rate through analysis
average time between order capture and settlement	measures time between order completion and external confirmation	quality check of external custodians

Fig. 7: Selection of KPIs for securities transfers

For these indicators virtual "probe heads" were placed in the process models. For a volume counter of executed process instances (orders) a single measurement point may be sufficient as shown in figure 8 by the top probe head. In order to discern STP instances from those requiring manual intervention two probe heads may discern the different edges that these instances may follow (probe heads in the middle). To derive throughput times the time span between two probe heads is measured (top and bottom probe head). KPIs are represented through appointment of measurement points and the derivation of formulae based upon them.

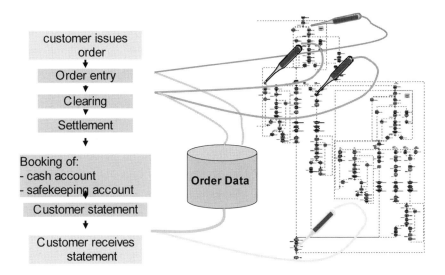

Fig. 8: Mapping of business process into IT processes

For securities transfers the final set comprised around 30 indicators and around 25 dimensions which contain the order specific information needed to identify the business process in the IT process as shown in illustration 8. With these indicators dash boards were set up which show relevant process information customized according to management levels.

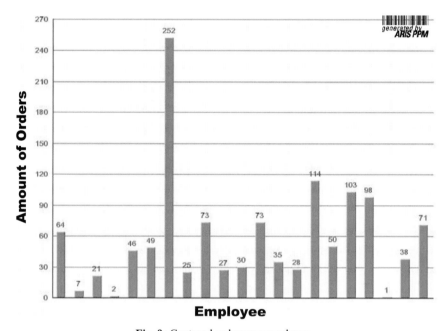

Fig. 9: Captured orders per employee

Figure 9 provides an example of a volume indicator showing the number of orders captured per employee. On one side this first picture provides an approximate overview of individual productivity. On the other hand interpretation must be undertaken with precaution since not all orders have the same complexity. Information revealing the complexity of the underlying orders may be contained in the other dimensions that process instances are enriched with or they may not be available in an automated form. However, reasonable interpretation requires a well founded understanding of the business.

Fig. 10: Cancelled orders per business unit

Figure 10 shows the number of cancellations of orders per business unit. Until the introduction of process performance management cancelled orders had not been known because the volume figures were based on customer statements produced. If an order was cancelled before the customer statement had been produced this became not visible.

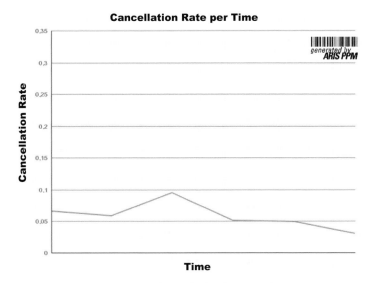

Fig. 11: Rate of cancelled orders over time

Figure 11 shows how the rate of cancelled orders evolves over time. The rate and not the absolute number is chosen because it is normalized by the total number of orders executed. Cancellations are a common phenomenon in the process of securities deliveries and may be due to internal or external factors. In any case, they reflect the quality of internal or external work. Until the implementation of ARIS PPM business had no means to measure cancellations because the system did not disclose them. A captured order which is cancelled later causes the same expenses as a successful order. Therefore they should be priced accordingly. Through the introduction of ARIS PPM the basis for a fairer allocation of costs among the different business units of Credit Suisse relying on securities operations' services becomes now available. For example business units with poor instruction quality leading to order cancellations could be charged accordingly giving them an incentive to improve the quality of their instructions through better training of employees. For securities operations this also new services available for the responsible managers, in order to provide its internal clients with analysis revealing the most common instruction errors and thus giving valuable input in which field of the delivery instructions additional training might be needed in front units.

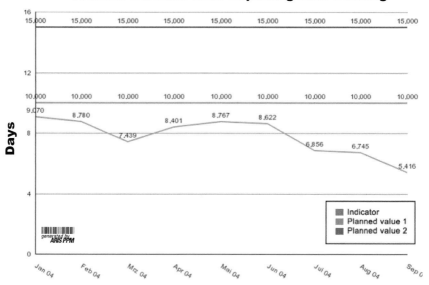

Fig. 12: Throughput time from order capturing
until booking of positions

As mentioned before, between the individual business units and securities operations service level agreements are defined. These SLAs include quality levels. Of course front units have a vital interest to monitor the service levels that they pay for. Process measurement now provides the opportunity to monitor time related quality indicators. Figure 12 shows the evolvement of throughput times over time (lowest line). Additionally an arbitrary line has been included in the chart to show the level of service quality agreed upon (top line). The line in the middle may serve as a lower threshold value for the process owner who of course would like to intervene before the upper line is crossed, if for some reason throughput times should begin to deteriorate.

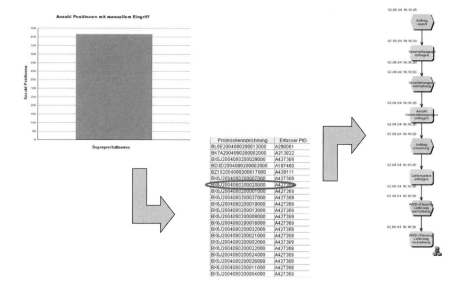

Fig. 13: Drill down to the individual order

While Figure 12 shows average values for throughput times by application of a time filter those orders not fulfilling the service level agreement can easily be separated. With just one mouse click a list of these orders can be generated and hence delivered to front units which then are informed which client's orders may not have fulfilled the service quality that Credit Suisse strives for (see figure 13). Moreover another mouse click reveals the process flow the order has pursued (depicted in the form of an event driven process chain).

For the safekeeping of securities it is common to work together with external custodians in the individual markets. If the suspicion arises that the services quality may be influenced by external factors, like e.g. a specific custodian, it is now easy to verify with hard facts if this suspicion proves to be true. Again, a lever for process optimization has become available.

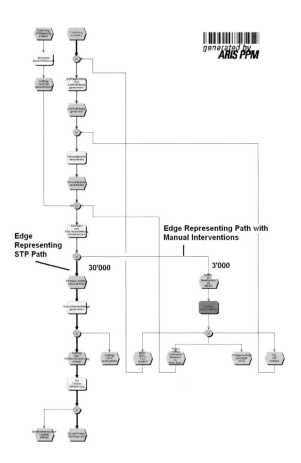

Fig. 14: Aggregated process instances

The column to the left in Figure 14 may also be represented in the form of a process. But instead of an individual event driven process chain the result will be an aggregated process model representing all the individual process chains. Such an empirical process model provides further insight into the process behavior. The edges represent the model paths which actually occurred. For every edge it is known how many instances have flown through it. In this dummy example for instance 30.000 orders were processed STP and 3.000 provoked a manual intervention.

The manual function in the process is the one to the very right. In addition, information on the average processing time of all functions is included by the color depth in this chart. Processing times of individual functions vary form milliseconds for a simple automated function (top left white function) up to close to an hour for the online function to the right.

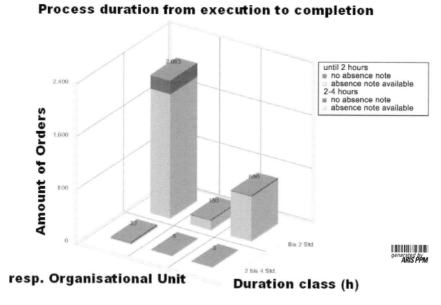

Fig. 15: Processing time of an online function

Figure 14 shows that the processing time for an online function quite naturally is larger than an automated one. For obvious reasons business is most concerned with online functions. Figure 15 may serve as an example for an analysis of an online function. A manager may be interested to know how long it takes until the reason for a halted order has been found out, corrected and order execution continued. And he may be interested to see, if different organizational units show differences in their processing times. The above illustration shows such an example which depicts in the columns additionally whether a note documenting the reason for the halt of the order has been captured.

While Figure 15 uses only two classes of processing time (0-2 hours; 2-4 hours) sometimes the actual distribution of orders over the processing time is of concern. Figure 16 provides such an example showing how many orders fell in which time class.

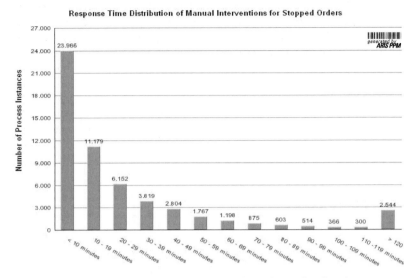

Fig. 16: Distribution of the processing time of an online function

6   Process Mining for Identification of Performance Shaping Factors

The throughput time of a delivery of securities may be influenced by many factors. In many cases the performance shaping factors are unknown. For these cases statistical analysis proves to be a powerful investigation tool. The statistics features in ARIS PPM are referred to as Process Mining functions.

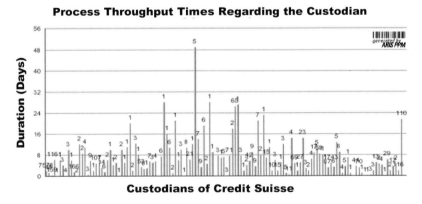

Fig. 17: Process throughput times in relation to the custodian

As mentioned before external factors can influence throughput times for securities transfers. A major performance shaping factor in this are the external custodians. Process mining allows for an analysis in which for a specified performance indicator a set of arbitrarily chosen dimensions is tested on its influence on the performance indicator. According to some boundary conditions chosen for the analysis ARIS PPM presents the dimensions which show a significant influence on the indicator. Of course causality has to be explained by business experts. Figure 17 depicts how external custodians influence the throughput times for securities transfers. Again the potential of process performance management for the optimization of business processes is evident.

7 Lessons Learned

The ability to scrutinize process execution down to individual performance shaping factors leads to a paradigm shift. While in the beginning business was reluctant to look thoroughly into the sometimes quite complex models for process execution the transparency brought by performance measurements has changed this. Now managers are aware of the meaningful performance indicators which have become available due to the process controlled order execution. Furthermore, following the path of an individual process instance (order) through the complex models facilitates people's understanding and internalization of process orientation. Performance of until now self-organizing employees becomes transparent to the management. Here emphasis is less on the comparison of work done by individual employees but rather on the performance of the front to end process. While smart self-organizing employees focus on finding the local optimum of how to do their work process performance management helps to find the global optimum of the overall process.

Different products vary in their execution complexity. Again process performance managements provides further insights. Obvious that these new insights can be used to identify products which tend to decrease process performance thus allowing for appropriate provisions for process improvements to be initiated. With the closing of the process control cycle improvement measures again can be assessed for their effectiveness as business process management is a perpetual mission.

The operation of processes inherently has some risks. While risk can not be measured directly, the measurement of the value of all open transactions, representing the exposure to risk, may serve as a proxy measure for operational risk.

From the point of view of the financial controller orders cancelled upon customer request can now be charged. With time a shift away from unit costs to activity based costing seems now feasible.

From the point of view of the clients of securities operations the quality levels can now be monitored.

In the process of separation of process from the business functionality of the applications some lessons had to be learned. For instance the processes contained in an application are much broader than individual business processes. As an example an application may serve for several organizational units as the ones in charge for in- and outbound securities transfers. It is quite obvious that the underlying application must serve both business processes. That means that processes on the IT level tend to be quite complex and this makes the mapping of business processes into them sometimes burdensome.

Process performance management leads to increased transparency. This transparency might not always be welcome and people investigating process performance, especially when related to staff, must do this with caution and be aware of the responsibility they carry.

As it is often the case the benefits of process performance management were not realized immediately. In the case of Credit Suisse it was the ability to measure the service level agreements which promoted the idea of process measurement.

Now that process measurement is becoming more and more familiar, all stakeholders welcome the fact that arguments concerning processes are based on real measurements delivering hard data.

8   Summary and Outlook

After the first implementations of the closed process control cycle Credit Suisse is convinced of the approach and propagation is ongoing. For every application which is modularized the definition of key performance indicators has become a natural supplementary step during the design phase of the processes. As a consequence the strategic initiative towards process controlled order execution is continued with another 10 application areas within securities operations.

Plans exist to include more manual steps which until now are not supported by IT systems. The extension of processes to front applications is another objective pursued. Once theses front to end processes can be measured continuously the focus of process optimization will solely be set on Credit Suisse's customer requirements.

Closing the Cycle – Measuring, Analyzing and Improving Processes, Performance and Workflows in the Insurance Sector

Herbert Oberländer
IDS Scheer AG

Frank Ossig
IDS Scheer AG

Michael Linke
IDS Scheer AG

Summary

Since the opening of the markets in the late 1990s, insurance companies have had to contend with global competition in which the abstract value "insurance protection" is the tradable commodity. Accordingly, optimizing organizational and IT processes and structures in this very conservative industry has now taken on greater priority, a very demanding task due to the highly sensitive data involved. With ARIS Process Performance Manager, a tool is available that enables reorganization and efficiency improvements, e.g. in application processing, to be measured and visualized for the first time. In several pan-European projects, it has led to a significant reduction in throughput times.

Keywords

Combined ratio, insurance industry, process map, legacy applications, business process analysis, weak points, throughput time, response times, QA phase, data extraction, process improvement, timestamp, policy drafting

1   Project Overview

1.1   The Environment

The golden age of the insurance industry came to an end in the 1990s, and the global players in this sector are now confronted by equally global problems. Where once profits could be taken for granted and company success was based on a handful of products, insurers are now finding life that much harder in the marketplace. Intense competition and turbulent times on the stock markets have meant that insurance companies must take concerted action to optimize their true core businesses (e.g. new products, lowering the combined ratio, leaner structures). This is one of the main reasons why the insurance industry is coming to grips more and more with the issue of Business Process & Performance Management. This involves defining the process portfolio within the company and which processes contribute what to the company's success or how important they are for the customer.

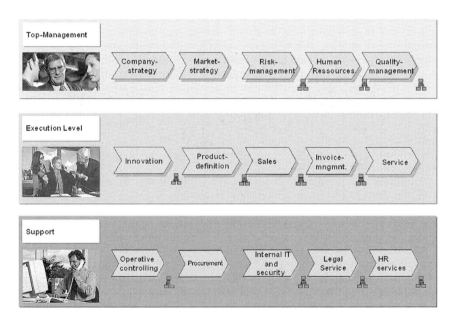

Fig. 1: Process map of an insurance company

In 2004 most of these core processes are handled with IT systems. Looking at these IT-supported processes in detail, it quickly becomes clear that the insurance industry has a highly heterogeneous and individualized IT landscape. Unlike manufacturing and retail for example, hardly any standard software (such as SAP) is used, the central master data and claims systems are mostly systems that have evolved over the years. These applications have been developed and supported entirely by the in-house IT departments for years, sometimes even decades.

In the recent past, these legacy applications have been augmented with more modern transaction and interface concepts using Enterprise Architecture (EAI) solutions, but in essence the core of the old systems has not changed and still serves as the basis for further upgrades.

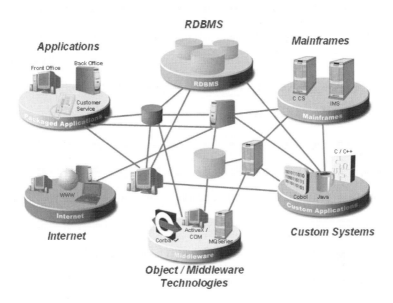

Fig. 2: Classic EAI infrastructure in the insurance sector

1.2   Description of the Problem

In the past, management gathered its knowledge about business activities from variables such as sales trends, cash flow, profit, earnings contributions etc. In other words it relied on information rooted in the past. Process-oriented consideration of the company's business was limited to business process analysis, ad-hoc recording of processing volumes and times noted by employees and retrospective work volume reports relating to a given term date.

The disadvantages of this approach are evident. A high degree of manual work falls to the operational employees in recording the data, and to others downstream in aggregating and analyzing the data. As permanent data collection is not possible, there is always a specific reason for doing so. This means it is hard to recognize trends, and changes cannot be detected early enough.

A further disadvantage is that whole ranges of questions relating to processes simply cannot be answered, e.g.:

- Are there new applications that have been delayed or even lost?
- How cost and time efficient are the various sales channels?
- Where are the weak points and bottlenecks in the workflows?
- How high is the average throughput time for a given product and what were the anomalies?

What was needed then was tool that measures IT-supported business processes. For example, the timely provision of quantity structures, processing and throughput times should enable process managers to estimate resource requirements. The chosen tool should also be able to show very quickly whether a technical/IT modification to a business process has really had the desired effects. And all this should entail less effort, not more.

The spectrum of processes considered ranged from new application processing (at HALLESCHE Private Krankenversicherung, Germany) to loss adjustment (RAS, Italy).

1.3   The Procedure

As a rule, the underlying projects in the insurance field were preceded by an approx. 3- to 4-month pilot project. The aim was to establish whether the information required could be extracted from the legacy IT systems. The pilot project was also intended to answer the question as to how much the information generated by ARIS PPM can support process managers in their work.

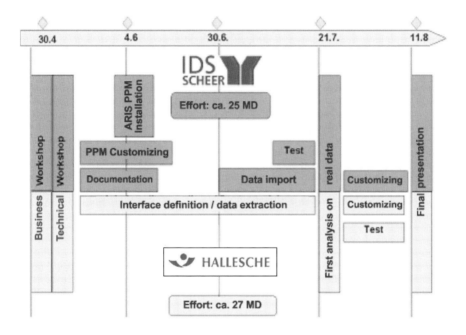

Fig. 3: High-level project plan

An appropriate pilot process was identified during the initial workshops, which were conducted jointly with the technical and application development departments. This process was then used to draw up the list of critical questions that needed to be answered with ARIS PPM. In addition, input was provided about the desired key performance indicators (e.g. processing duration, number of process steps, response times, throughput times per customer) and dimensions (insurance type, sales channel, regional allocation, policy status, etc.).

A review of the technical environment and relevant systems frequently revealed that a certain amount of effort would be required to obtain the necessary source data in each case. The customer-side application developers produced shell scripts for the mainframe and legacy systems to extract the required process data, which was then imported via ARIS PPM import routines into the ProcessWarehouse, where it was then processed. This was done in XML format, which enabled the

IDS Scheer consulting team to develop the import procedure (parsing) for the mainframe data without an unreasonable amount of work.

Following the successful initial import of the source data, it was now possible to generate the first graphic reports "ad-hoc" as it were, and to actively analyze the selected processes. The analysis specifically attempted to determine whether the important questions could be answered at all with the source data, or whether indications of possible behavior patterns could be given and so provide process owners with more transparency on the processes for which they were responsible.

It proved to be absolutely necessary to establish a QA phase that carefully checked for errors in the data delivered. Even minor errors (e.g. a single bit error during data extraction) can seriously corrupt data extraction and lead to irrecoverable acceptance problems for ARIS PPM.

The conclusion of the pilot projects was marked by a presentation of lessons learned and results achieved to the respective decision makers, conducted by the joint team of customer staff and IDS Scheer consultants.

1.4   The Solution

Even in the pilot projects, ARIS PPM provided the customer with more transparency regarding the business volume. Near real-time identification of trends was possible with the weekly updating of data in ARIS PPM. The evaluations that were conducted and the interpretation of results enabled the companies to analyze, control and even improve workflows. Now, individual functional units and their processes can be examined and evaluated so that specific process improvement measures can be adopted. The following slides are taken from a concrete example at a German health insurance company. They enable process owners to identify the weak points in the "New heath insurance application processing" process under review and where the process is carried out particularly quickly. The basis was formed by some 38,000 process instances from a selected representative period that were fed into ARIS PPM as an initial load. Specification and coordination were carried out in close cooperation between the operating organization (OO), the responsible technical department and the application development department (AD). As some of the necessary process steps did not have a timestamp (date and time) in the master data system, it was agreed to use the day as the smallest unit of time. This did not result in any unacceptable loss of information for the desired views.

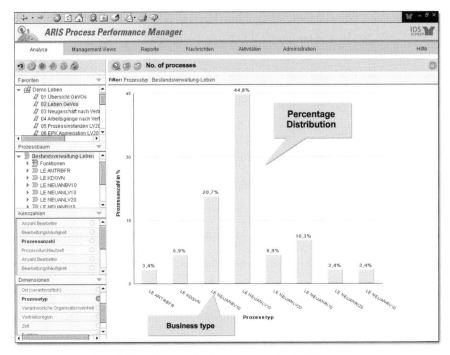

Fig. 4: Drill-down to business types in the "Life" segment

Desired key performance indicators included periods such as between application date and receipt of mail, customer to customer cycle through to policy drafting, and also the number of checks within a process and the number of processing steps. Dimensions such as insurance type, service center, sales unit, sales channel and policy status were chosen so that these key performance indicators could be better judged with respect to their origin.

2   Conclusion

Now that the customers have decided to purchase and establish ARIS PPM throughout the company, the next stage is to identify the suitable processes and prioritize the corresponding implementation projects. The stated aim of the "Insurance" BU is to advise and continuously coach the customer during these implementation projects so that they are ultimately able to use the tool relatively independently. The customer will also be supported in carrying out a weak point analysis and making the necessary corrections by the full extent of the business unit's expertise in the industry, including "best practice" approaches and the process reference model for insurance companies.

Performance Management in Power Stations - with openJET, openBMS and ARIS PPM

Bernd Heselmann
Gesellschaft für integrierte Systemplanung mbH

Peter Stängle
Gesellschaft für integrierte Systemplanung mbH

Andreas Kronz
IDS Scheer AG

Klaus Miksch
IDS Scheer AG

Summary

The integration of the ARIS Process Platform in the open product family of GIS mbH, one of the largest European providers of operations management systems for nuclear power station facilities, has now made holistic Business Process Management technically possible in the energy generation sector as well. The transfer of operations management data for a power station facility from the widely-used openBMS system to ARIS PPM enables users to identify potential improvements in times, quality and costs from extracted real data. Use of the same methodologies and XML structures has led to an integrated Performance Management solution that permits the design, implementation and controlling of process-oriented workflows in the power station environment.

Keywords

Operations management systems, openBMS, openJET, nuclear power station, malfunction and fault reports, occupational safety measures, facility description system, maintenance rate, processing duration, reporting obligations, safety system, indicators, early warning system, process costs, management view, workflow engine, XML import interface, PPM graph format, process typification, processwarehouse, workflow logic, UML (Unified Modeling Language, CORBA (Common Object Request Broker Architecture)

1   Initial Situation

Operations management systems have been used in nuclear power stations since the end of the 1980s. One such system is offered by GiS, and can now be found at many sites in German-speaking countries. The latest version is openBMS. Today it is more necessary than ever that a company continuously reviews its processes and so ensure sustained optimization. Of course, this is done for safety reasons, but also in a context of liberalized and deregulated markets and a depressed economic climate.

But which processes are running badly, where is there need for action? What needs to be done so ensure that power station management is supplied with all the information it needs, and quickly enough for it to institute appropriate measures? Before these questions are answered, the concept behind an operations management system merits a few words of explanation.

2   Operations Management

Running a nuclear power station is an extremely complex undertaking in which several hundred people perform thousands of mission-critical processes with innumerable individual activities each year in a coordinated, compliant and quality-assured manner on an interdisciplinary basis in order to maintain the facility in a defined technical target state at all times. A wide range of regulations, rules and guidelines have to be complied with to ensure the safety of the plant and the environment as well as that of the operators.

Keeping track of this immense workload and variety and still economically plan, execute and document the tasks involved demands an IT panoply that effectively supports and controls all the related processes.

The openBMS operations management system from GiS is equal to the challenge of interactively planning all operations management processes in the facility, as well as monitoring and documenting their proper execution. Conversely, it also ensures that nobody may carry out any maintenance work in and on the facility without a written order to do so. The rule is: "No order, no job". The openBMS occupational safety components efficiently integrate statutory requirements in business processes, thus minimizing risks for the company.

Violation of these environmental and occupational safety regulations can cause lasting damage to a company's image. The use of openBMS effectively supports regulation compliance and thus contributes significantly to achieving company objectives.

The maintenance processes are precisely described in the Maintenance Manual. Every employee can and must carry out exactly that work for which he or she has been scheduled and is responsible for, and the operations management system provides guidance and support so that all the pertinent regulations and guidelines are complied with. With these features, openBMS represents quality assurance in the best meaning of the term.

The system is used to process all the planned tasks of preventive maintenance and also unplanned tasks entered in the form of malfunction and fault reports. This provides for transparency regarding what is happening on the site at the moment and also a complete case history of all faults, repairs and maintenance activities for every component in the facility.

This information forms an ideal basis for damage statistics and analyses. Moreover, it represents a wealth of operational experience that can be tapped in repeat or comparable situations. Knowledge of the facility and its history has long been established as a company asset. Whenever required, a user looks for similar job orders in the system's memory, copies them, makes changes as necessary, and has then already completed the entire job planning. This not only saves a considerable amount of planning effort, it also leverages proven actions and processing mechanisms and exploits past operating experience. If this approach is applied consistently, it results in long-term company expertise that leads to continuous optimization, savings in maintenance costs, enhanced efficiency and innovation and thus provides the preconditions for sustained corporate success.

Thanks to openBMS, the degree of planning for all the tasks to be carried out is increased significantly, a enormous variety of site- and release-related tasks is logically combined, packaged and optimized with respect to resources and time. Each planned job order is greeted by a query as to what other planned tasks with the same release, same BOM, same transport media, lifting gear, personnel etc. can be carried out at the same time. The benefit of this aggregation has is that there are fewer job orders altogether, with fewer releases and better resource utilization. openBMS enables a considerably higher degree of planning with no extra effort for planning activities. This better planning also leads to better and more reliable work results.

A particular challenge for managers is the annual power station audit. A large number of jobs have to be carried out at practically the same time with due regard to all marginal conditions: safety, resources, deadlines, costs. In the days and weeks of the audit, the operations management system serves as the central coordinating tool. Every job, every release or standardization, all occupational safety measures, are effected via openBMS. Although detailed advanced planning is the foundation for a successful audit, careful attention must still be paid to change management.

Timely and extensive advanced planning of all work envisaged has another major advantage: in the event of a temporary stoppage, pending work that was actually scheduled for the audit can be brought forward at short notice. A key aspect of operations management is the facility description system, in which all facility objects (components) are recorded together with their spatial and technical data and described together with their procedural relationships to other objects. The facility description also includes the entire power and control engineering discipline at the facility. The importance of a consistent facility description for the operations management system should not be underestimated: the software system cannot not work effectively without it.

Operations management also means the close synchronization of an enormous diversity of functions such as document management, materials management or controlling. With openBMS, a degree of integration is achieved that removes the boundaries between the various IT systems. As the integration platform, SAP NetWeaver is particularly important here.

All in all, running German power stations nowadays cannot be imagined without openBMS. It plans and controls all activities on and in the facility, permits transparency in daily operations and ensures that QA-sanctioned procedures are established for the tasks of all participants at every hierarchical level.

3   Process Orientation in Operations Management

Power station operators realized very early on that operations management processes would have to be given workflow support. Process data and history have been recorded in the operations management system for years and now constitute a priceless source of information. For example, this information may relate to job order, release or fault reporting processes. The procedure for a fault report is outlined below as a typical example of such processes. Needless to say, these processes differ slightly from power station to power station:

3.1   Reporting and Recording Fault Reports

In general, all staff are encouraged to report malfunctions and faults as quickly as possible. In practice, these range from items left in places in violation of safety regulations to defective lighting and leaks in the controlled area, a very wide range of reports. The fault report is characterized in the operations management system by a damage description. Information on the time reported, the person reporting and his or her organizational unit, when noticed (e.g. housekeeping inspection, by chance etc.) and the operating state of the unit in question can be entered as codes to supplement the report. Digital photographs of the damage and documents can also be attached. Once the originator has entered a fault report, he or she completes the process with a digital signature and forwards it to the shift manager.

3.2   Evaluation by Shift Manager

The shift manager reads incoming fault reports on a current basis and particularly evaluates their impact on the facility and its target state. The assignment of a priority and a deadline is obligatory. Where appropriate, immediate action is initiated as a temporary response to the problem. In this case, a safety release is normally required. If the shift manager considers a particular technical department or member of staff to be responsible, this is entered accordingly. Otherwise, re-sponsibility for rectifying the problem is determined in a discussion with the power station and departmental managers and passed on to the persons in question via a workflow system.

3.3   Acceptance by Assigned Employee

Where appropriate, the assigned employee inspects the problem area and initiates a technical clarification to rectify the situation. This results in a new job order with corresponding planning, or orders that are already planned may be used to correct the fault. The job order constitutes a process of its own.

3.4   Closure of Fault Report by Assigned Employee

Once the problem has been rectified, the assigned employee is prompted by the workflow to describe how the problem was dealt with. Codes can be used in the report to specify the cause of the malfunction, description of the fault, precautions and rectification.

Of course, these business transactions can be controlled and monitored by the workflow system. This guarantees that the right information is processed at the right time by the right unit or person. However, it is also necessary to critically assess the process flow on a continuous basis: Is the defined workflow efficient? Could the work be carried out more cost effectively without any loss of quality?

An example of a new approach to process optimization in operations management is the integration of openBMS and ARIS PPM.

4   Process Analysis in ARIS PPM

The operational experience stored in openBMS (see openBMS ARIS PPM interface) is transferred to ARIS PPM. In other words, the business objects for maintenance and the corresponding workflow information are made available to ARIS PPM for analysis. ARIS PPM uses this information to determine essential indices. For fault reports, these may include for example:

- Number of fault reports relating to the safety system, with high priority for correction
- Number of fault reports that may need to be reported to public authorities
- Fault-related maintenance rate
- Number of fault reports identified during regular inspections of components
- Number of open fault reports
- Fault-related component downtimes, outages and malfunctions
- Downtimes of components covered by preventive maintenance
- Processing time for fault reports

Besides the continuous monitoring of permanent safety indicators, the benefit for operations management lies especially in the situational analysis of the process data. For this, ARIS PPM offers extensive capabilities. Process and maintenance managers are provided with a wealth of new analysis options:

- Can the process chain, i.e. the sequence of steps in a process, be shortened?
- Is all the information available in good time?
- Was there sufficient planning or did delays arise in job execution?
- Do problems arise more frequently in particular constellations?
- Does the process chain have a structural defect?
- Could steps be carried out more efficiently?
- How high are the process costs?

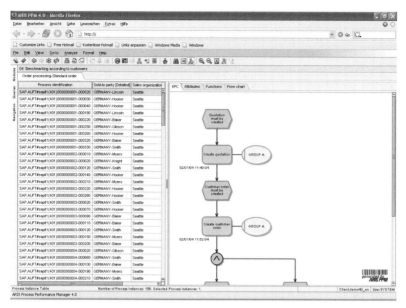

Fig. 1: Process analysis in ARIS PPM

Process optimization in operations management must be seen as a holistic strategy aimed at achieving the goals of improved safety and quality combined with cost minimization and is of course an ideal management tool.

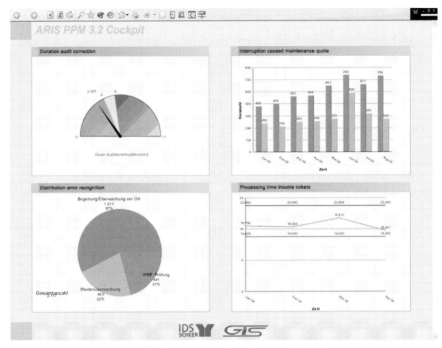

Fig. 2: Management Cockpit in ARIS PPM

Power station senior management defines clear corporate objectives. A failure to meet the defined targets must be made transparent as early as possible. The role of ARIS PPM is to aggregate all the relevant facts to key points so that top management at the power station can make the right decisions as quickly as possible with due regard for corporate strategy and all other marginal conditions. This purpose is served by the Management View, a condensed presentation of the relevant information in a type of cockpit display that can be used as an early warning system (see Fig. 2).

What does successful and feasible process management actually look like, without overambitious promises of success? What improvement potential can managers expect from ARIS PPM coupled with openJET?

5   Business Process Optimization in openJET

5.1   Architecture of openJET

openJET (JET = Java-based Engineering Tool) is a JAVA-based framework for the automated production of mission-critical applications. With openJET, mission-critical applications can be generated directly from the results of the technical analysis. This integrates the systems development phases from technical design through to running applications, thus reducing development and maintenance times.

openJET is based on the 'Model Driven Architecture' (MDA) philosophy. Various graphical editors are used to produce the platform-independent model (PIM). The major diagram types are supported by UML (Unified Modeling Language) for modeling the business logic. A generation process is applied to the PIM to produce and compile the Java source code and the corresponding Java class files. More information about MDA can be found at http://www.omg.org/mda/.

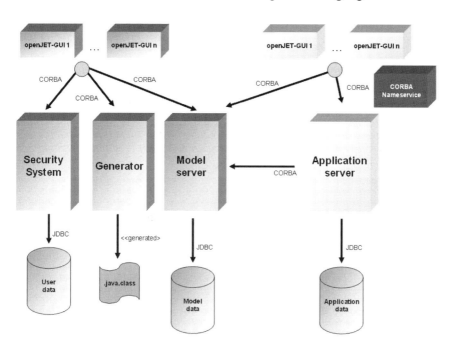

Fig. 3: openJET architecture

openJET provides both the modeling and the runtime environment. Thus openJET offers a complete framework for developing and executing distributed enterprise applications. The overall system has been realized as a classic multi-layer application.

Communication among the various components flows from the servers to the database via JDBC, communication between the servers and clients and between the servers themselves is assured by CORBA (Common Object Request Broker Architecture). The following overview presents the relevant system components:

- **openJET modeling client:**

  The openJET modeling client contains all the tools required to create an application with openJET.

- **openJET application client:**

  The openJET application client provides the environment for executing the created applications.

- **Security system:**

  The security system administers the privileges of the openJET modeling environment users.

- **Generator:**

  The generator automatically creates the necessary .java and .class files needed to run the application. These are stored in the file system.

- **Model server:**

  The model l- server administers the information on the modeled application in a relational database. This includes information about the business classes, for example.

- **Application server:**

  The application server is needed for running the application. It stores the application data in a relational database. This data includes the instances of the business classes, for example.

- **CORBA NameService:**

  The CORBA NameService is required so that components can communicate with each other.

During development, the modeler can concentrate solely on implementing the technical requirements. The following is a selection of the functionalities that openJET provides for modelers:

- Transaction service and object administration
  (caching, optimistic blocking procedure)

- Distributed calls using CORBA

- Object-relational mapping persistence service

- Configuration management layer model

- Workflow engine

5.2   Configuration Management – openJET Layer Model

With openJE, users can customize an existing application. Customizing can be carried out locally by the customer. So that customer changes are not lost during application software updates, openJET provides various modeling layers. There are a total of seven layers in openJET, although the principle will be explained here with only the three that are most significant for modeling.

The Reference Layer is used to develop the openBMS standard software, which is customer-independent. During a rollout of the software the specific customer requirements, especially its business processes, are mapped in the Adaptation Layer. After delivery of the modified application, the customer can make further changes locally in the Customizing Layer.

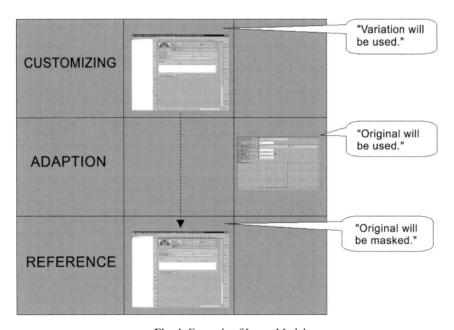

Fig. 4: Example of Layer Model

If a part of the delivered software is changed, a variant of the original is automatically created in a higher layer. During runtime, the highest variant of the software component is always applied and used. The variant masks the original, in other words removing the variant restores the original state. Of course, new software components can also be created in a higher layer. Fig. 4 shows an example of a variant for a GUI dialog.

Installing a new version of the standard software (Reference Layer) at the customer's premises does not affect or overwrite the variants in the superior layers. This guarantees that the customer modifications will still run after a version change.

5.3   Business Process Modeling in openJET

openJET has a workflow engine that is responsible for carrying out a business process during runtime. For the purposes of openJET, a business process represents the sequence in which various business activities (BA) are to be performed. A BA is a special GUI dialog with which a user can carry out a certain task, e.g. the entry dialog for a material master record or a dialog for releasing the material master record.

The workflow engine was designed in conjunction with the University of Erlangen and implemented using the results from GiS mbH. A business process can be modeled using the openJET Workflow Editor, a graphic environment for designing a business process.

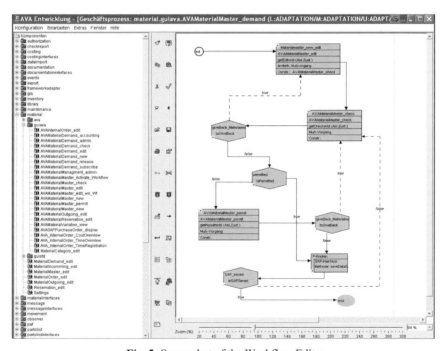

Fig. 5: Screenshot of the Workflow Editor

The following section describes some of the nodes types a developer can use to model a business process:

Operation Nodes

This is the central node type of a business process. An operation node bundles the information "what has to be done when and by whom". The "when" is defined by the position of the operation in the business process. The operation is not due for processing until all the upstream operations have been completed by a user. "Who" is defined by the derivation of a responsibility. The operation can be modeled on a functional, organizational or personal basis. "What" means that an operation node is assigned to precisely one business activity, which the user must process. Other settings can be made to the node that determine, for example, the operation type, whether processing the operation is obligatory or optional.

Decision Nodes

Decision nodes are used to model different paths in the business process, whereby only one is carried out at runtime. Decision values can be simple Boolean values or also integers. The path actually taken is determined by specifying a method that identifies the decision value at runtime.

Program Nodes

With a program node, any program can be executed at a given time in the business process. For example, after a material master record has been released, the data can be sent to an SAP system, where a material master record is also created.

Pause Nodes

A pause node can be used to interrupt a business process until a certain condition has been fulfilled. This means that while the business process is waiting there are no operations for a user to carry out.

Trigger Nodes

A trigger node can be used to "bring to life" a different business process. The business process thus prompted is recalculated and all pause conditions are retested.

Pause and trigger nodes are required to synchronize two or more business processes with each other. For example a maintenance order cannot be closed out until all the associated services have been concluded. In this case, the maintenance order business process waits for the maintenance service business process. Upon its completion, the maintenance service business process triggers the order business process, so that a further check is run to ensure that all services have now been completed.

5.4   Business Process Execution in openBMS

The user has a task list in the main menu. This list contains all the operations from various openBMS business processes that the user has to carry out. This means that the task list is the central entry point for users.

The operations in a user task list are derived from the responsibility modeled on the operation node. Thus, a user finds in the task list all those operations that have been assigned to him or her personally or to his or her organizational unit or to one of his or her functions. If operations are group based (organizational or functionally based), these events can be carried out by several users. Once a user starts processing the operation, it is removed from the task lists of the other group members. The user confirms that the operation has been processed by entering a password. Then the business process is recalculated and the task list is populated with the subsequent operations.

Thus, the Workflow Engine ensures consistent execution of the business process. While a business process is being carried out, the Workflow Engine administers all the process-relevant data in a relational database. The data stored for each completed operation node includes:

- User who completed the operation
- Date and time of execution
- Operation name
- Business object, e.g. material master
- Upstream event
- Downstream event

This data can be used to reproduce the actually completed business process for each business object. This Workflow Engine and business object data is fed to ARIS PPM for analysis purposes via the XML interface (see Fig. 6).

5.5   openBMS / ARIS PPM Interface

Basically, ARIS PPM can use two different procedures for extracting process data from the application systems. Both are based on an XML import interface for asynchronous importing of data to ARIS PPM.

The import interface can handle two different XML formats: PPM graph format and PPM event format. Fig. 6.1 shows these two import variants.

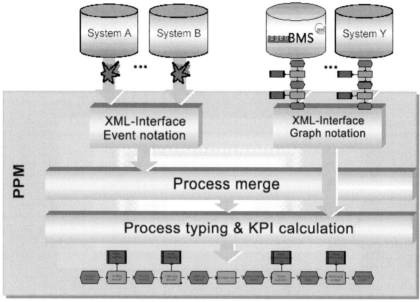

Quelle: IDS Scheer AG

Fig. 6: ARIS PPM XML import interface

The event format is used for all activity-oriented application systems for which the process-forming information (sequence logic) cannot be exported. The events or incidents in the source system are interpreted as process fragments. This is necessary whenever the source system is not workflow based and uses status-based emulation. The configuration effort within ARIS PPM is greater than with graph format as the individual process fragments have to be configured for the "Process merge" step.

PPM graph format is used to import already structured process data from process-oriented application systems (e.g. workflow systems). The openJET-PPM adapter generates XML files that describe business transactions, "process instances", including their workflow logic in PPM graph format. Unlike the PPM event format, complete process instances can be imported. There is no need to merge process fragments to form process instances via a business logic.

Within the ARIS PPM system, the graph format is used for universal exchange of process-oriented data. ARIS PPM uses the transferred process information to build a "ProcessWarehouse". First it categorizes the transferred process instance to determine whether it is, for example, a fault report (process typification).

Then the specific indicators for the fault report, such as duration or costs (key performance indicator calculation) are determined. The analysis is done online in the ProcessWarehouse at the evaluation time, for example the number of open fault reports on certain components.

As process-oriented application systems have been developed with openJET, the PPM graph format was used for the XML interface. The Workflow Engine is responsible for executing the business processes. It is independent of the technical business process and so can be used as the runtime environment for all business processes within openBMS. This enabled a universal openJET-PPM adapter to be created that can be used for all business processes modeled in openJET. Thus a single adapter can be used for exchanging process data on all existing and new business processes with ARIS PPM. Newly defined business processes can also be exported to ARIS PPM without additional configuration.

6   Conclusion

Process orientation and optimization are now key factors for operations management. The ongoing analysis of business processes and their optimized design are critical for future corporate success.

The transfer of operations management data from the openBMS system to ARIS PPM enables users to identify potential improvements in times, quality and costs on the basis of real data in nuclear power stations.

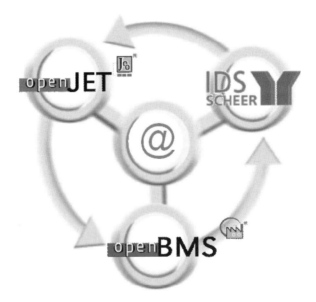

Fig. 7: Business Process Change Management

Business Process Management solutions based on openBMS, ARIS PPM and openJET thus serve to automate, rationalize and optimize complex operations management process sequences. The integration of process design, process execution and process monitoring enables the knowledge generated in the process to be used and made available for closed loop analysis. This optimizes the overall solution and its execution. With the openJET modeling component, processes can again be adapted to individual requirements quickly, simply and cost effectively. If an operations management process need changing or modifying, this can be done while openBMS is running.

In addition, the system permits pragmatic mapping of existing processes, as with the classic procedure using upstream business process analysis.
The ARIS PPM monitoring component permits users to identify the impact of new processes or changes on the existing processes in good time.

This Business Process Management (BPM) approach is enabling ever more companies to improve their operating efficiency. Nowadays, many business processes are mapped in heterogeneous IT systems. The business logic is hard coded in these systems. They lack the flexibility that is needed to carry out changes quickly. If the entire potential of BPM is to be exploited, the IT systems too must meet the demands of Change Management for business processes. With the combination of openBMS, ARIS PPM and openJET it is now possible to implement, analyze and optimize a business process-oriented IT system landscape. As a result, IT systems can be adapted constantly to the evolving experiences and needs of corporate operational processing organizations.

More than Figures – Performance Management of HR-Processes at Vodafone Greece

Petros Panagiotidis
Vodafone Greece

Phillip Knirck
IDS Scheer AG

Andreas Kronz
IDS Scheer AG

Summary

Early 2004 the first ARIS Process Performance Manager (ARIS PPM) pilot project in Greece was launched by Vodafone, with the objective to evaluate how quickly ARIS PPM can be implemented and what business value ARIS PPM can provide. Vodafone had lived and experienced the design and implementation phase of the business process life cycle. As next step Vodafone IT wanted to close the life cycle by implementing Business Process Controlling as final phase of their process-oriented IS Development methodology. ARIS PPM was chosen to close the loop between the realization, GoLive and support stages of the adopted process oriented IS development methodology in the context of systems continuous improvement. The ARIS Process Performance Manager provided Vodafone with a pilot process specific reporting functionality of recruitment processes. The scoped processes could be measured and analyzed by combining the configured test KPIs and dimensions or by analyzing automatically created visualized process patterns, using test data. The project was successfully conducted in a very short timeframe in collaboration with Vodafone Greece IT, the local IDS Partner Spirit SA and ARIS PPM Consultants from the UK and Germany The following pages will share with you how this opportunity emerged and the lessons learned. It will also show which approach was taken to achieve these two objectives and how the project team created added value for all participants.

Keywords

SAP HR, ARIS, recruitment, process extractor, customizing tool kit (CTK), costs per applicant, process mining, vacancy process, process cycle time, multinational team, pilot, test data, test KPIs, process oriented IS development

1   About Vodafone Greece

VODAFONE Group is one of the largest mobile telecommunication companies in the world, participating in private telephony networks in many countries amongst which is Vodafone Greece. In 2004 Vodafone Greece generated almost € 1,5 billion profit with more than 3,5 million customers.

During the eleven years of presence in the Greek market Vodafone has been established in consumers' minds as the leader in the field of mobile communication. Since the beginning of its operation it has traveled a long way, focusing on the application of the most advanced technology, on the development of innovative services and products and on substantial investments. Vodafone boasts the most extended and technologically advanced, durable and reliable against damage or failure, mobile telephony network in Greece, a fact that allows it to provide a wide range of coverage and communication of high quality. In addition to that, acknowledging the fact that its development is interwoven with the progress of the society in which it operates, Vodafone has offered work of great importance in fields pertaining to crucial social issues.

Fig. 1: Greek Vodafone Internet Site

1.1   About the IDS Scheer Partner SPIRIT

In the absence of an IDS Scheer subsidiary in Greece, Vodafone is supported by the Hellenic IDS Scheer Partner SPIRIT SA. SPIRIT offers integrated solutions and consulting services to address managerial challenges in the area of CPM. As much an engineering as a management consulting company, SPIRIT S.A. conceptualizes, develops and implements bottom-line solutions for business and IT transformation. Its core team has been involved with ARIS products and the ARIS methodology since 1998 under different company umbrellas. The company's core business is Business Process Improvement based on IDS Scheer products and the solutions designed around these products.

1.2   The History of ARIS at Vodafone

The ARIS PPM Project at Vodafone is the concluding step of a process which started roughly three years before the project was launched. Over a period of three years Vodafone Greece integrated different companies and business units into a new organisational structure, in order to align infrastructures to recent business needs. As a result the IT was faced with a very heterogeneous systems and application landscape. These technologies had to be integrated into core platforms such as the ERP and CRM systems. To counter this challenge a new "Information System Integration" team under the lead of Dr. Petros Panagiotidis was founded. Faced with this enormous integration task Panagiotidis was looking for a structured analysis tool, which supported a business driven approach instead of one focusing on technical parameters. Petros Panagiotidis, a Ph.D. in Business Systems Analysis evaluated the ARIS products as the best in class for the integration objective.

One application to be integrated was the HR system for which the future platform would be SAP. Around two years after the integration team has been formed the SAP HR system was alive. It had been blueprinted, designed, implemented and rolled out by the Integration Team. Now it had successfully passed both the design and implementation phase of the process life cycle. During the implementation Vodafone was supported by the Hellenic IDS Scheer Partner SPIRIT SA. However, Vodafone management through Dr. Panagiotidis ensured that the main focus was kept on the business issues.

From this business perspective the process life cycle was still in need of the third and concluding phase. The processes anticipated and designed in ARIS needed to be monitored and controlled. It was stressed that the process design and the required "to be processes" had to be linked with Vodafone's real life operations in order to serve as the information system for a continuous improvement cycle. The need to manage and possibly identify any gaps between described processes and real life operations led to the first ARIS PPM implementation in Greece.

Besides the need to measure the HR process, Vodafone wanted to test the ARIS PPM functionality and to get experience in using ARIS PPM. This would allow Vodafone to take forward the experience into further projects and IT systems and in the long run to be able to implement the entire process cycle on their own. As ARIS PPM was a new subject to Vodafone, it was decided to choose a process which could be implemented as a pilot, an approach proven successfully by many ARIS PPM customers before. Due to the sensitivity of HR data, it was agreed that all data used would be fictitious and therefore the KPI results would not represent real life operations. Altogether the project posed two objectives:

- Closing the process life cycle of the HR applicant process
- Testing ARIS PPM functionality and learning about ARIS PPM projects

1.3   The Environment

The recruitment process starts when a position is vacant in the company, and a successor has to be found (either externally or internally). Vacant positions are published in job advertisements. A job advertisement involves the publishing of one or more vacancies with the aim of attracting suitable applicants. The Planning and Recruitment Department checks the received applications in response to the advertisement and then ranks the employees using a profile match up of the job requirements and the applicants' qualifications. These applicants then go through a selection procedure, and a suitable employee is hired. This process is now run using the SAP HR system. It had been chosen as the pilot process for two reasons: first and foremost it was a process in need of a reporting and controlling functionality. Secondly a standard ARIS PPM content for SAP HR is available from IDS Scheer as an official product. This meant most of the reporting functionality needed came out of the box.

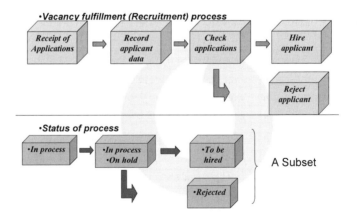

Fig. 2: Recruitment process at Vodafone

The Vodafone SAP HR application had been modified in order to adhere to Vodafone business requirements, this is an approach commonly used by SAP customers. ARIS PPM uses SAP information and thus had to be adapted to the SAP changes. This can be done without programming efforts by using the standard tools that come with ARIS PPM such as the PPM Extractor4MySAP and the Customizing Tool Kit (CTK).

1.4   The Approach

The general approach for the project consisted of three stages: conceptualisation, where requirements and measures where identified, implementation, where ARIS PPM was rolled out and training, where end users were trained and ARIS PPM explained in detail. The following paragraphs cover this approach in more detail.

The project team was formed by Vodafone's IT department, ARIS specialists from Spirit and ARIS PPM consultants from the UK and Germany. Whenever necessary the team got excellent support by Vodafone's SAP specialists. All major project activities were conducted onsite at the customer's premises in Athens. Before all project members met for the project kick off, Vodafone had already worked out, written down and distributed a presentation of their expectations and project requirements.

Project Matrix

Goal	Track and Control the overall time of the Recruitment Process in order to improve the response time to our customers
Component	Labor throughput per Process and per Status
Unit of measure	Time (days / hours)
Recruitment Process Metrics (KPI)	▪ Average no. of days for applicant processing ▪ Recruiting process time ▪ Marketing cost per applicant ▪ Average no. of days for status "In process" ▪ Average no. of days for status "On Hold" ▪ Average no. of days for status "To be hired" ▪ Average no. of days for status "Rejected" ▪ Number of CV processed per day per Recruiter ▪ Time per Decision"

Fig. 3: Overall project objectives and possible process measures as provided by Vodafone

As a result all parties involved were well prepared for the workshop, which made this project stage both effective and efficient. The remaining time was used to write the project charter and to install ARIS PPM. Using their comprehensive business and technical knowledge, Vodafone prepared in advance a document clearly showing their goals and requirements. This made this part of the project easy and fast. Their preparation was backed up with plenty of examples, one being a list of KPIs which they wanted to be implemented together with a technical description of where to find the data for these KPIs.

Description	SAP Table Field
Actions	P4000-MASSN
Status	P4000-APSTA
Advertisement	P4001-OFFID
Applicant Group	Q4000-APGRP
Family Group	P9400-ZEIDIK1
Vacancy	P4002-OBJID
Aplplicant Number	P4000-PERNR
Personnel Sub area	P0001-BTRTL
Personnel Area	P0001-WERKS
Layers	P0001-ZL2
Advertisement Costs	T750B-PCOST
Unsolicited Group	P4001-SPAPL

Fig. 4: Relevant fields in the SAP system

One workshop result was a list of measures to be controlled. Vodafone wanted to fully understand how these can be configured in ARIS PPM. It was therefore decided to conduct full-scale training at the end of the project. Experiences from similar projects as well as best practices were also presented and incorporated into the workshop.

During the workshop new requirements evolved. Some of the KPIs requested were not covered by the standard SAP HR content from IDS Scheer and had to be newly configured. Adding to this was the decision to perform the entire ARIS PPM Training, covering everything from end user application to customization, in order to give the customer a full understanding of ARIS PPM functionality. These new requirements were considered and incorporated into a revised project plan.

At the end of this phase all project members returned to their home bases having created a detailed project charter and performed the first data import into the ARIS PPM system. This thorough preparation ensured a quick start for the ARIS PPM roll out during the second get together.

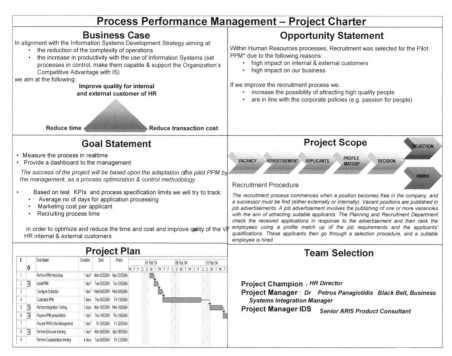

Fig. 5: The Project Charter, a result of the workshop

Before this pilot ARIS PPM had never been used to process Greek information and was therefore only available in German, French and English. However, some of the SAP content contained Greek characters. This issue was tackled in two ways. For the short term solution all Greek information was automatically transformed into English during import using a standard ARIS PPM functionality. Following enhancement a new ARIS PPM Version was implemented which fully supports Greek and any other multi-byte characters (such as Chinese or Japanese). The second meeting was dedicated to configuring ARIS PPM to fulfil Vodafone's requirements and to adapt it to the specifics of Vodafone's SAP system. Two major challenges were encountered: Time constraints and access to the SAP system that was open within set timeslots.

These challenges were resolved through the close collaboration between the experts of Vodafone, Spirit and IDS Scheer. The project team was given free access to any SAP specialist, this access was needed to understand the Vodafone specifics of the SAP system and information structure. Here the technical expertise of Vodafone proved to be an important key to success again.

The team also worked in parallel. One part focused on data import and ARIS PPM configuration while the other one created the preconfigured process analyses, management views and prepared the final presentation.

By adopting this approach the client's requirements were met. All KPIs, dimensions and requested results were delivered on time. Implementing the reporting functionality for an entire process within one week is quite an achievement, and consequently the project team, including Dr. Panagiotidis, was thrilled.

Some measures have the nature of belonging to several processes. One KPI Vodafone had required was not tied to the application process alone: marketing costs per applicant, a measure which is part of the vacancy process. A vacancy can be advertised and the costs of this advertisement can then be divided through the number of applicants who applied as a direct result of it. With the selected applicant process the marketing costs per applicant could only be used in a limited way, i.e. the KPI could only be combined with a certain set of dimensions. In order to work comprehensively an additional process, the vacancy process, was needed.

This scenario was used for the training. Implementing the vacancy process as well as its KPI & dimensions was supposed to be the exercise for the participants of the technical and customization training. The participants were to create something new and provide a real benefit to the project while learning ARIS PPM customizing at the same time.

A Vodafone-specific training scenario was prepared. This new scenario had an additional advantage: its process was much simpler than the application process and therefore would fit a training scenario much better in the sense that it was easy to comprehend by the participants.

The training was divided in user-specific parts. Business personnel and users attended the one-day end user training. The customization training was carried out for users who knew ARIS PPM functionality and were likely to be included into future ARIS PPM projects. The data import training was attended by users with SAP knowledge.

The project management was highly involved in the training and received ongoing summaries. In return its feedback was incorporated into the training. This management involvement and the customised training plan ensured a thorough understanding of the ARIS PPM functionality.

2   Achieved Results

As the goal of the project for Vodafone was twofold (to learn about ARIS PPM and ARIS PPM projects and to close the process cycle of the SAP HR process) the results have to be looked at from these two angles.

Understanding ARIS PPM functionality was achieved through:

- Intensive training with a custom-made training scenario

- Close collaboration between all participants during the entire project course

- Management involvement in conducting process analysis and working together to adhere business values

These measures allowed Vodafone to gain a comprehensive understanding of the added value ARIS PPM can provide and effective use of its potential.

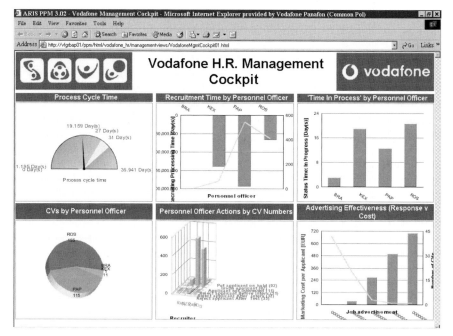

Fig. 6: Management view with detailed analysis about employees and advertisements

In the training the customer understood the attributes and influencing factors, which have an impact on the success of an ARIS PPM implementation project. This knowledge is shared between several persons at Vodafone according to their specialties and background. Project members learned on the job by supporting the ARIS PPM consultants during customization and roll out.

Gradually more and more work was taken over by the project members from Spirit and Vodafone. Therefore Vodafone did not just learn but experienced the work required for ARIS PPM projects.

The management involvement and the accustomed effective training plan as well as the resulting knowledge and experience will allow Vodafone to evaluate what business value future ARIS PPM projects can provide as well as how much effort will be needed to achieve this. In addition to the requirements further benefits were achieved. The standard customization was extended by more than a dozen measures and more than half a dozen dimensions. To facilitate process analysis, favourites were created, allowing instant access of key analyses, many of which were created by Vodafone and Spirit. The most important views were put into two management views in the design of Vodafone's Corporate Identity.

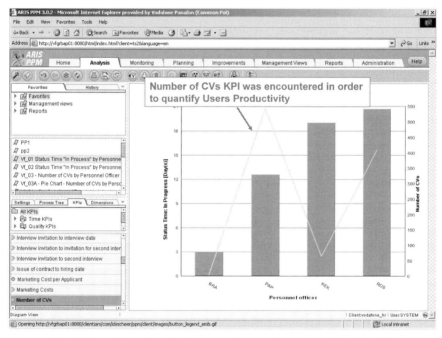

Fig. 7: Quantities and cycle times to analyse performance and productivity

To facilitate process analysis, favourites were created, allowing instant access of key analyses, many of which were created by Vodafone and Spirit. The most important views were put into two management views in the design of Vodafone's Corporate Identity.

The implemented KPIs can be categorized into these categories:

- Volumes and Quantities
- Process Cycle Times
- Costs

The first group was mainly represented by the number of CVs which enables Vodafone to analyse how many applications are being processed in combination with any dimension, e.g. time, employees etc. The number of CVs gives an overall impression of productivity. It allows Vodafone to see their "champions" in terms of which employees are processing most of the work at a certain time. Volumes are also used to understand and explain performance variations in terms of processing time. They show whether the amount of applications handled influences the processing time in a positive or negative way.

"Process cycle time" is the category to which most KPIs implemented belong. The process throughput time as a whole and the duration of parts of the process are analysed with different KPIs of this category. In conjunction with the overall process duration, cycle times for all process states were configured. This gives the opportunity to see overall durations of applications as well as to analyse which parts of the process take how many resources. For example: it is now possible to see how long applications are being processed or how long chosen candidates decide to accept or reject offers. This will help focusing on weak points in the process chain by monitoring closely and improving.

Costs are measured through the marketing costs per applicant. This measure shows the effectiveness of job advertisements. Vodafone now knows how many applicants an advertisement produces and how much it has to pay for each applicant.

Exactly 29 dimensions have been implemented in total, fifteen of these are project specific, meaning they are not part of standard HR customization and have been added by request. Typical examples of dimensions are Recruiter, Processor, Status, Actions, Training, Contact Medium, Recruitment source etc. These dimensions provide different angles and perspectives to view and understand the KPIs performances.

3   Resume and Outlook

The experience of the first ARIS PPM project in Greece produced results and learning experiences in several ways. A complex pilot was executed within a short period of time, including one week entirely dedicated to training. The project has also proven that ARIS PPM works abroad and can overcome even critical issues quickly, as shown by the new multi-byte functionality.

Vodafone's comprehensive understanding of the added value of business process controlling as part of business process management was key to the quick success of the project. From the IDS Scheer perspective, Vodafone's desire to understand how object oriented data is being transformed into process-oriented information was very encouraging. Together with Spirit, Vodafone will now be able to conduct future projects on its own.

The project showed that establishing process controlling will not require huge projects, but by focussing on key business areas and using predefined content such benefits can be realized quite quickly.

Corporate Performance Management in Logistics and Procurement – Focused Identification of Weak Points with Supply Chain Controlling

Steffen Drawert
IDS Scheer AG

Summary

The increasing integration of logistics chains within and between companies offers significant cost advantages, albeit at the expense of higher complexity and loss of transparency. Supply Chain Controlling based on holistic Corporate Performance Management is an approach for restoring clarity. Actual relationships with suppliers can be automatically monitored and documented on the basis of ARIS PPM. A Management Cockpit permits automatic graphic localization and flagging of weak points in the logistics network for further optimization. Evolving the in-house reporting system towards end-to-end process benchmarking with a CPM-based solution approach is then the logical next step to create the basis for establishing Logistics Process Management. Purchasing and procurement thus become the "enabler" for the logistics ability of a company.

Keywords

Supply chain controlling, ABC analysis, delivery backlog, material price stability, delivery reliability, service level agreements (SLA, Supplier Controlling, SLA controlling, root cause analysis, just-in-time, just-in-sequence

1   Why Does Logistics Need Supply Chain Controlling?

The growing complexity of logistical networks within and between the value-added chains of different companies, from the Just-In-Time (JIT) approach of the mid 1990s through to the present Just-In-Sequence (JIS) method, can lead to a drastic reduction of costs, but it may also reduce the transparency in logistics networks, e.g. in the automotive industry. Sustained customer loyalty depends increasingly on market-responsive logistics services from the companies involved. Optimum logistics service as the outcome of intelligent Supply Chain Management can only be assured through optimum coordination of the links in the logistics chain.

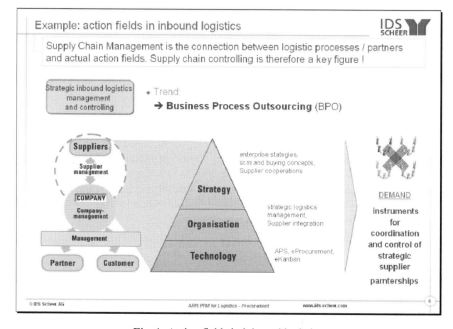

Fig. 1: Action fields in inbound logistics

Despite a rapid development in the field of logistics optimization, many issues relating to efficient planning and controlling of supply chains remain open and unanswered, such as:

- How productive are material inventories today and tomorrow?

- What are the real causes for poor supply service?

- Do suppliers really deliver as desired?

This has been borne out in IDS Scheer's many years of experience. Industry studies reveal that many logistics and purchasing managers complain about a lack of control options in the integration of logistics partners even as the marketplace demands swift responses, and also about a lack of performance transparency within the supply chain, though real-time information could minimize supply delays.

The major deficit is an effective and needs-oriented system for reporting and monitoring solutions to provide near real-time status checks of supply chain processes. Exploiting logistics improvement potential and providing decision support in strategic and operational action fields demands focused analysis that delivers answers to the question: "Where can potential be leveraged to create sustained competitiveness?" This becomes more important than ever when contemplating cooperation with and integration of logistics partners (e.g. suppliers).

2 How Do Companies Benefit from a Process-Oriented Solution Approach?

Effective support for decisions concerning planning and controlling of logistics transfer relationships can only be achieved with a needs-driven transparency in intra- and inter-company processes. Action-oriented reporting solutions are required that enable near real-time management of business processes by not only providing information efficiently but also by effectively triggering and monitoring appropriate improvement actions. The aim is to establish solutions that go beyond the traditional scope of reporting solutions.

This can only be achieved by establishing a direct relationship between the "process" performance and measurement object and "information" based thereon in the form of analyses and cockpits. Only this linkage will ensure focused identification and analysis of relevant deviations (effects) on the basis of possible process and flow breakdowns, i.e. the actual causes. In logistics management systems of this kind, such consistent linking ensures efficient performance and cost measurement and also leads to qualitative and quantitative process transparency throughout the Supply Chain Management system.

In order to meet all these logistics and procurement management requirements, IDS Scheer has leveraged ARIS PPM, its proprietary Corporate Performance Management solution, to create a preconfigured "Logistics" content module for the procurement side (inbound) of the value-added chain, which for the first time permits root cause analysis based on the lived ACTUAL processes.

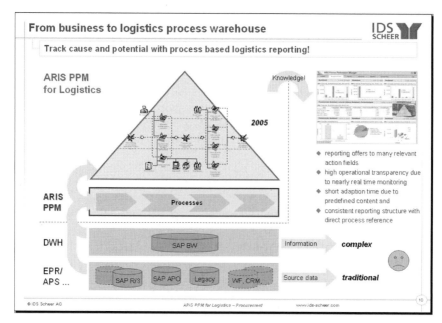

Fig. 2: Logistic Process Warehouse

Starting with the specific action fields and issues at the strategic and operational levels of purchasing and procurement, relevant information requirements were derived and examined for reporting purposes. Not only does the solution permit efficient performance and data management, it also enables the identification and analysis of improvement potential.

3 What Does an Effective and Integrated Overall Solution Look Like?

In order to be able to make the best use of the flexible and adjustable reporting structures provided by the ARIS Process Performance Manager, it made sense to augment the patented Process Mining technology with an industry-specific analysis and reporting solution including a logistics-specific content package.

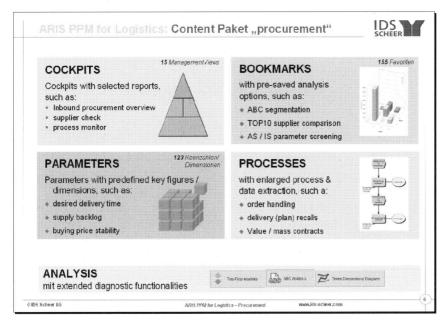

Fig. 3: Content and function scope of the "ARIS PPM for Logistics – Procurement" - industry solution

The primary purpose was to establish a state-of-the-art "Logistics Process Warehouse" with the following outstanding features:

Completely preconfigured ARIS PPM Content Module for

- end-to-end and balanced evaluation of inbound logistics performance,
- practice-related use in procurement and purchasing and
- fast adaptation of an efficient reporting solution.

Comprehensive content coverage of strategic and operational purchasing issues by means of

- user-specific management cockpits,
- application-compatible evaluation and favorites structures and
- multidimensional key performance indicator analyses.

Completely data-oriented expansion of the extraction scope to include

- analysis-relevant characteristics fields,
- purchasing-specific process types and
- preconfigured settlement logics.

Expansion of the analysis and functional scope compared with the standard version to include

- ABC classification/top-flop lists,
- multistage filtering and
- new chart and list types.

For example, Service Level Agreements (SLAs) with suppliers can be controlled with split-second accuracy and consistently integrated in any legacy reporting system. Such monitoring of logistics transfer relationships frequently leads to a higher degree of partner integration and acts as a driver for continuous process improvements. The provision of relevant key performance indicators such as supply backlogs, material price stability or delivery reliability as part of preconfigured analyses accelerates purchasing processes, improves the quality of planning and optimizes supplier performance for the long term.

4   What Can CPM for Logistics Offer Companies?

To show the effectiveness of preconfigured process reporting solutions such as "ARIS PPM for Logistics – Procurement", there follows a discussion of their practical application.

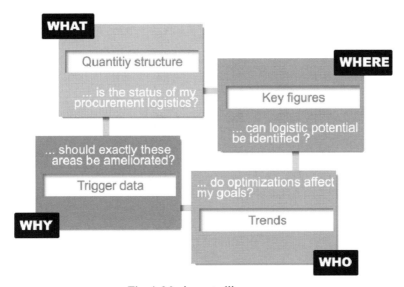

Fig. 4: Magic controlling square

The process-based measurement of logistics performance in procurement and suppler management mostly involves four steps. (see Fig. 4), as explained below. The insight derived should be fed directly into supply chain optimization and drive a continuous improvement process.

4.1   WHAT – Determination of Purchasing Status

The first step is to determine the quantity and value volumes I order to obtain a qualitative and quantitative view of the logistics processes under analysis and to identify action fields and potential. This data pool is formed for example by:

- recording purchasing-related quantity volumes
- identifying logistics-intensive purchasing segments
- clustering in supplier/plant or supplier/material combinations
- detailed analyses according to corporate specification

4.2   WHERE - Measuring Performance Capability

An end-to-end view of procurement based on fully data-based process analyses creates transparency and permits near real-time identification of logistics potential. The performance capability and flexibility of suppliers, for example, can be analyzed both at the time the measurement is taken (snap-shot analysis) and over a period of time (trend analysis). A meaningful, easily comprehensible visualization of the real, i.e. "lived", purchasing process supports understanding of the actual performance (e.g. delivery reliability) of suppliers, so that weak points can be identified in concrete terms This is demonstrated by the following "ARIS PPM for Logistics - Management View" as an overview of logistics and procurement management.

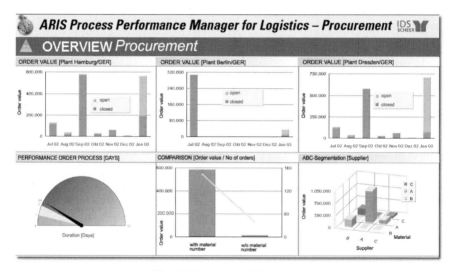

Fig. 5: Magic controlling square

A Management Cockpit like this places the purchasing, logistics and plant managers in the position to make analyses with a wide range of relevant purchasing parameters such as:

- Supply backlog and key performance indicator overview for individual plants

- Strategic process and target/actual comparisons

- Special material/supplier combinations in the form of ABC segmenting

4.3   WHY - Verification of Potential

In order to convert this newly achieved transparency into concrete optimization efforts, the greatest leverage must be brought to bear on the potential concerned In this context, purchasers received automated support in the form of preconfigured segmenting and driver analyses that deliver an initial improvement action package straight away. In addition, flexible target/actual comparisons can be used to establish an efficient early warning system (e.g. email or SMS messages sent as soon as a target delivery date is missed) that draws the attention of managers to the relevant deviations through alert and exception controlling. There is also a flexible ad-hoc reporting module for identifying specific performance drivers.

Detailed diagnosis of critical purchasing processes with respect to structural or individual performance drivers permits verification of the improvement potential in this phase. The following figure shows a typical evaluation of significant planned/actual delivery time deviations for purchaser groups that enables this need for action to be addressed directly to the process owner. This sharpens purchasers' optimization focus, which is assisted in no small measure by the consideration of various process parameters at interfaces with upstream and downstream activities.

4.4   HOW - Support for Improvements

The focused and – based on ARIS PPM Process Mining technology – completely automated visualization of the logistics chain as it actually works delivers methodological and content support for modern purchasing issues such as optimized integration strategies with suppliers (SMI) and also for operational process harmonization.

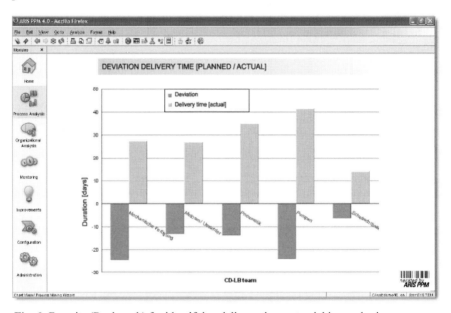

Fig. 6: Favorite (Bookmark) for identifying delivery time potential in purchasing processes

Periodic monitoring of running workflows, processes and procedures enables logistics managers to spot changes and trends early. This permits end-to-end target achievement controlling, e.g. for SLAs. This in turn drastically enhances the performance and visibility of purchasing and also promotes the process-based integration of logistics partners.

5   What are the Concrete Benefits to Purchasing of a CPM System?

The business management and logistics benefits that can be derived from the results of process-based logistics reporting are many and varied, with regard to the identification of causes and potential and also as a key to the practical establishment of an improvement system. The following specific improvements, which have all been proven in real-life projects, can be gained by using a Corporate Performance Management solution:

- Provision of predefined logistics reporting contents for individual user groups
- Fast adaptation to customer requirements (preconfigured, fast rollout)
- Transparency through full data basis for cause and potential identification
- Action-oriented reporting concept down to operational process/records level
- Use of snap-shot analyses also as a tool for continuous process controlling
- Multidimensional process evaluation and deviation analysis possible
- Efficient early warning system through alert controls
- Support for parameter management through full data and plausibility checks
- Effective and end-to-end target achievement controlling possible
- Improved delivery quality by suppliers thanks to split-second controlling of SLAs.

The logical next step is then to use a CPM-based solution approach to evolve the in-house reporting effort into an end-to-end process benchmarking system, and thus create the basis for establishing Logistics Process Management. Purchasing and procurement thus become the "enabler" for the logistics ability of a company.

Continuous Measurement and Analysis of Operations Management Processes – ARIS PPM at E.ON Kernkraft GmbH

Karl Ramler
Kernkraftwerk Unterweser
E.ON Kernkraft GmbH

Jürgen Schwarzin
Kernkraftwerk Unterweser
E.ON Kernkraft GmbH

Andreas Kronz
IDS Scheer AG

Klaus Miksch
IDS Scheer AG

Summary

The Unterweser Nuclear power station (KKU), owned by E.ON Kernkraft GmbH decided at an early stage to establish an end-to-end Performance Management System (PMS). The PMS was realized as an end-to-end control system and set up on the basis of a clear strategic focus derived from E.ON Kernkraft GmbH target specifications. The IDS Scheer Corporate Performance solution, which was added to the deployed SAP BW Business Intelligence solution to include process-oriented analysis functions, achieved the goal of anchoring and implementing process management in the company.

Keywords

Nuclear power, energy, KKU operations management system, performance-related process indicators, SAP BW, Performance Management System (PMS), cockpit, browser-based, Malfunction and Fault Reports (MFR), deadline overruns, corporate performance management, operational key performance indicators, ACTUAL costs, PLANNED costs, main drivers

1   Outline Presentation of E.ON Kernkraft – Unterweser Nuclear Power Station (KKU)

Based in Hannover, E.ON Kernkraft GmbH (EKK) is the operator of or shareholder in a total of thirteen nuclear power stations in Bavaria, Lower Saxony and Schleswig-Holstein. This makes it the largest private nuclear power utility in Europe. The installed net output of all plants including the shares in shared ownership nuclear power stations is more than 8,500 megawatts (MW).

Fig. 1: Unterweser nuclear power station

EKK is the operator and sole shareholder of Unterweser Nuclear Power Station (KKU), which is situated ten kilometers south of Nordenham on the lower reaches of the River Weser. The nuclear power station commenced commercial operation in September 1979. A pressurized water reactor generates a net output of 1,345 MW, representing a significant contribution to the reliable and environment-friendly production of electricity for Germany.

By October 2004, the power station had generated more than 230 billion kilowatt hours. This generation achievement is unequaled by any other nuclear power station in the world. In 1980, 1981 und 1993, KKU was the generating world champion. Since coming onstream, Unterweser nuclear power station has achieved an average availability of some 90%. This places it among the best pressurized water reactors in the world. Its high availability also serves as proof of the reliability and operating safety of the power station, as well as the high technical standard and expertise of its workforce. With its 320 employees, Unterweser nuclear power station is an important economic factor for the entire region.

The KKU mission is to generate electricity. It is one of the base load power stations that are onstream around the clock. Base load is the volume of electricity that must be available day and night without interruption.

1.1 Technical Data:

Gross output:	1,410 MW
Net output:	1,345 MW
Therm. output:	3,900 MW
Electricity generation 2003 (gross):	9,747,671 MWh
Availability 2003	88.34 %

2   Initial Situation

None of the operational control systems and analysis tools commonly used for controlling today is capable of promptly and permanently identifying weak points in business processes. Analysis and optimization projects are normally of a one-off nature, the data capture and optimization methods chosen are too time-consuming for permanent use, data is entered manually and usually has no interfaces to operational systems. The recording and analysis of performance-related process indicators is a precondition for holistic process management and forms the basis for end-to-end and continuous process optimization. Process Performance Management is based on the measuring of operational key performance indicators which until now could not be captured at all or only with great effort. Performance-related process indicators are derived from the operational control systems and presented as user-oriented evaluations. Identifying key performance indicators for process-oriented controlling of a company presupposes that a technical concept has been defined that renders the controlling relevance (meaningfulness) of the key performance indicators transparent and enables IT-technical implementation.

For the first time with the "ARIS Process Performance Manager (ARIS PPM)" software tool developed by IDS Scheer, the objective of permanently anchoring process management in a company and supporting it with credible data can be achieved.

The following article describes the integration of ARIS PPM in the KKU operations management system and serves as an example of how the ARIS PPM analysis capability can be used.

3   Integration of the Process Performance Manager (ARIS PPM)

KKU decided at an early stage to establish an end-to-end Performance Management System (PMS). The PMS was realized as an end-to-end control system and set up using a clear strategic focus derived from the EKK target specifications. Figure 2 illustrates the primary PMS system functions.

Functional Scope of the Performance Management System

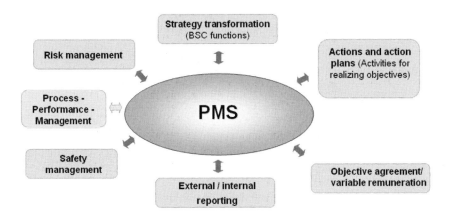

Fig. 2: KKU Performance Management System

The role of process performance management within the PMS is to monitor all important process flows and is thus a key component in the implementation of the entire control system at KKU. ARIS PPM, manufactured by IDS Scheer AG, is used for continuous process performance measurement. ARIS PPM was integrated in the IT system structure and organizationally in the PMS.

3.1   IT Integration

The key performance indicators managed in the PMS are administered in the SAP Business Warehouse (SAP BW). The SAP BW administers the definitions and the movement data (target-actual values and traffic-light thresholds) for each key performance indicator but not the raw data itself. In other words, SAP BW is used as the display, administration and definition component. The provision and calculation of the actual values from the operational level depends on whether or not the process is IT-assisted. Monthly key performance indicators captured manually or processes without IT support are entered via an intranet entry system that stores the results directly in SAP BW. For the IT systems used by KKU

- operations management system (OMS),

- document and event management system (DMS / EMS) and

- business management systems (SAP R/3)

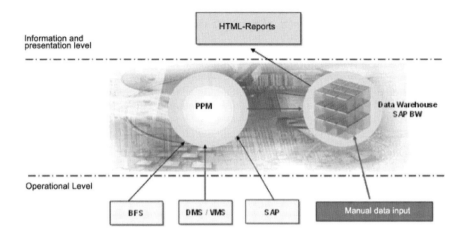

Fig. 3: IT system structure

the key performance indicators are recorded with ARIS PPM. This data is automatically transferred from ARIS PPM to SAP BW via configurable interfaces so that all the results are available in a uniform manner in SAP BW. New key performance indicators require only additional configuration of the interface between SAP BW and ARIS PPM. Users can access HTML evaluations via a Management Cockpit at the information and presentation level. For further analysis, they can then jump to the ARIS PPM analysis component. The following figure is a diagram of a typical IT system structure.

The advantage of this architecture is the fast entry and easy expandability of processes and the use of comprehensive analysis capabilities in ARIS PPM. The key difference between ARIS PPM and the DataWarehouse is the deliberate structuring of the data extracted from the operational systems in predefined process structures. This enables automated performance measuring of running business processes and so enables the efficiency of company procedures to be evaluated on the basis of measured PMS key performance indicators for the purposes of proactive process controlling.

At the same time, in SAP BW have a globally uniform interface for querying and viewing basic key performance indicators. Local entry of manual key performance indicators is possible and also simple to expand.

For all the processes carried out with OMS, DMS / EMS and SAP, the data is generated with ARIS PPM. The following figure shows the processes that have been implemented.

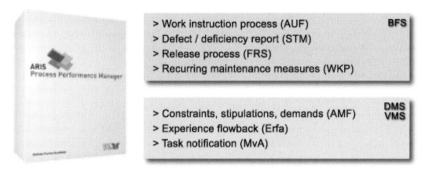

Fig. 4: Processes implemented in ARIS PPM

Over 100 key performance indicators are already being determined for the seven realizable processes. Further evaluation options are currently being assessed for the SAP processes. The process performance indicators obtained form a part of the input information for management assessment.

3.2   Organizational Integration

The ARIS PPM organizational integration is effected by management assessment. At KKU, it is done in stages as shown in Figure 5. This self-check is carried out on a monthly basis by departmental managers. This involves evaluating the target achievement of the PMS and initiating corrective actions where required. Level 1 management assessment is normally carried out on a quarterly basis by the facility manager (FM) as part of the status meetings with the departmental managers. The aim here is to ensure inter-departmental target achievement and effectiveness of the PMS. Level II management assessment must be carried out annually by the facility and departmental managers.

This addresses the suitability and appropriateness of the PMS, annual target achievement and coordination of the following year's target values.

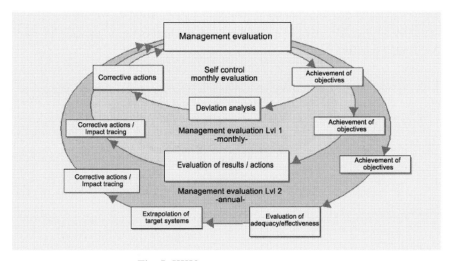

Fig. 5: KKU management assessment

The PMS key performance indicators can be reprioritized and recalculated and are quickly implementable thanks to the flexibility of the IT system structure.

For all the PMS process performance indicators in which the targets have not been achieved, managers receive a detailed ARIS PPM evaluation (called the Management View) in preparation for the management assessment. Below is a typical example of an ARIS PPM Management View on missed deadlines for malfunction and fault reports (MFRs).

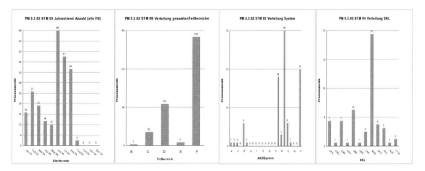

Fig. 6: Detailed evaluation for management assessment

These detailed evaluations help the managers in question to analyze the deviations. If necessary, they can then call up further analyses for identifying the causes. Other options provided by ARIS PPM will be explained in the following example of deadline tracking for malfunction and fault reports.

4   Process Analysis with Process Performance Manager (ARIS PPM)

A favorite is defined in ARIS PPM to map a process performance indicator. A favorite is a standard evaluation comparable to using a browser bookmark for an analysis that has been saved and can be called repeatedly at any time. Favorites are the starting point for evaluations and can be refined with selection criteria (dimensions), filter settings etc. The options available in ARIS PPM are demonstrated in the following example.

4.1   Analyzing "Deadline Tracking of Malfunction and Fault Reports (MFRs)"

As mentioned above, analysis starts from a favorite. The following figure shows the favorite "MFR_04.1 Proportion of missed deadlines" for the MFR process. The y-axis in the data window shows the number of processes as a percentage and the x-axis whether the processing deadline was exceeded or not.

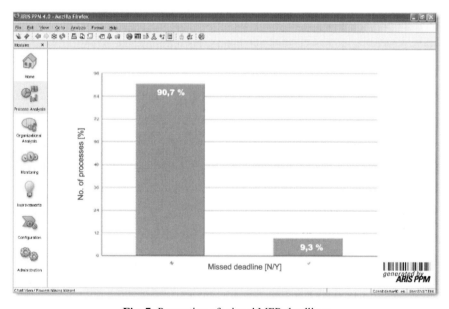

Fig. 7: Proportion of missed MFR deadlines

In 2004, 90.7% of the malfunction and fault reports (MFRs) were completed on time and 9.3% were late. The next question is then by how much.

The analysis shows that the missed deadlines were in a range from 1 to a maximum of 14 days. A more detailed analysis (see Figure 7) shows that of the 9.3% late MFRs (see Figure 8) about 83% were less than 3 days late. 16.2% were between 3 and 7 days late and only 0.7% were more than 7 days late.

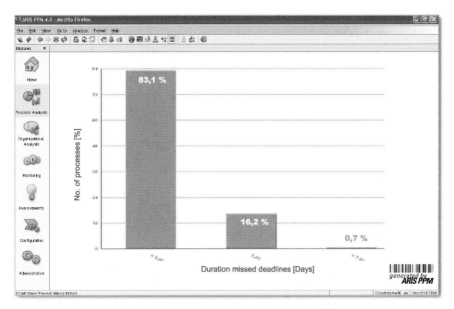

Fig. 8: Detailed evaluation of the duration of missed deadlines

Every malfunction and fault report has a lead organizational unit that is responsible for the MFR and its rectification. This then raises the question whether there are organizational differences in carrying out MFR processes and whether there are lead organizational units (OU) that cause more missed deadlines than others.

Analysis (see Figure 9) shows differences in the distribution and a buildup of missed deadlines at OU F. The reasons for this can now be examined, especially for purposes of comparison with OU G, so that best practices can be copied or a better distribution of MFRs for a more even workload. The greatest potential for optimization seems at to be at OU F with 47%.

This means that improvements can be introduced at the right place. After completion of the analysis for this organizational unit, the causes can be identified and presented at the next management assessment.

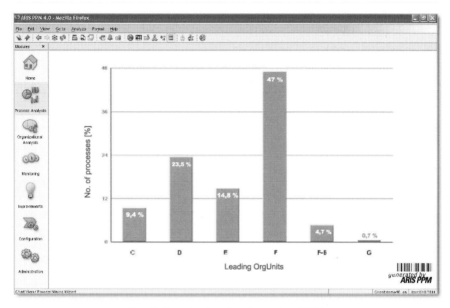

Fig. 9: Organizational units causing MFRs

It is very important that the resources responsible be addressed with objective figures. In this way the resources primarily responsible for missed deadlines can be convinced to examine the deviations in detail and work on a solution to the problem.

A further consideration for the analysis is which process-technical systems (see Figure 10) are affected by the missed MFR deadlines. KKU process-technical systems are designated by facility identifiers (FI) and aggregated over several levels in components and component groups.

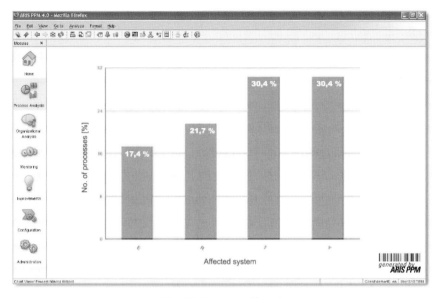

Fig. 10: Systems affected

An analysis is thus normally refined across the systems' various hierarchy levels. Figure 10 shows a predominance of MFRs with missed deadlines in systems T and Y (30.4%).

What is the distribution in System T?

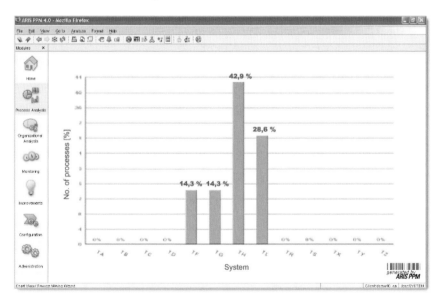

Fig. 11: Distribution System T, TH System Part 1

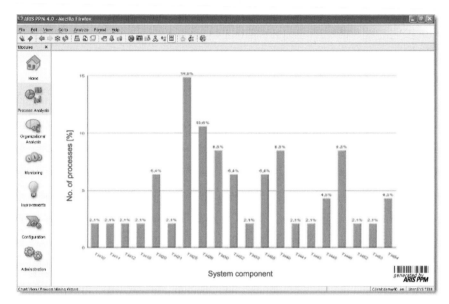

Fig. 12: Distribution System T, TH System Part 2

As can be seen from Figures 11 and 12, the peak is in System TH (approx. 43%). Within System TH, this can be broken down to subsystem TH25 with approx. 15% and TH26 with approx. 11%. The next step is to clarify the problems that led to the deadlines being missed. One possible cause might be a lack of spare parts for these components.

Appropriate modification of inventory strategy could then rectify this deadline problem. This example clearly demonstrates how the analysis can be used to systematically eradicate individual weak points.

4.2   Analyzing the Urgency of Malfunction and Fault Reports

An urgency is stipulated for dealing with MFRs. The urgency of an MFR can be adjusted if the situation at the facility permits this. This then influences the specified deadlines for the MFR and thus the missed deadline key performance indicator.

In fact, there are situations in which it is necessary to change the urgency of an MFR. However, changing the urgency comes at the expense of impacting process efficiency. The following figure shows how often urgencies were changed in 2004. The urgency of about 14% of MFRs was changed.

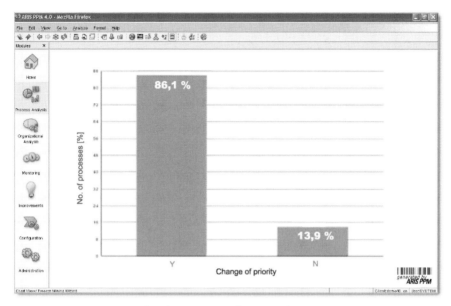

Fig. 13: Frequency of urgency changes

As with missed deadlines, the next step is to analyze the distribution of changes according to the organizational units that trigger them. The approximately 14% urgency deviations were caused by the organizational units as shown in Figure 14.

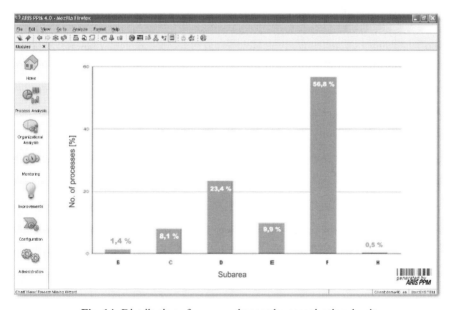

Fig. 14: Distribution of urgency changes by organizational unit

4.3   Analyzing Open Malfunction and Fault Reports

Another important aspect relating to missed deadlines is the number of open MFRs. The number of open MFRs must not be allowed to become too large, otherwise this could impact facility availability.

At the time the analysis was run, 173 MFRs were still open across the lead organizational units, as shown in Figure 15:

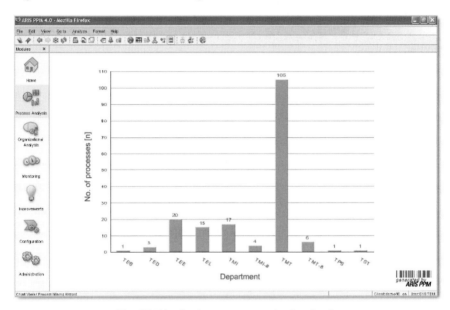

Fig. 15: Distribution across organizational units

Again, organizational unit F seems to be resource primarily responsible. Despite the high rate of urgency changes, OU F still has the largest number of open MFRs. If deadline reliability in the processing of MFRs is to be maintained, it is absolutely essential to rectify the causes of F's missing deadlines in a permanent manner.

Key performance indicators should never be considered in isolation, as they mostly reflect just one aspect of a process without horizontal relationships and dependencies. For example, controlling MFRs should look at both missed deadlines and also the number of urgency changes key performance indicator. Only by considering these key performance indicators together and the way they affect each other it is possible to achieve a corporate optimum defined on the basis of the target specifications.

Following the rollout of ARIS PPM, the processing of MFRs was tracked on a regular basis. From 2002, there was a steady downward trend. The quota of missed deadlines fell from a maximum of about 37% in 2001 to its current level of approx. 10%. 98.4% of MFRs are completed within a tolerance of three days.

The rigorous analysis of the causes for missed MFR deadlines led to a considerable reduction in the number of missed deadlines.

The tracking of malfunction and fault reports example impressively shows that the use of ARIS PPM has materially improved punctuality in MFR processing. This translates to better quality and improved efficiency.

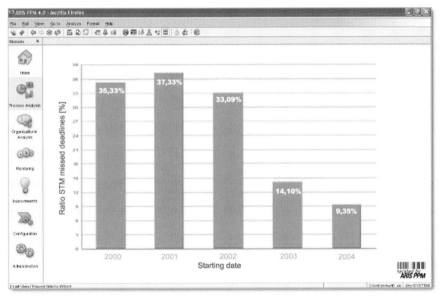

Fig. 16: Trend from 2000 to 2004

5   Summary

With the PMS control system, KKU has created an efficient tool for continuously evaluating and optimizing the operational management of its plant. One of the most important elements is the analysis of business processes, realized with ARIS PPM and integrated in the PMS. Now that the system has been in live operation for some time, the integration and use of ARIS PPM in the KKU control system has been deemed a great success. Further processes have been integrated in the PMS without any problems. The benefits of ARIS PPM were clearly demonstrated.

ARIS PPM is a flexible tool for mapping process performance indicators without a high level of effort. Transparency for managers regarding process performance and the identification of process weak points has been significantly improved. The technical departments are now in a position to conduct detailed analysis of their processes using real data from the operational systems without extensive work or calling on the IT department.

The options provided by ARIS PPM for identifying weak points or root causes of problems in processes from the key performance indicator are shown in the following figure.

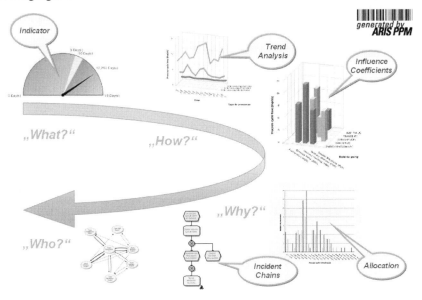

Fig. 17: Capabilities of ARIS PPM

The consideration of trends, influencing factors and distributions enables the causes for deviations in a given key performance indicator to be determined. ARIS PPM provides the basis for deriving corrective and improvement measures and thus contributes significantly to improving process quality and efficiency.

Analysis and Optimization of the Credit Application Process at DaimlerChrysler Bank

Lars Müller
Daimler Chrysler Bank

Frank Gahse
IDS Scheer AG

Summary

DaimlerChrysler Bank is one of the leading German auto-banks and for years has been expanding at a rate well above the sector average. Fast and fault-free business processes with low process costs are a key success factor for long-term retention of satisfied customers through new profitable financial services. A year ago, DaimlerChrysler Bank decided to implement ARIS Process Performance Manager. This article discusses the procedure and the experiences gained during the rollout of process measurement for the credit application process. It ends with a look at future uses for the tool.

Keywords

Process performance management, measuring and analyzing process performance indicators, process automation, service level management, customers' business processes, return on investment in IT

1   Presentation of DaimlerChrysler Bank

With a balance sheet total of EUR 14.2 billion, DaimlerChrysler Bank is Germany's second largest auto-bank.

Its product line includes financing, leasing, insurance and fleet management for Mercedes Benz, smart, Chrysler, Jeep and Setra vehicles. In Germany, DaimlerChrysler Bank gets more than 40 percent of all new DaimlerChrysler cars and 50 percent of utility vehicles rolling. Since mid 2002, the bank has also been offering overnight money accounts, fixed-interest-rate deposits, savings plans, investment funds and credit cards for private customers. DaimlerChrysler Bank services more than 900,000 customers, half of whom with leasing and financing transactions with a contract value of over EUR 13 billion.

			2003		
No of Customers			845.080		
No of Employees			1.488		
			2003	**2002**	**2001**
Balance Sheet Total	According to US-GAAP	Mio €	14.213	12.173	10.781
Turnover	According to US-GAAP	Mio €	3.697	3.420	3.079
	Leasing and Financing				
	Accounts	Units	655.346	613.468	570.078
	Contract Asset	Mio €	13.222	12.192	11.298
Deposits					
	Accounts	Units	147.166	43.429*	-*
	Deposit Volume	Mio €	3.138	768*	-*
Funds					
	Subscription volume	Mio €	90**	-**	-**
Credit Cards					
	Units		248.351	12.974	-*

* Launch deposites and cards 01.07.2002   ** Launch funds am 01.07.2003

Fig. 1: Development of DaimlerChrysler Bank in figures

2   Process Performance Management at DaimlerChrysler Bank

2.1   Initial Situation

In the past, company management and thus controlling was highly profit-oriented. Financial metrics such as interest revenue, costs, operating profit or return rate on equity were used by senior management to assess the overall business situation. Growing and more diverse customer wishes, tougher competition and not least the rising importance of information technology have all led to sharply increased demands facing company management over the past few years.

As part of its strategic focus, the aim of DaimlerChrysler Bank is to be the best financial service partner for customers and dealers in close cooperation with the DaimlerChrysler brands. In order to reflect the shifting demands on the company's objective system, 2003 saw the launch of a project to develop a detailed balanced scorecard (BSC). Along with the financial metrics, BSC also measures goal achievement in the customer, process and potential perspectives.

DaimlerChrysler Bank customers expect their mobility requirements to be met and their financial flexibility ensured. Excellent service and high quality are the keys to success. Customers and dealers need a fast response to credit applications. In particular those business processes with direct customer contact must be designed in a way that ensures fast and reliable processing. Optimal processes can only be provided, however, if they are continuously monitored. That is why, in the autumn of 2003, DaimlerChrysler Bank decided to add process performance to its controlling approach by including the ARIS PPM software solution from IDS Scheer.

2.2   The Objectives

The underlying objectives of DaimlerChrysler Bank in the process-oriented development of its controlling system were:

- Ensuring high-quality and efficient business processes
- Creating transparency on actual processes
- Identifying optimization potential in process flows
- Visualizing the impact of process changes over time
- Meeting the demands on the balanced scorecard

- Replacing or consolidating decentralized reporting
- Organized distribution of process know-how

3   Implementation with ARIS PPM – *easyline* Pilot Process

Before deciding on ARIS PPM, a test installation using the credit application process as an example was carried out to determine the suitability of this tool. An initial prototype with real data was available within a short space of time. With relatively little effort, the selected process data (status information, timestamp, evaluation dimensions) were imported from the operational systems to the PPM database.

The initial results were so convincing for all those involved in the project that a decision was taken to acquire the appropriate PPM licenses and to use the test installation as the basis for implementing a pilot project to measure the performance of the *easyline* process.

3.1   Process Description

The *easyline* process is part of the credit application process in DaimlerChrysler Bank's leasing/financing product area. In general, car dealers can submit a credit application in two different ways: either by fax or the "submit button" in their proposal/costing program. The latter case involves the *easyline* process.

The "happy path" in the *easyline* process is as follows: A customer in the dealer's showroom has chosen a car, e.g. a Mercedes-Benz CLK. But the dealer can only complete the order when the financing has been arranged. To do this, he or she records the customer's data and sends the financing application to DaimlerChrysler Bank using the submit button. This results in automatic prechecking before the application is stored in the agreement management system. Then a suitable scorecard based on the customer and agreement data is used for an automatic credit check (point evaluation) and confirmation. The positive credit decision is sent back to the dealer via the feedback interface. The dealer has had to wait less than a minute for this positive credit decision. The prospective customer feels that he or she has been well advised and signs the contract for the dream car.

In reality, the process often does not follow the optimum path for any number of reasons. On the one hand, the dealer might have overlooked some data, so that the application is returned for completion. Or the data is complete but does not meet all the criteria for automatic processing. For example, individual repayment is to be agreed. Even if *easyline* has been able to create the application, the credit check may fail or require manual checking – e.g. if the scoring system ranks the customer as not or not fully creditworthy or the response from the automatically consulted credit agency has not been received. In such cases, DaimlerChrysler Bank may require further information from the dealer or the customer, or the case is sent to the support center for manual checking. Or the customer may want an alternative financing plan or even put off signing the contract until later.

The actual performance of the *easyline* process is to be continuously measured with ARIS PPM. A technical process model with specific measurement points was defined in a technical requirements workshop. The process to be measured comprises four functions or subprocesses that can produce a wide range of events. Along with the timestamp, the individual events also contain the information as to whether a function was completed automatically or whether manual processing was necessary.

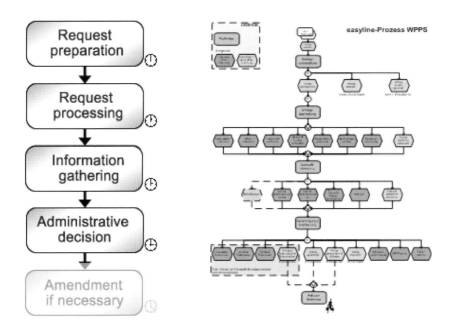

Fig. 2: *easyline* credit application process with defined measurement points

3.2   Technical Architecture

ARIS PPM uses probes to extract the information from the individual *easyline* process instances. The extracted information must contain all the attributes required for calculating and presenting the defined measurement variables. The event timestamp is the key information for ARIS PPM so that it can understand the sequence of the individual steps in an end-to-end process instance. This is how

ARIS PPM converts unstructured information into business processes. The standard extraction format is XML. The process instances are stored in a database known as the ProcessWarehouse.

OLAP technologies are used to query the ProcessWarehouse. The results can be illustrated in more than 30 different business graphics. The probes are normally applied to critical processes, such as transitions in the organization or system interfaces. In the DaimlerChrysler Bank case, data extraction was relatively easy. This was thanks to the use of EAI (Enterprise Application Integration), a process automation technology. The company opted for BusinessWare from Vitria for the process automation level. BusinessWare collects the business process information from the individual operational systems and controls the operational flow. All the relevant process information is transferred from the EAI layer to ARIS PPM. The advantage of this is that only one interface for PPM needs to be implemented and maintained for the *easyline* process.

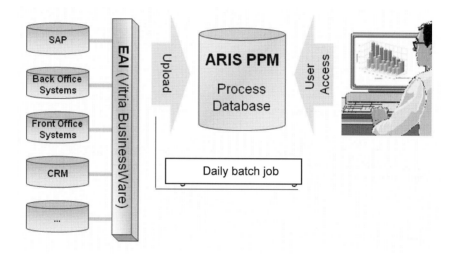

Fig. 3: Integration of ARIS PPM in the DaimlerChrysler Bank system architecture

3.3   Measurement Variables and Dimensions

A number of measurement variables were defined for the ARIS PPM pilot that express various process performance criteria (time, quantity, quality, efficiency). Cost-related measurement variables have not been analyzed so far, though this is possible with ARIS PPM.

The measurement variables are generally broken down by process and function levels. For example, whereas there is only one possible occurrence for each of the considered measurement variables for a credit application at the process level (e.g.

number of manual interruptions), the same measurement variable can have several occurrences at the functional level – depending on which function is being considered.

The following tables show the measurement variables implemented:

KPI	Type	Business content / explanation
Number of processes	Quantity	Absolute number of request processes. Multiple display of the same request on a repeated cycle
Manual break	Quality	Average number of manual breaks in the *easyline*-process. Every event which results in a manual intervention is counted as a break (e.g. manual customer classification)
Automation Level	Efficiency, Quality	Percentage of requests which ran through the whole process without being manually broken
Cycle Time	Time	Total cycle time of a process from the first to the last event. The cycle time changes as long as the whole process is not finished. Thus the use of this category makes only sense if the analysis is limited to finished processes. The basis for the 'KE-quota' KPI
KE-quota	Time, Service level	Percentage of those credit checks that were reported back to the seller within 15 minutes for *easyline*-processes in consumer business. (Processes with a cycle to of <= 15 minutes in relation to all processes)

Table 1: Measurement variables at the process level

KPI	Type	Business content / explanation
Function Cycle Time	Time	Total cycle time of a process from the first to the last (current) event. The cycle time changes as long as the observed function is not finished. Thus the use of this category makes only sense if the analysis is limited to finished functions.
Processing frequency	Efficiency, Quality	Average number of process steps per function. Tells how often a function is ran through at average (hint to loops)
Manual Breaks	Quality	Average number of manual breaks per function (see corresponding measurement category of the same name)

Table 2: Measurement variables at the functional level

Various evaluation dimensions were defined as part of the technical concept so that process owners can trace the causes of any deviations from planned values. For example, an increase in the throughput time of the overall process could be caused by a clearly distinguishable problem in the commercial business process of a particular dealer. Only this knowledge permits focused process optimization and fault rectification.

The dimensions too can be categorized by process and functional level. The following dimensions were defined for measuring the *easyline* process:

Dimension	Explanation / Example
Process type	Order processing
Process status	Event where the process is currently located
Business area	Retail, Fleet
Product	License, Financing
Usage of contract	Commercial, private
Region	North, South
Service center	Munich, Hamburg
Dealer organization	Car dealer, who made the request (e.g. office in Stuttgart, sales representative Maier)
Car	Cars (MB, Chrysler, smart), Commercial vehicle (HGV, busses, transporters,...)
Time	Time of incoming request (scaleable from hour to years)
Contract / order number	Search dimension

Table 3: Dimensions at the process level

Dimension	Explanation / Example
Function	Term for an observed process step
Processing status	Events which were passed by a function (very important dimension)

Table 4: Dimensions at the functional level

When selecting the required evaluation dimensions, attention must paid to ensuring that only those dimensions are defined for ARIS PPM that actually influence the process flow or are required for qualified cause identification. Here is an example from the pilot project:

The contractual type of use (private, commercial) depends on the customer's legal form and is thus an important customer-dependent feature that affects the process flow. The reason for this is that a commercial customer is subject to different credit check standards than a private customer. This results in a different expectation for the throughput time until the credit decision is received. At the beginning of the pilot, the customer's industry was also defined as an important evaluation dimension. However, it transpired that this has no influence at all on the process. Therefore this dimension can remain hidden in the future.

3.4   Project Chronology

Implementing ARIS PPM for the *easyline* process took less than six months from start of the technical concept until going live. The technical workload came primarily at the beginning of the project (producing the technical concept) and at the end (testing, acceptance).

Based on the experience of the DaimlerChrysler Bank project, the duration of an ARIS PPM project depends greatly on the following factors:

1. Availability of the required process data: do the source systems need upgrading?

2. Format of the process data: It is better if the data already has a process-oriented format in the source systems. Here DaimlerChrysler Bank uses the EAI integration platform.

3. Degree of detailing or process measurement requirements (number of measurement points/events).

4. Complexity and number of the measurement variables requiring special calculation: ARIS PPM comes supplied with a set of standard measurement variables (e.g. total throughput time). If this is insufficient, additional measurement variables have to implemented via customizing.

5. Where possible, thought should be given in any process/system design project in the company about the subsequent measurement of the process under review and so define the optimum measurement points for them.

6. Training/communication: Project participants must receive focused information about the objectives, procedure and concept at the beginning.

3.5   Organizational Participants

A wide range of DaimlerChrysler Bank departments connected in some manner or other with the process to be measured were involved in the project. Process knowledge is frequently highly dispersed in a company. The correct presentation of the process in ARIS PPM calls for detailed knowledge of the defined and actual flows. The integration of all the departments affected is a significant factor in the sustained success of an ARIS PPM rollout, as active participation in the technical concept and testing ensures identification with the philosophy and the tool and also the capabilities it offers even before the software goes live.

Department	Role
Operations	Process responsibility (central)
Sales	Process user (local)
Business Process Management	Method responsibility for process management and documentation
Controlling	Overall project management, technical coordination, key performance indicator development, management reporting
Information Technology Management	Technical process responsibility, implementation responsibility, operation

Table 5: Departments involved in the project

Since the productive start, some 10 members of staff in the various departments have been regular users. The main users are currently the Operations department, regional service centers (sales), and controlling, whereby the departments have different requirements with respect to the measuring of the *easyline* process performance (see following graphic).

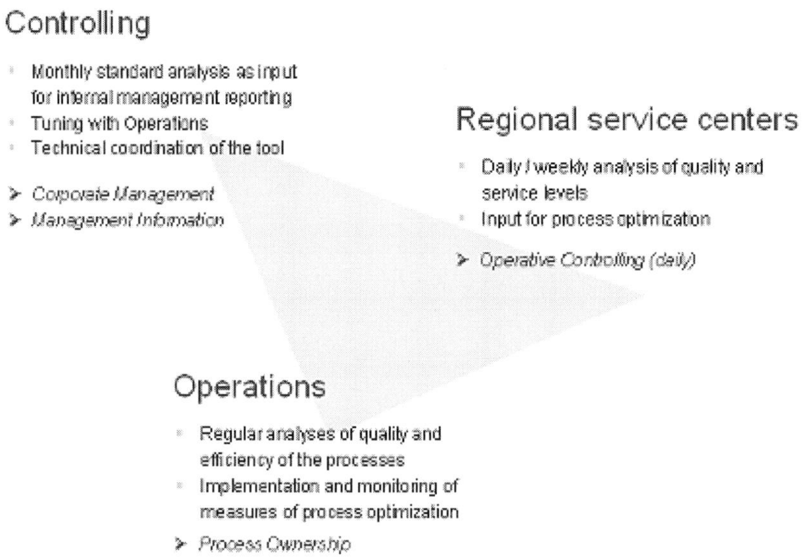

Controlling

- Monthly standard analysis as input for internal management reporting
- Tuning with Operations
- Technical coordination of the tool

➤ *Corporate Management*
➤ *Management Information*

Regional service centers

- Daily / weekly analysis of quality and service levels
- Input for process optimization

➤ *Operative Controlling (daily)*

Operations

- Regular analyses of quality and efficiency of the processes
- Implementation and monitoring of measures of process optimization

➤ *Process Ownership*

Fig. 4: Current use of ARIS PPM

4   Initial Findings and Actions

The several months of "test operation" have led to some valuable findings with respect to both the handling of the project and also for optimizing the *easyline* process.

4.1   Experiences from Working on the Project

There is no standard recipe for implementing an ARIS PPM project or conducting a pilot introduction. Nevertheless, various success factors are worth mentioning which from the DaimlerChrysler Bank viewpoint contribute to a successful project and the avoidance of errors.

Besides the time factors already mentioned in the previous chapter, the inclusion of the affected departments and IT in the technical concept phase is strongly recommended and this is a key driver for the quality of the implemented solution.

The process model defined for measurement should be complete but with a focus on what is important so that the business process is comprehensible for all employees. In this context, a meaningful limitation of the key performance indicators and dimensions to the required level is advisable. As the project managers are entering new territory with ARIS PPM, the slogan "the less the better" is particularly apt in the early stages. It is quite common for the significance of further important details to be revealed only after the first process performance data becomes available, details that were not given suitable consideration in the technical concept phase. An iterative approach is developed.

Therefore, the project planning must accept right from the start that change requests are essential. These iterations are all the more necessary in more complex processes. On the other hand, it tends to be these processes that offer enormous optimization potential.

The organizational responsibility (roles in process management) should be clarified before the introduction as far as possible. A side effect of the convincing actual process data provided is that ARIS PPM often serves as an implementation driver towards a more process-oriented organization.

4.2   Replacement of Legacy Reports

The introduction of ARIS PPM was by no means DaimlerChrysler Bank's first encounter with the issue of process optimization. The use of such a solution also creates efficiencies through the systematic identification of process weaknesses.

The *easyline* process too had been the subject of intensive analysis by DaimlerChrysler Bank employees with a view to optimizing the process, even before the introduction of ARIS PPM. For example, the Saarbrücken customer service center, which deals with private customer business, kept daily tally lists of the reasons for interruptions in the *easyline* process before ARIS PPM was available. The data was then aggregated in an Excel file as the basis for time series analysis of the manual interventions in the process.

Today, this analysis is carried out in a matter of seconds using a predefined standard report (favorites) in ARIS PPM. This enables prompt identification and initiation of improvement actions. Simple exporting of data to Excel for further processing is also possible.

4.3   Identification of Optimization Potential

The introduction of ARIS PPM has already led to the identification and rectification of various weak points in the business procedures analyzed. The findings are continually leveraged for actions to optimize the process. In some cases, immediate actions can lead to rapid systematic improvements with relatively little effort.

Apart from fundamental process weaknesses, specific issues can be addressed, e.g. regional differences in the degree to which the automated process is used. Dealers are not obliged to submit a credit application electronically. They can also be printed out and faxed, which results in manual processing of the credit application at DaimlerChrysler Bank. Now the "Dealer organization" dimension can be used by ARIS PPM to analyze which dealers are not yet using the much more cost-effective *easyline* process to the desired degree. These dealers can then be contacted, and perhaps given further encouragement or training.

The key measurement variable in the credit application process is the throughput time from receipt of application to the credit decision. The shorter the waiting time for the customer, the higher the probability of a successful signing of a deal with lasting customer satisfaction. The throughput time depends on the degree of automation in the process, which in turn is determined by the causes of manual interruptions and their frequency. Only a systematic and complete analysis of these causes enables users to understand and optimize the process. These and other initial findings have led to the initiation of corresponding improvement measures for a sustainable improvement in throughput times. Regardless of whether it is an organizational initiative (e.g. training selected car dealers) or technical process optimization, the success can be measured with ARIS PPM immediately after implementation.

5   Conclusion / Outlook / Next Steps

DaimlerChrysler Bank decided to use ARIS PPM for particular reason that it can continuously monitor and optimize mission-critical core processes. Reducing mistakes and minimizing throughput times pay dividends in the form of higher customer satisfaction and also positively affects the bottom line by ensuring efficient business processes. The findings to date lead to the conclusion that investment in setting up the corresponding organizational and technical infra-structure will amortize itself quite quickly.

DaimlerChrysler Bank intends to consistently expand its process controlling with the support of ARIS PPM. The further development is already proceeding at top speed. The Balanced Scorecard project on the one hand and the operational requirement on the other result in requirements that can in future be met by the tool. Currently, it is being expanded to include manual applications reaching DaimlerChrysler Bank by fax rather than the *easyline* interface. In addition, continuous screening of the submission quality of the documentation required for the credit decision is being planned so that the throughput time can be differentiated and evaluated even better, thus enabling the identification of further weak points in the process. A follow-up project will take a closer look at the credit disbursement process.

The selection of suitable processes is primarily determined by their focus on the mission-critical procedures in the company. There is already a wealth of ideas at DaimlerChrysler Bank that also seem to be ideal candidates for implementation in ARIS PPM. The issues have yet to be assessed and prioritized, however. Examples include CRM processes in customer processing, contract termination processing, and also support processes such as accounting (throughput times for records) or receivables management, to name but a few.

Literature

Hagerty, J.: IDS Scheer elevates Importance of Process Performance Management. AMR Research Inc., Nov. 2002

Horvath, P.; Mayer, R.: X-Engineering: Neue Potentiale der Prozess Performance erschliessen, in Information Management & Consulting, Oct. 2002

IDS Scheer AG (Hrsg.): ARIS Process Performance Manager. White Paper, Saarbrücken 2004.

Kaplan, R., Norton, D.: The Balanced Scorecard – Measures that drive Performance. Harvard Business Review on Measuring Corporate Performance, P. 123-145. Harvard Business School Press 1998

Kühl, M.: Geschäftprozesse unter Beobachtung; in Computerwoche no. 10, March 7, 2003

Kronz, A., Renner, A., Ramler, K.: Prozess Performance Measurement im Auftragsbearbeitungsprozess; in BWK Das Energie-Fachmagazin; Nr. 11/ 2002, S. 48-51.

Loes, G.: Prozessorientierte Einführung und Controlling von CRM-Systemen am Beispiel von Service-Level-Agreements; in A.-W. Scheer, W. Jost (Hrsg.) ARIS in der Praxis: Gestaltung, Implementierung und Optimierung von Geschäftsprozessen, S. 241-265; 2002

Scheer, A.-W., Kirchmer, M.: Business Process Automation – Combining Best and Next Practices, in Scheer, A.-W., Abolhassan, F., Jost, W., Kirchmer, M.: Business Process Automation – ARIS in Practice. Berlin, New York, and others 2004, P 1-16

Westermann, P., Gahse, F.: Excellence in Vehicle Financing, in Scheer, A.-W., Abolhassan, F., Jost, W., Kirchmer, M.: Business Process Automation – ARIS in Practice. Berlin, New York, and others 2004, P 83-106

Increasing Customer Satisfaction with Visualized Root-Cause Analysis – CPM Success in the Mass Market at British Telecom

John Bird
IDS Scheer UK Limited

Summary

BT implemented a Corporate Performance Solution in order to increase the number of satisfied customers. In the first step of this strategic project it was necessary to identify the cause of customer dissatisfaction. Amongst other ARIS Process Performance Manager analysis features, the patented Process Mining Wizard was used to visualize areas of concern by analyzing data from more than 20 different BT-specific Helpdesk-Systems.

Keywords

British Telecom, customer satisfaction, root-cause-analysis, helpdesk, customer service center (CSS), EDCSM (event driven customer satisfaction measures), oracle RDBMS, internal measures, repeated fault calls, estimated repair times, post faultcalls, revenue generation, early life failure, process performance management

1   Project Review

1.1   About British Telecom

Generating £13 billion annual revenues and with 21 million customers and 48,000 employees, BT Retail is a major force in the communications market. It has a well established strategy that puts customers firmly at its heart, vigorously defending its core business and growing new market opportunities. This strategy is underpinned by effective cost transformation and people programmes.

BT Retail have three main customer groups, consumer, business and major business or corporate for whom they provide everything from traditional telephony services, mobile technology, internet access and web-based services, through to help and advice.

In the consumer market BT Retail have developed and delivered innovative propositions (BT Talk Together, Entertainment, BT Answer). Their biggest and most important offering to date however is BT Broadband.

For business customers they offer bespoke solutions and advice on key areas of business strategy. They also provide a practical understanding of business issues and comprehensive knowledge of all business communications needs and issues.

In addition to this, Field Service comprising an engineering team of 17,000 is truly at the forefront of the business providing that crucial interface between the company and its customers. It plays a key role in bringing to life BT's vision of 'connecting your world completely' by delivering a world-class provision and repair service to all BT's 21 million customers.

Other areas of operation include: BT regions, customer contact centres, products and enterprises and transformation and technology.

1.2   Project Background

The company BT Retail wanted to increase the usage of the ARIS Toolset within the organisation, mainly to map their processes and to distribute these to all employees on the intranet using the ARIS Web Publisher component.

Following initial presentations and acceptance, it was agreed that high-level sponsorship was required to ensure the project had a high profile. To this end, a second presentation and demonstration was made to a senior BT Retail director at which the entire ARIS product portfolio was outlined.

When ARIS PPM was discussed, the director soon realised the potential of the product and the probability of a 'quick-win' by using ARIS PPM with live data to model his processes, rather than build them from scratch using the ARIS Toolset.

These processes are very complex and to ensure that ARIS PPM was 'up to the job', it was decided to run a proof of concept based on one business process – Business Highway.

This proof of concept started on 13 September 2002. The data to be used came from three separate source systems and covered a four week period. The main transaction data came from the CSS (Customer Service System) system, Internal Quality data also came from CSS and finally, a third party input stream relating to Customer Satisfaction, this data is known as EDCSM (Event Driven Customer Satisfaction Measures).

As mentioned earlier, the process to be analysed was 'Business Highway', this encompassed some 9 different process types, 2,800 jobs, 7,000 orders and 53,000 activities. There were 6,500 Internal Quality transactions and 80 EDCSM transactions. ARIS PPM was configured with 81 Key Performance Indicators and 23 Dimensions.

2   Project Objective

The project focus was to be in the area of 'Consumer Repair' with an emphasis on identifying the root cause of 'Customer Dissatisfaction'.
This objective embraced several BT Retail overall objectives of improving levels of satisfaction and reducing dissatisfaction amongst BT Retail customers by:

- Identifying what causes customer dissatisfaction

- Cross-linking the customer view with the process view – the idea here was to try to see the problem from the customer's perspective

- Creating the necessary improvements to the processes and planning the programmes to implement the changes

- Implement the programmes in the field

3   Project Approach

3.1   Project Structure

A preliminary planning meeting was held on 9th January 2003 to identify the scope of the project; the team members required; data involved and timescales.

The project was structured around nine 'Work Packages' identified in the meeting, each of these was represented by one or more people on the project team, some people having a dual role. These 'Work Packages' were:

- Project Management
- End to End Root Cause Analysis
- Customer Acceptance Test & Training
- Management Information Solutions
- ARIS PPM Platform
- ARIS PPM Configuration, Administration & Maintenance
- ARIS PPM Consultancy & Technical Support
- Field Engineering
- Call Centres

There was a further person involved who was responsible for project coordination. In all, the project team consisted of ten people.

3.2   Workshop

Once project funding had been obtained, the majority of the project team assembled at the end of March 2003 to discuss the data in more detail and to define the processes involved. In total some 22 separate processes were identified within the 'Consumer Repair' Process Group. Once these had been decided the KPIs and Dimensions were determined. The main transaction data was to be extracted from 28 regional CSS databases and to complete the end-to-end transaction details, a further 8 extract files were generated from CSS and additional application systems. These contained data covering the Fault details, CSS Internal Measures, Repeated Fault Calls, Estimated Repair Times, Post Fault Calls, Revenue Generation and Early Life Failure. A final data set was assembled from the EDCSM data which is obtained from a third party organisation that undertakes the surveys to ensure impartiality.

Nine standard ARIS PPM KPIs were retained and a further 75 identified. Four standard ARIS PPM Dimensions were retained and a further 52 identified.

During development of the Pilot, a new release of ARIS PPM took place which introduced both Search Dimensions and Process Independent KPIs. As a result of this, 7 Search Dimensions were identified and 9 Process Independent KPIs were introduced.

3.3   Project Schedule

A high level project schedule was developed and agreed by all parties. This took into consideration any possible problem areas and contingency was built in to allow for any such events occurring.

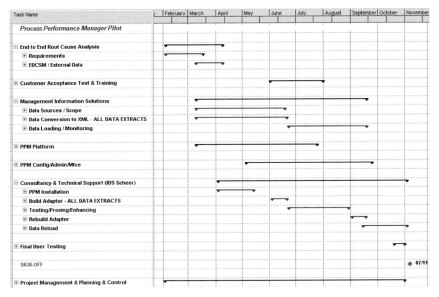

Fig. 1: Projectplan

Certain unforeseen circumstances caused us to deviate from the schedule during the middle of the project, these revolved mainly around hardware specification, availability and location. This delayed the loading of the data by a couple of weeks. From IDS Scheer's perspective, there was a prolonged period of inactivity during April and May whilst BT Retail ensured that the data could be obtained from the sources identified. Eventually this proved to be both feasible and practical and so the ARIS PPM configuration activities began. This work was undertaken in the IDS Scheer offices as the hardware issues mentioned above had not yet been resolved.

As can be seen from the schedule, Customer Acceptance testing was to be undertaken throughout June and July but Final User Testing was at the end of October. This may seem unusual, but the reason for this large gap was to allow both BT Retail and IDS Scheer to make changes to the data and to the ARIS PPM configuration should the first testing phase find any discrepancies.

In actual fact, this was not the case, Customer Acceptance Testing proved that the data was correct and the ARIS PPM configuration was giving the correct results.

3.4   Hardware

In conjunction with BT Retail IT, a two tier hardware platform was agreed. Two server machines were made available, one was to act as the Database Server and the other as both ARIS PPM Server and Web Server.

The ARIS PPM Front-ends were a mixture of PCs running Microsoft Windows and Internet explorer.

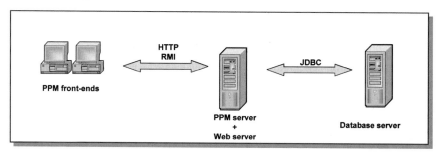

Fig. 2: Server-Architecture
The combined ARIS PPM Server & Web Server had 3 GB RAM,
two Xeon 2.4

GHZ processors and was running Microsoft Windows 2000 server service pack 2 and Microsoft Internet information server 5.0. The Database Server also had 3 GB RAM, two Xeon 2.4 GHZ processors and 150 GB Raid 1 Disk for data and fault tolerance. This machine was running Microsoft Windows 2000 server service pack 2 and Oracle 8I Enterprise Edition. The ARIS PPM Server/Web Server was linked to the Database Server via a high-speed (100 MBit) network.

3.5   Data Retrieval

The responsibility for Data Retrieval lay entirely with BT Retail. IDS Scheer provided BT Retail with an output specification which detailed the XML formatting required for the data and BT Retail wrote several Visual Basic programs to extract the data from their source systems. Several test iterations of the output were read into ARIS PPM before totally clean data was obtained.

It was intended that data import would be on a weekly basis, unfortunately, this could not be undertaken at a week-end for various reasons, the major factor being that a significant amount of data would not be ready for use at that time. All data would be ready for processing by the Tuesday evening of each week.

Although we had a good idea of the volume of data ARIS PPM needed to handle, it was only when this phase of the project began that the exact volumes became known. The main transaction data ranged from 110,000 per week to 185,000 with an overall average of 130,000 EDCSM data was approximately 800 to 900 transactions per week.

At the time of writing, the system has been operational for some 11 months and held approximately 17 months data, this means that approximately 10 million records are available for analysis.

3.6   Training

An intensive Training Programme was devised which included several one-day ARIS PPM appreciation sessions for line managers, system evaluators and team leaders who would be involved in the project. These sessions provided the attendees with an overview of ARIS PPM functionality and the application of ARIS PPM to their own data. It was essential that these people understood the capabilities of ARIS PPM so that the Pilot system could move forward with their support. Two End-User training courses of two days duration were scheduled, the first was for those people who would be close to the project, but not actually true 'End-Users' this was to ensure that they had a firm understanding of what ARIS PPM could do and how it was achieved.

The second course was for the End-Users and this took place on a BT Retail site just prior to going live. In total some 45 people were trained, 18 of whom were End-Users.

3.7   Testing, Issues and Corrective Action

At an early stage it was recognised that testing needed to be very thorough. The project schedule was tight and the project could not afford to waste valuable time reconfiguring ARIS PPM and, more importantly reloading data.

Testing was undertaken in several areas. Firstly data integrity was checked; this soon highlighted an area which caused us to rethink our approach.

Our chosen approach had been to run the XML import and immediately follow this with the PPM import. This is standard practice, what we had failed to realise however was the impact if errors were found on the XML import, in extreme cases the import would be aborted for the file containing the error. Our XML import would read all nine weekly files in one pass. Normal errors, such as invalid data formats were ignored and processing continued, but if invalid characters were found, the import of the file concerned stops at that point and the next file is read. Surprisingly these invalid characters were more common than we realised due to the fact that there were several fields in the BT Retail data which were pure text entered by end-users and engineers in the field, thus reserved XML characters such as ampersands, apostrophes, quotes, etc were frequently present. Once these errors were corrected, the XML import and PPM import could be run again. We also discovered at this point that our PPM import was taking longer due to the duplication of the data which had been accepted in the first XML import.

All this of course wasted valuable time and so the BT Visual Basic programs were amended to eliminate these reserved XML characters. Furthermore, as a precautionary measure it was decided that we would create a dummy ARIS PPM client to run the XML import against until all errors were corrected and the data was clean. At this point we could now run the combined XML and PPM imports.

Additional testing was carried out to ensure that the transaction fragments were being assembled in the correct sequence to form complete end-to-end process instances (we were using the "sortmerge" functionality for this).

Finally, our testing ensured that the KPIs were being calculated correctly and that the Dimensions were being populated as expected.

4   Going Live, Issues and Corrective Action

BT Retail did not want to go live with a small amount of data, so it was agreed that 6 weeks of data must be loaded before the users would begin their ARIS PPM analysis work.

Approximately four weeks before going live, a new ARIS PPM Release became available giving us the ability to use Search Dimensions and Process Independent

KPIs. BT quickly recognised the advantages of these new features and requested that they be included in the Pilot system.

This request coincided with us experiencing performance issues, particularly in the area of data import. As mentioned earlier, we did not have the luxury of being able to do the weekly import over a week-end, our SLA was to have this available each Wednesday morning. The other performance issues related to some of the more complex queries being run by the end-users which took some time to complete, especially when several weeks worth of data was being queried. This was having a detrimental effect on user perception, even though by traditional means these results would have taken far longer too obtain.

We needed to be proactive and acted quickly to address the issues, the pressing one being query response times. A short term fix was achieved by adjusting the ORACLE parameters to increase block-buffer sizes.

In conjunction with members of the ARIS PPM development team in Saarbrucken, we examined the ARIS PPM configuration and determined that several changes could be made to improve data import times. These involved converting some of the KPIs into Dimensions (which speeds up data import as less calculation is needed) and more importantly isolating the more heavily analysed data (the EDCSM specific transactions). This latter action was achieved using ARIS PPM's hierarchy functionality which essentially created a separate process group for the EDCSM transactions whilst retaining links back to the original transaction data. In this way queries could be run against the EDCSM data extremely quickly because of the lower volumes involved.

Also by doing this, we were able to configure ARIS PPM so that the Dimensions which were EDCSM specific were only available for the EDCSM process group, this also contributed to speeding up the data import

To save time whilst the BT Retail hardware was being reconfigured, the ARIS PPM configuration was being modified and installed on an IDS Scheer Server. All data which had been previously imported on the BT Retail platform was made available to IDS Scheer and batch jobs created to import these. Once the IDS Server was fully loaded with the BT Retail data, the ORACLE instance was backed up and made available to BT Retail.

Over a two day period, one of the BT Retail server machines was reconfigured so that the ARIS PPM Server, Web Server and Database Server were all on the one machine, RAM was increased to 6 GB and Windows Advanced Server was installed this allowed ORACLE to access more RAM. Then the new ARIS PPM configuration was loaded and the ORACLE backup restored.

From that point onwards, there was an immediate increase in the speed of Data Import and network traffic was reduced significantly. Queries were also faster as a result of these changes. Section 5 User Acceptance Criteria contains the results in detail.

Also, because the data import was now taking approximately 9 hours as opposed to the earlier 12 to 14 hours, it was felt that a second data import could be run during the week to load historical weekly data going back to the start of the BT Retail financial Year.

On a day-to-day basis, BT Retail uses the full range of ARIS PPM functionality to evaluate the Consumer Repair processes. There are several standard queries run for regular reporting/statistical requirements, but a large part of the analytical work is triggered by the EDCSM results each week and therefore is of a random nature because of the variety of responses obtained.

5   User Acceptance Criteria

As a result of the performance issues identified during Customer Acceptance Testing a series of Benchmark queries were devised as part of the overall User Acceptance Criteria. These were to be run each day for a minimum of two weeks the benchmark queries were stored as Favorites and were run at approximately 7:30am each day, this was a deliberate decision made to avoid higher network traffic during the course of the day which might have distorted the figures. Additionally, ARIS PPM caching was turned off thus ensuring that the queries were run directly on the ARIS PPM database.

- The "System Benchmarks" – comprised three queries run against one, six and 13 weeks data.

- The "User Benchmarks" – consisted of six typical/representative user queries also run against one, six and 13 weeks.

- Based on the performance experienced and expectations from the system improvements, an 'Ideal Response Time' was set for each query.

- Each query was run separately and the response time was recorded to enable assessment of the percentage within target and the distribution of the responses.

These queries were run over a prolonged period and average Response Times calculated. The results are shown in the table below, for completeness the column headed "Original Response Time" shows the responses experienced before the hardware and adapter changes were made.

The maximum expected response times for the queries for both types of benchmark were agreed and are shown in the table below, along with the responses achieved:

Weeks Under Analysis	Original Response Time	Ideal Response Time	Actual Response Time
One Week	22.5 secs	15 secs	6 secs
Six Weeks	2 mins 15 secs	1 min 30 secs	7 secs
13 Weeks	6 mins	4 mins	7 secs

Fig. 3: Computing times

As can be seen, the "Actual Response Time" far exceeded the "Ideal". Overall Pilot Acceptance was determined through the following criteria:

- System availability to users - 95% during office hours (08:30 - 16:30)

- Data import delivers consistent overnight performance, i.e. less than 13 hours for each week loaded (see table below for results)

- Response times are within the maximum agreed for 90% of all benchmark queries using the final system configuration released to users

- System availability enables benchmark testing to be carried out for a minimum of ten working days

- Two instances of two, four and six concurrent query/flood testing are carried out by users, each running one of the user benchmark queries, for one six and 13 weeks, and the results recorded

	Transactions	Import Time
Minimum	108,623	5:25:24
Maximum	185,077	13:06:10
Overall Average	130,111	9:28:35

Fig. 4: Transaction and import times

5.1   User Testimonials

The Pilot passed all the necessary Acceptance Criteria with ease and resulted in some very complimentary comments:

"The figures include the results of flood testing carried out …… with a group of seven users; these were also excellent, with a maximum time of only 23 seconds for the last query to run in all the tests carried out." – BT Retail PPM Implementation Project Manager.

… were very pleased with the performance of ARIS PPM and there was general appreciation, and more importantly belief, that the newly implemented configuration means that we now have a truly useable system." - Root Cause Analysis Manager (Consumer).

"I have no doubt that we have concluded testing with all thumbs up, and that we will be able to close the action plan and effectively the Pilot of ARIS PPM with positive sign-off from all of the key project and user representatives." - Management Information Solutions Manager.

"…the benchmarks. All are within target and showing an exceptional performance against the target set for each of the benchmarks." – BT Retail PPM Implementation Project Manager.

"…performance exceeded our expectations. Well done to all concerned." ." - Root Cause Analysis Manager (Consumer).

6   Benefits

BT Retail acknowledge that ARIS PPM has contributed to the identification and some of the key areas of dissatisfaction within the Consumer Repair Process and pinpoint areas for further detailed analysis.

It has helped them begin to understand the potential of ARIS PPM to chart the process followed against the process documented, at the individual fault level, and track a job from the customer's point of view as well as being able to see the process itself. However, the process mapping functionality delivered in Version 3 has not yet enabled BT to reach its goal of being able to chart the aggregate repair view. This view is something that BT looks forward to seeing implemented in the medium term to more accurately chart and monitor deviation from the documented process and assist in the development of corrective actions.

An added bonus is the ability to monitor dissatisfaction levels over time and against differing Dimensions and against target levels.

The major overall benefits are

- BT Retail now have a more in-depth view of the customer experience for the Consumer Repair process, linking the customer view and the process view enabling them to drill down to root causes.

- The Analysis process has been accelerated; they can identify areas where Customer Dissatisfaction is high in a fraction of the time it took previously.

- ARIS PPM has brought a wider scope and provided more versatile tools and techniques to the Root-Cause Analysis team.

Monetary Assessment of Performance Management in the Health Care System – Process Cost Analysis at Marienhospital Herne

Holger Raphael
Marienhospital Herne

Hendrik Schenck
Marienhospital Herne

Summary

Together with IDS Scheer, the Catholic Hospital Foundation Marienhospital Herne launched a pilot project for the operational intensive care station to meet the challenges of the flat rate payment system with process cost accounting (PCA), opting for ARIS Process Platform as IT support so as to ensure the best possible cost-driver accounting.

Keywords

DRG, Process Cost Analysis, clinical paths, healthcare system, case rates, descriptive QM, performance-amount induced (pai) and performance-amount neutral (pan) processes, Process Cost Accounting, Cost Driver, eEPC, ARIS Process Platform, Hospital Information System (HIS), InEK raw case costing

1   Why Process Cost Accounting in Hospitals?

1.1   The Hospital Environment

In response to increasing cost pressures caused by economic and demographic developments, legislators have produced more reforms for health than for any other sector of the economy. The reform of the compensation system for inpatient treatment and its price-like lump sums is designed to reduce healthcare costs, and hospitals are now being forced to act. Unlike the previous system of compensation by daily rates, the new DRGs[1] offer little incentive for wasting resources.[2] Therefore hospitals must render their services at the lowest possible costs while still complying with quality standards.[3]

Cost accounting in particular now plays a much greater role as a management tool because "the hospital shall maintain cost and performance accounting that permits operational controlling and an evaluation of its efficiency and effectiveness (...)".[4]

Hospitals find in general that revenues are capped by the negotiated budget. Thus, only the costs remain as an object of an assessment[5]. One method of fundamental cost analysis is to evaluate the individual process steps. The focus here should be on those subprocesses that stand out either for their higher costs (e.g. major HR expense) or frequency of execution within the process. The cost drivers of the workflow, i.e. the influencing factors that determine the nature of the cost development, have to be identified and analyzed. There follows an explanation of why process orientation is required, then the principles of process cost accounting will be introduced. That will be followed by a description of the procedure adopted in the pilot project for the Catholic Hospital Foundation Marienhospital Herne and its results. A conclusion rounds off the presentation.

---

[1] Diagnosis Related Group.

[2] See Breyer, F. / Zweifel, P. (1999), P. 353 ff.

[3] The options for revenue optimization are not dealt with in this article.

[4] Hospital Accounting Regulation: Section 8 Cost and Performance Accounting.

[5] This assumes that up-coding is not an option for boosting revenues, as it is with DRGs.

1.2   Process & Performance Orientation in Hospitals

Because of specialization and the wide range of tasks, hospitals are organized along functional, hierarchical lines.[6] As a result, processes are split up across various organizational units and tasks are distributed among many task centers, contrary to the logical sequence. The economic and efficient treatment of a patient thus depends greatly on the coordination of the service-providing units in the hospital.

This issue is currently being discussed with respect to the quality of treatment under the heading of Clinical Paths[7]. A treatment path is a control instrument. The clinical path describes the optimum path of a specific patient type with key diagnostic and therapeutic services and its chronological sequence.

Interdisciplinary and interprofessional aspects are covered along with elements for implementation, control and economic evaluation.Process orientation is an important tool for ensuring the quality management (QM) required by law. With case rates, there is a strong incentive to reduce treatment quality below the optimum by rendering (too) few individual services [8] or not to comply with the minimum standard (in figurative terms: "discharging bleeding patients"). Therefore, hospitals are required by Section 137 Social Code V to maintain a documented quality management system. Looking at quality standards such as ISO, KTQ or EFQM, the first step concentrates on proof in the form of documenting quality in manuals and reports. This is followed by the process of continuous improvements to hospital workflows.

Of course, the more descriptive QM tends to have synergy effects with process cost accounting which must be exploited. In an optimum situation, the processes documented in QM can be evaluated using process cost accounting, thus providing a new source of information for process optimization.

---

[6] Compare this context and below, Scheer et al. (1996), P. 77.

[7] Other terms used include clinical pathways, critical pathways, patient path, treatment path.

[8] See Breyer, F. / Zweifel, P. (1999), P. 354

2   Basis of Process Cost Accounting

Process cost accounting is a term that has recently begun to inform discussions and the design of cost accounting. Process cost accounting considers the idea "that even in industry, costs that are demonstrably attributable to production are now very low compared with the fixed overheads that are attracted as lump-sum payments in the form of surcharge and settlement rates."[9] The main tasks of process cost accounting include revealing the performance-related links between the use of production factors, processes and treatment in hospitals in the context of the high overheads.

At the same time, process cost accounting is not a radically new cost accounting system; rather, it applies traditional cost category and cost center accounting. The starting point for process cost accounting is the question as to the main influencing factors for cost accounting. These variables are called cost drivers.

Process cost accounting can be seen as the basis for a number of use cases. The main ones are:

- Process management

- Performance costing

- Contribution-based cost accounting

- Target costing[10]

- Cost management.

In general, a process is a chain of activities directed at rendering a performance output.

---

[9] S. Schmidt, A. (2001), P. 220; Coenenberg emphasizes the strategic aspect of process cost accounting with the presence of three effects: the allocation effect, the complexity effect and economies of scale effect. Cf.. Coenenberg, A. G. (1999), P. 235 ff.

[10] Target costing cannot be applied directly to hospitals. Market orientation in the sense of concentrating on customer wishes must be limited as patients, doctors and health insurance funds are the customers, and in most cases patients do not demand the services voluntarily, are seldom able to judge the medical treatment themselves ,and do not pay the direct price. Thus conjoint analysis can therefore not be applied for calculating the target price. See Schlüchtermann, J. / Gorschlüter, P. (1996), P. 107.

A process has the following features[11]:

- Quantifiable service provision,

- of a given quality,

- with analyzable throughput or processing times,

- requiring measurable resources to produce it (costs)

- can be traced to certain cost-influencing factors (cost drivers).

As a rule, a multi-layer, a hierarchical process model is assumed.[12] At the sub-process level, a distinction is made between performance amount-induced (pai) and performance amount neutral (pan) processes.[13] In the case of performance amount induced subprocesses, the time and associated costs are proportional to the quantity of output. In contrast, performance amount neutral subprocesses represent the basic cost of the cost center. Experts have yet to come up with a definitive answer as to how pan processes are to be settled.[14]

The following assumes a broad definition of process cost accounting[15] according to the basic concept of cost-related process evaluation as a pragmatic approach to project implementation. In this context, process cost accounting is seen as offering a possibility of tactical/operational planning on a partial cost basis. However, the term process-oriented accounting is suggested to provide a linguistic distinction from process cost accounting, which is generally understood to be based on full cost accounting.

In this article, the presentation of the general situation in German hospitals and the methodological principles of process cost accounting is followed by a discussion of the way process cost accounting was implemented at the Catholic Hospital Foundation Marienhospital Herne.

---

[11] See Horváth, P. / Mayer, R. (1993), P. 16.

[12] Presentation differs in the literature. A wide range of terms and differentapproaches are used concerning the number of process hierarchy levels.
See Reckenfelderbäumer (1994), P. 33.

[13] Cf. here and below Mayer, R. (1990), P. 307 f. and Mayer, R. (2002), P. 1623 f.

[14] See Götze, U. (1997), P. 167

[15] This and other terms are often used as synonyms (see Coenenberg, A. G. / Fischer, M. (1991), P. 21 f.).
Whereas some authors justify this use of synonyms on the grounds of the identical fundamental idea (see the work just quoted as a case in point), other authors make an explicit distinction between the terms, particularly rejecting any use of the term Activity Based Costing as a synonym (see for example Mayer, R. (2002), P. 1622 f.).

3   Marienhospital Process Cost Accounting Pilot Project

3.1   Framework Conditions at Marienhospital

Marienhospital has been using process management with a focus on QM and certification (DIN EN ISO 9001:2000) since 1999. A strategic decision was taken at an early stage to use a process-oriented tool as IT-side support. Criteria for selecting the software included in particular a central data pool for efficient management in the use phase and the most extensive possible reuse of modeled processes. This included the direct transfer of processes by Controlling to process cost accounting and also the option for customizing a workflow-oriented hospital information system (HIS).[16]

Based on the Marienhospital's annual participation in InEK raw case costing[17], a hospital-specific DRG evaluation on a full-cost basis is already being used for controlling in the internal reporting system. As InEK costing works with rough keys in respect of hospitals' performance data, more detailed information about cost drivers is required.

The Operational Intensive Station (OI)[18] was chosen for the process cost accounting pilot project for several reasons. On the one hand, considerable costs[19] arise here, the need for information is high. On the other hand, the intensive station workflows are very complex, so that a positive outcome of the pilot project would prove the general applicability of the method and the tool.

---

[16] Introducing a workflow-oriented HIS, which was developed with a particular focus on the requirements in primary performance delivery, i.e. the treatment of patients, involves enormous adaptation effort and requires the hospital's legacy workflow structures. In the past, all the HIS systems on the market were originally developed from the billing requirements. A workflow-oriented HIS called Soarian has been announced by Siemens.

[17] The hospitals' umbrella associations, Verband der Privaten Krankenversicherung [Private Health Insurance Association] and the Deutsche Krankenhausgesellschaft [German Hospital Society] founded the Institut für das Entgeltsystem im Krankenhaus [Hospital Compensation System Institute] (InEK GmbH) on May 10, 2001. The Institute provides member partners with support for self administration and the bodies they formed for the legally mandated introduction and continuous development of the DRG System based on Section 17 b Hospital Financing Act (KHG). Further information can be found at http://www.g-drg.de.

[18] Interdisciplinary intensive station for the surgery, vascular surgery, hand surgery, gynecology, pain therapy, urology, and neuro-urology departments.

[19] As a result of inadequate mapping after the introduction of DRGs, many hospitals regarded their intensive station as a major loss-maker.

And not least, access to the expertise of a specialist involved in the process was assured by the leading physician obtaining a doctorate in the field of process cost accounting.

3.2   Procedure

3.2.1 Objective

The business key performance indicators, their calculation formulas and evaluation options were defined in a two-day workshop. The workshop also identified the information sources and modelling conventions for the software. For more detailed evaluations, the cases were initially grouped at the 1st level by main diagnosis and by DRG at a 2nd level.[20] The agreed objective was 5-level contribution accounting and a contribution benchmark diagram.

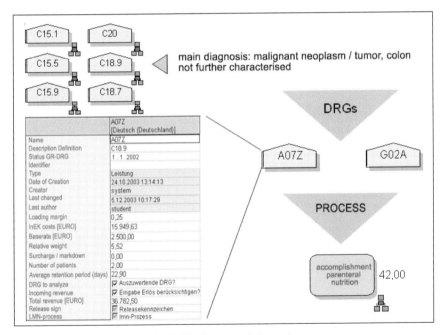

Fig. 1: DRG process information

---

[20] As DRGs essentially determine revenues as an aggregate of many case-related attributes, there is frequently little point in comparing them with the case costs. In theory, the main diagnosis attribute can be used anywhere.

Contribution accounting initially takes into consideration the 3 directly attributable cost categories before considering pan costs and the administration overhead. The pan costs are allocated on the basis of care days. If Contribution Accounting III is negative, the corresponding DRG is to be avoided in the short term.[21] If Contribution IV or V are negative, there is a medium-term need for action.

Revenues per DRG
./. medical supply costs
= DBI
./. personal costs
= DB II
./. operating costs
= DB III
./. LMN costs
= DB IV
./. loading margin
= DB V

In the Contribution Benchmark diagram, not only is Contribution V shown but the identified costs are also compared. The reference value is taken from the InEK raw case costing.[22] The OI (case) costs determined in process cost accounting are compared with the costs of cost centre group 2 (intensive station) of the corresponding DRG from the InEK costing[23]. This diagram allows for the fact that there are DRGs whose revenues do not fully cover the average costs determined by InEK. Thus a hospital's cost structure may appear positive compared to that of other hospitals but it still makes a loss.

---

[21] To the extent that this is permitted under the terms of the treatment mission.

[22] Of course, the objection may be raised at this point that InEK costing cannot determine comparable cost-driver allocated costs owing to the methodology and options available, and so does not lend itself entirely to benchmarking. The InEK Benchmark Index should be seen as a rough guide and used only with due allowance for possible variations due to its methodology. The problem of comparability is intrinsic to benchmarking.

[23] As the OI assessment covers only part of a DRG performance delivery, cost center group 2 is used. Evaluating a DRG requires consideration of the complete course of treatment.

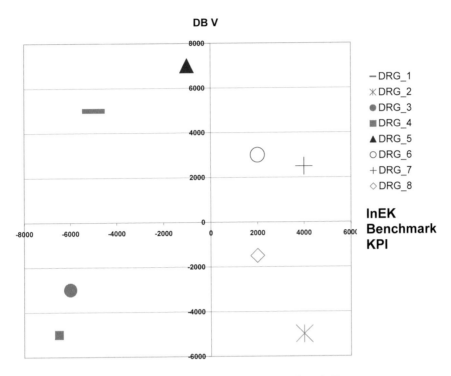

DB V

- — DRG_1
- ✳ DRG_2
- ● DRG_3
- ■ DRG_4
- ▲ DRG_5
- ○ DRG_6
- + DRG_7
- ◇ DRG_8

**InEK
Benchmark
KPI**

Fig. 2: Contribution-based cost accounting benchmark diagram

Apart from these specific key performance indicators, others have also been developed, e.g. the degree of utilization.

3.3   Software Support from ARIS Process Cost Analyzer

Technically, the realized solution envisages the ARIS PCA[24] controlling tool, which is an ARIS Process Platform component along with ARIS Process Performance Manager, importing the processes that have been modeled in the ARIS database. Then the desired key performance indicators are calculated on the basis of freely defined rules via the object attributes maintained in the ARIS database. This results in transparency of both calculation and costs. In addition, freely defined analyses can be run beforehand, with the results displayed graphically and exported for further processing. The advantage of having a separate imported database is that what-if scenarios can be generated by changing the attributes in the tool itself. The essential structure of the ARIS database, including the Organization, Control and Performance views, is obtained. The calculation of the key performance indicators is transparent thanks to the drill-down function in all key performance indicators.

3.3.1 Activity Recording

The detailed analysis of personnel costs required the approval of the staff representative committee (SRC) on the anonymized recording of work and time taken. The QM processes could not be transferred directly because this presentation sets different priorities and so does not adequately map the origins of costs.

Whereas in the past procedures were modelled top down solely by QM representatives and physicians, this time all ward staff were asked to make a complete list of their activities. The next step was to group these activities and aggregate them in workflows. The uniform wording and degree of abstraction demanded detailed technical and process knowledge. The advantage of this method is that the real actual state is recorded and not a desirable target one. As a more differentiated allocation was not possible, the only differentiation was between doctors and nursing staff.

The subprocesses were organized in a way that made them constant with respect to the cost driver. This enables the treatment expense of a given DRG to be derived by simply multiplying the usage quantity by the evaluated subprocesses.

---

[24] Process Cost Analyzer.

3.3.2 Personnel Costs

The processing times were determined for the identified activities using a minute-based multi-moment time recording procedure. The personnel cost rates were determined in ARIS PCA on the basis of salaries, holiday entitlements, overtime and illness-related absences.

3.3.3 Costs of Medical Needs

As there was no electronic patient-related documentation of the medical needs available, models and allocation keys were developed so that the actual costs could be allocated to the individual processes as accurately as possible with respect to the cost drivers. Medical needs encompasses the three subgroups blood, medication and other medical needs.

3.3.4 Equipment Costs

The calculation of equipment costs includes (imputed) depreciation and also the identified costs of the medical equipment. In order to minimize the modelling workload, equipment used together for treatment was aggregated in systems.

3.3.5 Determination of Input Quantities

The input quantities (number of times the treatment modules were carried out) were determined by analyzing the patient files. The input quantities were entered in a Microsoft Access database. The automatic transfer of the data to ARIS was not yet implemented, so parts had to be modelled. In future, usage quantities will be entered and maintained whilst the patient is in the hospital. This points up the need for workflow-oriented systems that permit comprehensive, analyzable documentation of medical services.

3.4   Modelling in ARIS

The individual DRGs are modelled as services and the associated subprocesses are assigned to the functions of a product/service tree as eEPCs[25] . The usage quantity of the subprocesses is stored in the functions. The pan processes are modelled parallel to this. The attributes for calculating minute cost rates and capacities are stored in the application system type diagrams for equipment and in organizational diagrams for personnel. The costs of consumable materials, the average processing time and the deployment factor of the functions are stored in the individual eEPCs.

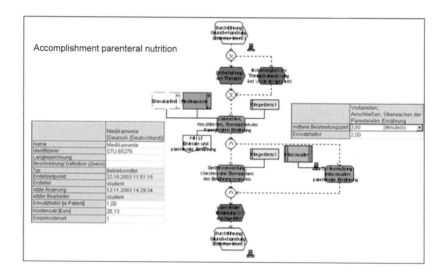

Fig. 3: ARIS EPC

---

[25] Extended event-driven process chains.

4   Results

The first result that must be shown is the modified ARIS PCA. This enables navigation through the various views and display of the corresponding key performance indicators. If key performance indicators are shown in white, this means that they have been taken from the ARIS database and can be edited for scenario analyses. Key performance indicators shown in blue can be used for navigating through the calculation. Exportable evaluations and graphics have been produced for the individual hierarchies – main diagnoses, DRGs, processes.

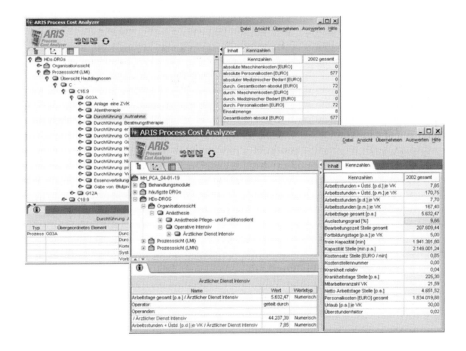

Fig. 4: Modified ARIS PCA

Now the economic aspects not only of individual subprocesses but also of entire[26] DRGs can be analyzed for business purposes. The user-definable grouping function also permits cases to be analyzed for a wide range of determinants through external processing of the data available in the HIS.

---

[26] The pilot project only dealt with a partial performance of a complete treatment path.

5   Conclusion

The process cost accounting-appropriate mapping of complex and in some cases scarcely structurable workflows can be regarded as a success due to the choice of a high degree of abstraction.[27] The greatest limitation lies in the legacy information system landscape. This determines the possible accuracy of the patient-related cost allocation, the effort required to obtain information and thus directly the economic success of process cost accounting. This underscores the economic necessity of digital and thus analyzable patient files.[28]

A critical success factor is close coordination with QM. Early consideration of process cost accounting in QM reduces the workload and creates greater acceptance, as certified processes are available for costing purposes.[29]

Another area of use where process-oriented costing has proved its worth is in investment decisions. A major benefit is the intuitive cost transparency that enables discussions with medical experts.

But process cost accounting also serves as an essential foundation for further analyses. Besides from the general ability to carry out detailed case costing, it can provide answers to other questions. A central point is the grouping of case data for strategic planning and control, because in many cases the case numbers do not allow solid statistical conclusions to be drawn. The determination of systematic differences between InEK costing and process cost accounting may also be of interest[30].

In conclusion, it may be stated that process cost accounting is an important but time-consuming cost accounting method whose success depends greatly on the concrete situation.

---

[27] Owing to the aggregation, the potential for process optimization is lower than for routine processes with a fixed order of activities.

[28] The existing situation in which on the one hand doctors spend a large part of their working time on documentation which on the other hand is often not in a form that lends itself to financial analysis, is clearly untenable from a planning and control viewpoint.

[29] A possible conflict of goals should be pointed out here. Whereas a complete workflow overview is desirable for QM, process cost accounting tends more to subprocesses that are homogenously influenced by cost drivers.

[30] This question is necessary for a definitive evaluation of the benchmark approach chosen here; this definitive answer will probably also influence the future behavior of both hospitals and health insurance funds.

Literature

Breyer, F. / Zweifel, P (1999): Gesundheitsökonomie, 3rd edition, Berlin and elsewhere, 1999.

Coenenberg, A. G. (1999): Kostenrechnung und Kostenanalyse, 4th edition, Landsberg/Lech 1999.

Coenenberg, A. G. / Fischer, T. M. (1999): Prozesskostenrechnung – Strategische Neuorientierung in der Kostenrechnung, in: DBW, Vol. 1, 1999, pp. 21-40.

Götze, U. (1997): Einsatzmöglichkeiten und Grenzen der Prozeßkostenrechnung, in: Freidank, C.-C. / Götze, U. / Huch, B. / Weber, J. (Hrsg.): Kostenmanagement: aktuelle Konzepte und Anwendungen, Berlin and elsewhere 1997, pp.141-174.

Horváth, P. / Mayer, R. (1993): Prozeßkostenrechnung. Konzeption und Entwicklungen, in: krp, Special issue 2, 1993, pp. 15-28.

Mayer, R. (1990): Prozeßkostenrechnung, in: krp, Vol. 5, 1990, pp. 309-312.

Mayer, R. (2002): Prozesskostenrechnung, in: Küpper, H.-U.; Wagenhofer, A. (Hrsg.): Handwörterbuch Unternehmensrechnung und Controlling, 4th edition, Stuttgart 2002, pp. 1621-1630.

Reckenfelderbäumer, M. (1994): Entwicklungsstand und Perspektiven der Prozessrechnung, Wiesbaden 1994.

Scheer, A.-W. / Chen, R. / Zimmermann, V. (1996): Prozeßmanagement im Krankenhaus, in: Adam, D. (Hrsg.): Krankenhausmanagement, Wiesbaden 2004, pp. 75-96.

Schlüchtermann, J. / Gorschlüter, P. (1996): Ausgewählte Aspekte eines modernen Kostenmangements im Krankenhaus, in: Adam, D. (Ed.): Krankenhausmanagement, Wiesbaden 2004, pp. 97-111.

Schmidt, A. (2001): Kostenrechnung: Grundlagen der Vollkosten-, Deckungsbeitrags- und Plankostenrechnung sowie des Kostenmanagements, 3rd edition., Stuttgart and elsewhere 2001.

Monitoring ITIL Process Performance at DAB Bank

Simone Sulzmann
iET Solutions GmbH

Summary

The productivity of a service department depends greatly on the ad hoc ability to analyze processes in detail and immediately initiate any change actions required. This closes the loop of operational activities, process and cause analysis and implementation of suitable optimization measures. DAB Bank has introduced an ITIL-based process structure in order to boost its service quality. This flexible analysis of detailed flows is the final logical component for a rounded-off concept.

Keywords

Service process, service quality, key performance indicator system, process definition, SLA monitoring, call volume, hotline, solution times, IT helpdesks, problem management, net processing time

1   Service Department Work as per ITIL

Today, the management of IT service processes is confronted with two challenges which at first sight seem to be contradictory: strict cost orientation and a focus on customer satisfaction. The ITIL guideline shows how both can be achieved. It supplies the foundation for successful IT Service Management (ITSM). This entails the process for planning, managing and controlling the quality and quantity of IT services rendered. The abbreviation ITIL stands for Information Technology Infrastructure Library. This is a collection of methods for organizing IT. The guideline comprises a number of modules or disciplines and provides guidance on how to set up a service-oriented IT department, but without direct instructions. More than 40 books have since been published containing proven real-life methods as "Best Practice for IT".

2   Introducing ITIL Processes at DAB Bank

DAB Bank AG supports savers, investors and traders in Germany and Austria. The largest direct broker in terms of its customers' securities holdings, DAB offers a full portfolio of services for wealth building, securities and asset protection. In corporate-customer business, the bank is a partner to asset management companies, investment fund brokers, investment advisers and also commercial and savings banks. Founded in 1994, the Munich-based bank started with some 10,000 customers; today it manages some EUR 13 billion for more than 462,000 accounts. It regards "1-A quality at the lowest possible costs" as one of its key strengths in the banking business. The in-house IT department operates its IT Service Management (ITSM) along the same lines. With the seamless, de-facto standard ITIL-based ITSM solution from iET Solutions, the bank succeeded in improving the quality of its IT services noticeably over an implementation period of 12 weeks.

2.1   Conception

The strategic impulse for adopting ITIL was the initiative in the IT department to consolidate systems and optimize processes.

The IT initiative requirements for DAB Bank raised the question as to whether the legacy helpdesk software could cope with the restructuring of the service organization. It was soon revealed that modifying the legacy system would be too expensive, an ITIL-compliant application was called for to replace it. For his bank, explained Marcel Comans, head of IT Service&Support, there were quite clear decision criteria: scalability, end-to-end ITIL basis, low modification workload and excellent value for money compared with other vendors simplified his decision for iET ITSM.

What applies for the entire IT initiative was also used as the yardstick for selecting the new IT Service Management System (ITSM). The tool had to be the state of the art and enable IT department staff to influence the application development themselves. Only then can DAB Bank ensure even at the helpdesk that changes to processes are immediately implemented in the ITSM application as well. "We just have a living process to which we make minor adjustments quickly and easily every week in iET ITSM," is how Comans describes his experience. Because one of the key objectives was to provide sales units with optimum support, and it is precisely here that flexible and fast responses are a must.

Fig. 1: ITIL-aligned processes help to provide a cost-oriented structure for the IT Service

The plan was to be turned into reality as quickly as possible. "Once a decision had been taken for ITIL-compliant IT Service, we were keen to roll out and implement the changes fast," recalls Marcel Comans, responsible for Incident Management. Consultants experienced in ITIL helped him to define the flows. Together they conducted workshops with internal customers from the bank's technical departments and IT staff. This formed the basis on which the project group designed the processes. DAB Bank wanted more customer-oriented controlling of IT services and processes from the new ITIL orientation. Of particular importance for the bank were:

- Standardization of procedures in IT

- Definition of interfaces to other areas

- Measurability of processes

- Documentation of all faults arising

- Conclusion of Service Level Agreements

- Reusability of problem solutions.

2.2   Incident Management – Reporting of Problems and Bottlenecks

Requests to replace a faulty keyboard or a problem with bank systems are recorded in Incident Management, as are warning or error reports generated in the Monitoring System. The ticket generated is classified and prioritized using various service categories; after all, not every incident is equally important and urgent. The five helpdesk staff are provided with active support by the system. An error in a particular system category can only be assigned certain priorities. In turn, these are couple to the service levels. Marcel Comans sees clear advantages in this: "My helpdesk colleagues find things much easier with iET ITSM and in the event of escalation we ensure that only relevant cases are presented to management."

Looking back, Marcel Comans is highly satisfied with the outcome: "Everybody who was affected was involved right from the start; this ensured the high level of acceptance we have today. Together with our customers, we defined recovery times that were then agreed in the corresponding service levels and are monitored with iET ITSM. Our customers are pleased that they now have only one point of contact." Regardless of whether they report the incident via the telephone hotline, intranet or email.

If a Service Level Agreement stipulates contacting the customer within 24 hours, the employee is given a timely reminder. The introduction of ITSM now permits sending email notifications and escalations to the employees responsible and to management.

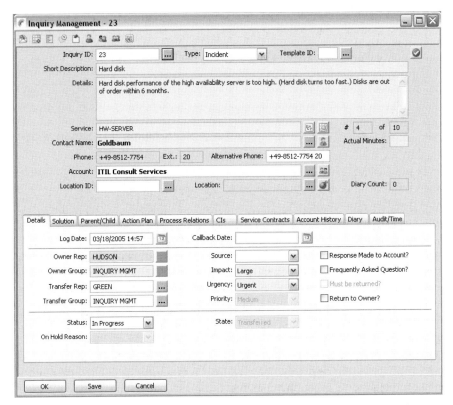

Fig. 2: A clearly designed screen is critical for fast and structured incident entering

The intranet interface is also an innovation much used by internal customers for standardized messages. "This enabled us to significantly reduce the number of initial calls to the hotline. With the queries over the intranet we are simply that much faster," comments Comans on the success. The helpdesk team processes some 200 incidents a day.

2.3   Problem Management – Tracking Down the Causes

IT department customers are more interested in having their problems solved. At the same time, Problem Management deals with analyzing and deriving solutions for similar incidents; this means that several incidents can be addressed in one go. Second-level Support at DAB Bank, IT Operations, is responsible for operating the systems such as the trading application or the account management system. The various system owners are the first point of contact when similar incidents arise. They analyze the incidents affecting their systems for repetitions and parallels. If they or a helpdesk team member notice a conspicuous frequency of comparable tickets these are linked to form a problem case.

The product owner draws up a solution along with the appropriate solution documentation.

This extra effort pays dividends, because the helpdesk team immediately has the right solution to hand if such an incident occurs again.

Depending on the problem, guidance on how to rectify the incident may suffice – or detailed tracing of the cause may be called for. In the latter case, the product owner puts together a team of experts to deal with the problem according to its urgency and importance. "The product owner ensures that a solution is found and documented. Normally the solution is communicated to the customer via a central point of contact at the helpdesk.

In more complex cases, the product owner contacts the customer directly. In this way we ensure that our customers receive prompt help without communication breaks," explains Klaus Hintermayr, Head of Problem Management. His team too is bound by particular recovery times. "Even now, so soon after rollout, we can say that iET ITSM has improved our service quality," sums up Hintermayr. "Thanks to the standardized processes, our staff work together extremely efficiently; everybody knows how valuable good information from colleagues is and so everybody plays their part."

2.4   Change Management

Solving a problem often entails major changes to systems. Accordingly, third level support, the "IT Systems Infrastructure" team, is responsible for Change Management. Under the project control of Alexander Venzke, Head of IT Systems Infrastructure, the relevant processes are set up as per ITIL. The second area besides IT Production, IT Solutions, is becoming progressively more involved in the work. Then, about 20 other employees will be using iET ITSM for their daily work. Step by step, DAB Bank is establishing a system that provides integrated mapping of all its individual service processes and is used jointly by all in-house IT units.

3   Process Performance Management in IT Service

3.1   Key Performance Indicators for Service

As the head of IT Operations, Klaus Hintermayr is responsible not only for the quality but also the efficiency of his department. Practically with a mouse click in iET ITSM, he generates reports on incident handling, throughput times and how long it takes to trace the cause of a problem. Since the rollout of the iET Solutions software, his colleague Marcel Comans also generates his own reports just as quickly. The open interface to the database enables him to answer questions quickly with a few clicks.

So he always has to hand queries about the number of incidents with a given priority for a given application. The iET ITSM add-on module, iET Process Analyzer, combines classic reporting with detailed analysis capabilities for tracing causes at the process level.

For Marcel Comans, this tool provides a clear bonus compared with the old way of processing data in a spreadsheet: "With iET Process Analyzer I always have graphic reports straight away. I can use Favorites to save model reports and then customize them using Drag-and-Drop and a few clicks of the mouse."

It is particularly exciting for him when quality performance indicators are involved. Questions about the initial solution rate and how many cases could only be completed with the help of the 2nd or 3rd Level are very helpful indicators. Also important is the question of compliance with Service Level Agreements. Here, the iET Process Analyzer comes supplied with comprehensive standard reports. It compares target and actual times for the processes.

"The evaluation options in the standard report already meet 95% of our requirements," explains Comans with satisfaction. "We merely augment them with a few key performance indicators to provide information on the results of our escalation process."

The quality of Problem Management can be measured with key performance indicators such as average time taken to solve a problem or the number of incidents related to a certain problem. Every process step can be linked and shown with cost rates or prices. Also advantageous is the direct link to the data from the operational system, iET ITSM. This does away with time-consuming customizing, mapping or synchronization processes. Ease of use was another reason why DAB Bank installed iET Process Analyzer. "We simply save so much time. I am faster with my own reports. And my colleagues who have no knowledge of the database structure can nevertheless "click together" their own evaluations and no longer have to rely on me," explains Comans with a smile.

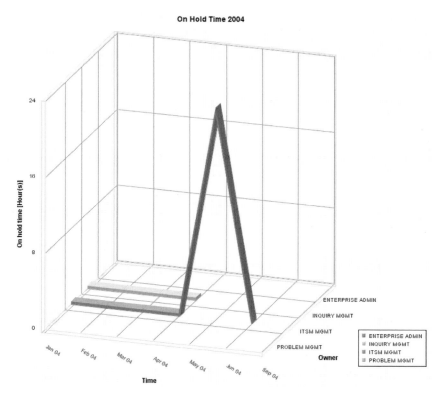

Fig. 3: Example of a standard iET Process Analyzer report:
The "outlier" in May/June shows unusually high waiting times.

3.2   Tracing Causes with Process Mining

When it is a matter of rooting out the causes of variances, iET ProcessAnalyzer really comes into its own. As a rule, the analysis process begins with the time dimension. The key performance indicators from Incident Management are first retrieved on an ad-hoc basis and then evaluated for a given period of time and may be compared with other periods. This might illustrate for example how many calls were taken per month by how many staff or how high the throughput time was over the last 6 or 12 months. If "outliers" are found, then the detective work begins.

If Comans, Hintermayr and their colleagues establish a noticeable variance, they can immediately "drill-down" to find the underlying reasons. Double-clicking on the graphic takes them further into the problem and presents a list of the processes affected. For each individual case, they see a visualized flow of all the steps of the actual process in an EPC diagram. This makes it easier to pinpoint the special case. A glance at the attributes shows the corresponding process values.

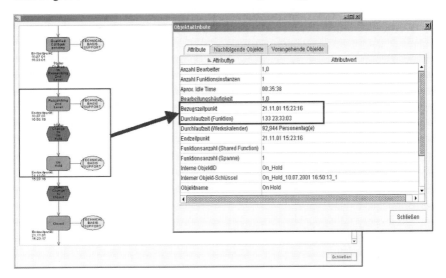

Fig. 4: EPC detail presentation

Figure 4 and the corresponding attributes show the reasons for the variation. In this example, the transaction was left unattended for a very long time owing to resource bottlenecks in the vacation period.

3.3   Ideal Decision and Planning Principles

The retrospective analysis of problems and their causes is extremely important. The derivation of the right actions for the future is the next key step. Here too, graphical evaluations help to show the optimization potential. They show where efficiency in a process can be boosted. Only an integrated cost analysis helps to draw the right conclusions from the historical data. For example, priority must be given to tackling those outliers that cause the highest costs. In addition, the evaluations are an ideal planning tool. For example, the multi-dimensional analyses help to produce better estimates for future resource requirements on the basis of the historical values. Marcel Comans at DAB Bank hopes that in future greater use will be made of iET ProcessAnalyzer to monitor running processes. "We don't have to wait until we receive a flood of incidents or escalations. Every IT team leader who regularly looks at iET ProcessAnalyzer can track whether there are signs of a problem emerging in his or her area. Then early remedial action can be taken."

4   Summary and Outlook

Comprehensive process work has paid off for DAB Bank. "What ITIL promises has been delivered," concludes Comans with satisfaction. Needless to say there were initial reservations in the various teams, says the project leader, but now everybody has been convinced. His colleagues have more breathing space for their daily work; they can concentrate on providing optimum solutions. At DAB Bank people are aware that the IT systems provide major support for the bank's strategy. Thanks to top-quality applications and new processes, the bank is ideally positioned to undertake future growth with confidence.

Annex: The Authors

Barth, Winfried
Senior Manager
ARIS PPM Product Consulting
IDS Scheer AG
Altenkesseler Straße 17
D-66115 Saarbrücken

Bauer, Tino
Manager
Business Unit Chemie/Pharma
IDS Scheer AG
Lindwurmstraße 23
D-80337 München

Bird, John
Senior Consultant
ARIS PPM Product Consulting
IDS Scheer UK Limited
Vienna House
Starley Way
UK-B37 7HB Birmingham

Blickle, Dr. Tobias
Senior Manager
ARIS PPM Development
IDS Scheer AG
Altenkesseler Straße 17
D-66115 Saarbrücken

Drawert, Steffen
Manager
Core Service Supply
Chain Controlling
IDS Scheer AG
Zimmerstraße 69
D-10117 Berlin

Dreißen, André
Manager
Business Unit Utilities/Telecom
IDS Scheer AG
Heinrichstraße 169A
D-40239 Düsseldorf

Gahse, Frank
Senior Manager
ARIS PPM International
IDS Scheer AG
Altenkesseler Straße 17
D-66115 Saarbrücken

Heinrichs, Rainer
Head of Call/Billing
Süwag Energie AG
Brüningstr. 1
D-65929 Frankfurt

Heselmann, Bernd
Signatory, Head of
Product Development
Gesellschaft für integrierte
Systemplanung mbH
Softwarezentrum
Junkersstr. 2
D-69469 Weinheim

Heß, Dr. Helge
Director
ARIS Business Process Engineering
IDS Scheer AG
Altenkesseler Straße 17
D-66115 Saarbrücken

Jost, Dr. Wolfram
Member of the Board
IDS Scheer AG
Altenkesseler Straße 17
D-66115 Saarbrücken

Klein, Dr. Olaf
Ass. Vice-President
Credit Suisse Zürich
Paradeplatz 8
8070 Zürich

Knirck, Phillip
Consultant
ARIS PPM Product Consulting
IDS Scheer AG
Altenkesseler Straße 17
D-66115 Saarbrücken

Kogelschatz, Dirk
Business Project Leader
Credit Suisse Zürich
Paradeplatz 8
CH-8070 Zürich

Kronz, Dr. Andreas
Senior Manager
ARIS PPM Product Consulting
IDS Scheer AG
Altenkesseler Straße 17
D-66115 Saarbrücken

Kruppke, Helmut
Member of the Board,
Spokesman of the Executive Board
IDS Scheer AG
Altenkesseler Straße 17
D-66115 Saarbrücken

Linke, Michael Peter
Product Marketing Manager
ARIS PPM
IDS Scheer AG
Altenkesseler Straße 17
D-66115 Saarbrücken

Loes, Gregor
Senior Manager
Customer Interaction Center (CIC)
IDS Scheer AG
Altenkesseler Straße 17
D-66115 Saarbrücken

Miksch, Klaus
Global Account Manager
IDS Scheer AG
Lindwurmstrasse 23
D-80337 München

Müller, Lars
Head of Process and
Quality Controlling
DaimlerChrysler Bank AG
Siemensstraße 7
D-70469 Stuttgart

Oberländer, Herbert
Director
Business Unit Insurances
IDS Scheer AG
Lindwurmstraße 23
D-80337 München

Ossig, Frank
Senior Consultant,
Core Service Technologies
IDS Scheer AG
Lindwurmstraße 23
D-80337 München

Panagiotidis, Dr. Petros
Dr. Petros Panagiotidis
Business Systems Integration
Manager
Vodafone Panafon S.A.
GR-15231 Halandri

Ramler, Karl
Technical Manager
E.ON Kernkraft GmbH
Kernkraftwerk Unterweser
Dedesdorfer Str. 2
D-26935 Stadland

Raphael, Holger
Head of Administration
Stiftung Katholisches Krankenhaus
Marienhospital Herne
Klinikum der Ruhr Universität
Bochum
Hölkeskampring 40
D-44625 Herne

Reif, Robert,
Corporate Management
Sales Control
E.ON Bayern AG
Heinkelstraße 1
D-93049 Regensburg

**Scheer, Prof. Dr. Dr. h.c. mult.
August-Wilhelm**
Head of the Institute for Econimic
Information Technology, University
of the Saarland; founder and Chair-
man of the Supervisory Board
IDS Scheer AG
Altenkesseler Straße 17
D-66115 Saarbrücken

Schenck, Hendrick
Controlling
Stiftung Katholisches Krankenhaus
Marienhospital Herne
Klinikum der Ruhr Universität
Bochum
Hölkeskampring 40
D-44625 Herne

Schwarzin, Jürgen
Divisional Head
Process Controlling
E.ON Kernkraft GmbH
Kernkraftwerk Unterweser
Dedesdorfer Str. 2
D-26935 Stadland

Stängle, Peter
Head of the Coaching Team
Gesellschaft für integrierte
Systemplanung mbH
Zepplinstr. 11
D-91052 Erlangen

Sulzmann, Simone
Marketing Manager Worldwide
iET Solutions GmbH
Boschetsrieder Str. 67
D-81379 München

von den Driesch, Markus
Senior Manager
ARIS PPM Development
IDS Scheer AG
Altenkesseler Straße 17
D-66115 Saarbrücken

Printing and Binding: Strauss GmbH, Mörlenbach